Flesh and Text

First published in the UK in 2025 by
Intellect, The Mill, Parnall Road, Fishponds, Bristol, BS16 3JG, UK

First published in the USA in 2025 by
Intellect, The University of Chicago Press, 1427 E. 60th Street, Chicago, IL 60637, USA

© Signed texts, their authors
© Rest of the book, the editors

Copyright © 2025 Intellect Ltd
All rights reserved. No part of this publication may be reproduced, stored in a retrieval system, or transmitted, in any form or by any means, electronic, mechanical, photocopying, recording, or otherwise, without written permission.

No part of this book may be used or reproduced in any manner for the purpose of training artificial intelligence technologies or systems without written permission from the publisher.

A catalogue record for this book is available from the British Library.

Copy editor: MPS Limited
Cover designer: Tanya Montefusco
Front cover image: *Model Love* (Arnolfini, Bristol, 2008): performers Tom Wainwright and Catherine Dyson. Photo: Edward Dimsdale.
Back cover image: *Life Class* (Lakeside Arts, Nottingham, 2019): participant Barbara J. Clark, performers Morven Macbeth and Graeme Rose, participant Beth Holland. Photo: Scott Sawyer.
Production manager: Debora Nicosia
Typesetter: Debora Nicosia

Hardback ISBN 978-1-83595-071-5
Paperback ISBN 978-1-83595-090-6
ePDF ISBN 978-1-83595-073-9
ePUB ISBN 978-1-83595-072-2

Printed and bound by Halstan

To find out about all our publications, please visit our website.
There you can subscribe to our e-newsletter, browse or download our current catalogue and buy any titles that are in print.

www.intellectbooks.com

This is a peer-reviewed publication.

Flesh and Text

Devising Performance by Bodies in Flight

Edited by
SIMON JONES AND SARA GIDDENS

Bristol, UK / Chicago, USA

Playtext

Series editor: Patrick Duggan
Print ISSN: 1754-0933 | **Online ISSN:** 1754-0941

The Intellect Playtext series publishes innovative performance texts under three inter-related strands: new writing (scripts), performance writings ('non-traditional' forms such as choreographic scores, devised performance texts, performance documentation), and translations (writing that is new to English-speaking audiences). The Playtext series makes available performance texts that are aesthetically and stylistically innovative as well as those that explore the socio-cultural and political contexts of their making. Each volume includes the performance texts alongside contextual essays that examine the processes of development, writing and performance as well as critical essays that discuss the texts from political, social, cultural and theoretical perspectives. Intellect's Playtext are concerned also to present volumes that engage with the wider historical and performance contexts of the work through, for example, the inclusion of production photographs, design sketches, historical documents and/or typographical design. The series celebrates critical writing, adaptation, translation, and devising processes and provides a forum for textual performance practices-as-research. From 2002 to 2013 the Playtext series was edited by Roberta Mock.

In this series:

Flesh and Text: Devising Performance by Bodies in Flight, edited by Simon Jones and Sara Giddens (2025)

Schechner Plays, edited by Richard Schechner (2025)

Following the Score: The Ravel Trilogy, edited by Michael Pinchbeck and Ollie Smith (2024)

A Holocaust Cabaret: Re-making Theatre from a Jewish Ghetto, edited by Lisa Peschel (2023)

Performing Collaboration in Solo Performance, edited by Chloé Déchery (2022)

Lightwork: Texts on and from Collaborative Multimedia Theatre, edited by Andy Lavender and Alex Mermikides (2021)

Acts of Dramaturgy, edited by Michael Pinchbeck (2020)

The Hour of All Things and Other Plays, edited by Caridad Svich (2018)

Plays in Time, edited by Karen Malpede (2017)

András Visky's Barrack Dramaturgy: Memories of the Body, edited by Jozefina Komporaly (2017)

Freaks of History, edited by James MacDonald (2017)

Justitia, edited by Paul Johnson and Sylvia Dabowska (2016)

JARMAN (all this maddening beauty) and other plays, edited by Caridad Svich (2016)

Ivar Kreuger and Jeanne de la Motte, edited by Barbara Tepa Lupack (2016)

Utopia, edited by Claire MacDonald (2015)

This book is dedicated to Sara Giddens (1965–2023).

MAN: It's a window ... isn't it? ...
WOMAN: ... that opens.
MAN: But it's just a spell of time ...
WOMAN: ... a little spell.
MAN: I'm glad you got in my way ... and stuck ...
WOMAN: ... for the time being ...

Life Class (2019–22)

Bodies in Flight

Contents

About Bodies in Flight — xiii
   Simon Jones and Sara Giddens
Foreword: Marking the Times: Experiencing Bodies in Flight — xix
   Andrew Quick

1. Unconcealing This Maker's Voice — 1
   Sara Giddens

1989–1995: THE FIRST SERIES: — 8
Performance as Energy, Ideas and Provocation — 10

2. *Deadplay* (1989) — 12
3. Playing Dead … Becoming Professional — 16
   Rachel Feuchtwang
4. *Exhibit* (1990) — 20
5. Controlled Chaos — 24
   Barnaby Power
6. *Love Is Natural and Real but Not for You my Love* (1990) — 26
7. My (Other) Other Collaborator: Philosophy Alongside Practice — 30
   Simon Jones
8. *iwannabewolfman* (1991–92) — 38
9. Working Alongside — 42
   Sara Giddens
10. *Rough* (1992–93) — 50
11. From Fan-Boy to Programmer – Memories of a Relationship with Bodies in Flight — 62
   Richard Dufty
12. As if for the First Time — 66
   Graeme Rose
13. Speaking in Texts: Writing Beyond Meaning — 72
   Simon Jones
14. *Beautiful Losers* (1994) — 78
15. Hearing Bodies in Flight — 90
   Darren Bourne
16. *Littluns Wake* (1995) — 96

1996–2009: THE SECOND SERIES:	100
Performance as (Non-)Collaboration Across Media	102

17. *Do the Wild Thing!* (1996) — 104
18. The Magnificent Minutiae — 115
   Sara Giddens
19. *Constants* (1998) — 124
20. Set-up and Situation – Dramaturgy as Transformation — 128
   Simon Jones
21. *DeliverUs* (1999–2000) — 134
22. A Dialogue at the Globe Theatre (London) — 143
   Polly Frame IN CONVERSATION WITH Simon Jones
23. Dialogues & Duets — 149
   Josephine Machon
24. *Double Happiness* (2000) — 158
25. *Beautiful Losers* Re-worked — 162
   Kaylene Tan
26. *Flesh & Text: A Document* (2001) — 168
27. *Skinworks* (2002–03) — 170
28. Being In-Between: Collaboration as Non-Collaboration — 182
   Simon Jones
29. *Who By Fire* (2004–05) — 190
30. *Who By Fire*: Very Slow Decay — 196
   Sleepdogs: Tanuja Amarasuriya AND Tim X Atack IN CONVERSATION
31. *Triptych* (2005) — 202
32. The Transmediated Image — 204
   Tony Judge
33. *The Secrecy of Saints* (2006) — 210
34. *Model Love* (2008–11) — 222
35. Rendering Visible — 231
   Paul Geary
36. Finding Suspension — 237
   Sara Giddens
37. Performance/Photography/Photography/Performance — 243
   [And On/And On]
   Edward Dimsdale
38. *Hymn* (2009) — 254

2009–PRESENT: THE THIRD SERIES: 256
Opening Out Towards Co-creating the Portfolio Work   258

39. *Dream→Work/Dream→Walk* (2009–16)   260
40. *Gymnast* (2011–13)   264
41. A Place That Is Intelligent, A Little Bit Punk Even …   268
But Always Human
Suzannah Bedford
42. Mayfest and Mayk: From Festival to Co-creation   272
Matthew Austin IN CONVERSATION WITH Simon Jones
43. *Do the Wild Thing! Redux* (2012)   278
44. *Still Moving: Moving Still* (2012–18)   280
45. Developing a Portfolio   282
Sara Giddens
46. *Life Class* (2019–22)   288
47. Making and Breaking, Failing and Faking   300
Morven Macbeth
48. The Dare of Other Voices – From Verbatim to Co-creation   305
Simon Jones
49. *Unbox Me!* (2023)   312

Afterword   315
Paul Russ
Postscript   319
Simon Jones
List of Figures   321
Index   329

Bodies in Flight

Sometimes to name the deed is enough. Isn't it? Just to give the instruction. Or not even to name it as instruction. Simply to say it out aloud. Or in my special whisper. To know you have done such a thing at such and such a time and place in the undocumented past. To imagine you could do such a thing, if so instructed, in some indeterminate future. That's enough. On quite a few occasions. But then. When confronted with the deed, who knows what'll come to one? When it's done, before me. That very complicated place. When all the talking, the instructing and the describing's done. And it is done.
[…]
Do it then. Go on, do it. Only kidding.
[both, shift]

Do the Wild Thing! (1996)

FIGURE F.1: *Constants* rehearsal (Arnolfini, Bristol): Patricia Breatnach, David Gilbert, Darren Bourne, Sheila Gilbert, Caroline Rye, Sara Giddens and Simon Jones.
Photo: Edward Dimsdale.

About Bodies in Flight
SIMON JONES AND *SARA GIDDENS*

BODIES IN FLIGHT, co-directed by Sara Giddens and Simon Jones from 1990 to 2023, make performance *where flesh utters and words move* that challenges and re-energizes the conventional relationship between audiences and performers, and audiences and place. Based in Bristol and Derbyshire, our work comes from the careful and rigorous development of interdisciplinary and collaborative methods, often with new technologies in cutting-edge venues. We insist on the buzz of ideas, on philosophy and poetry, using words and images, movement and stillness, voices and bodies, through which we aim to move audiences emotionally and spiritually.

Since 1989, we have made over twenty performance and installation works and published many documents and reflections on our practice. Looking back now on over 30 years of performance-making, this book describes three broad series of our work and a set of deepening concerns: the company's early professional practice; the development of its practice-as-research methodology working across a range of collaborations; and its recent work collaborating with different communities. Of course, these series are not discrete, concerns and strategies carrying over from one to the next, blurring and accreting as methodologies complexify and collaborations mature. Nevertheless, attitudes to and handling of material shift; compositional tools, moods and tactics have emerged and endured as distinctive aspects of our flight over the decades. As with all historical shorthand, these series are useful only up to a point: each work still moves, sings and speaks in its own specificity of making, showing and thinking, which this book aims to elucidate.

PERFORMANCE AS ENERGY, IDEAS AND PROVOCATION: Our first shows (1989–95) thrilled to the energy and excitement of the late 80s and early 90s UK experimental performance scene where physical and dance theatre encountered performance and live art when challenging work in body art mixed with experiments in multimedia. These shows were high-energy, action-based, erotic and political; they increasingly involved poetic text and choreographed movement. They pastiched both popular and esoteric forms; they were irreverent, slyly provocative and unremittingly satirical. They consistently prodded at theatre's capacity to make meaning, affect its audiences and comment on the world.

PERFORMANCE AS (NON-) COLLABORATION ACROSS MEDIA: In 1996, with our eighth show *Do the Wild Thing!*, we formalized these concerns with a specific research imperative: to explore how performance achieved these affects. We began to deconstruct and examine what we called the *mixing of flesh and text*, which we understood as performance's unique contribution as an art form. We achieved this through a series of collaborations with sonic and visual media artists (1996–2009), developing a strategy of duetting between bodies and technologies, texts and spaces. We extended our interest in siting performances in specific places, including the virtual online environment. We took these collaborations across continents and cultures so that bodies with radically different experiences were brought together in the work. And yet, in each new work, the concern remained to explore *how we mix* in the event of the performance itself, however and wherever that might be.

OPENING OUT TOWARDS CO-CREATING THE PORTFOLIO WORK: Our current series of work (2009–present) extends further our collaborations to include working with different communities, some of place, others of skill sets, for example – choirs and gymnasts, taking the work to global cities, seaside towns, galleries and gymnasia, mixing different kinds of expertise with different kinds of personal investment. In these ways we have increasingly opened out our practice to different understandings of everydayness: how commonplace experience might help us fashion a new idea of community, however realized in the performance event itself. This opening out has often involved extending the envelope of what each work can do by re-making 'editions', sited in different locations and responding to producers' different priorities; by re-mediatizing material to reach new audiences; and by returning to and 're-entering' previous material to find new meanings in new contexts and media.

ABOUT THE BOOK

All archives are timely, both full of *times* and *of* their time: a mixing of hapless memories, wayward gestures, technological tricks, deep socio-cultural narratives and personal-political manoeuvrings, all 'retrospectively' organized into a seeming logic, a history, *the* account. This book seeks to capture some of the happen-chances and designs that have shaped our work; and acknowledge both the value and the provisionality of constructing a history and a methodology from these memories, records and ongoing, embodied practices.

The ghosts of this activity – Bodies in Flight's twenty or so performance works, so painstakingly and pleasurably done over these 30 years, are the only real things to remain, once the arranging and sifting, this archiving has been revealed as the partial truth we always knew it was. The memory and the trace are what will be left of us, and that persists most splendidly in the minds and fleshes of everyone with whom we have had the honour to make work, and every audience-spectator who has honoured us with their attention at our performances. By commissioning reflections from a range of collaborators and interested others, we want this book to express the richness of that collective endeavour, in essence, to represent how all performance is made out of such complex artistic, personal and socio-cultural constellations. The differences and shifts of voice, register and concern evidence the breadth and depth of energies, knowledges and passions that come together to make a performance: the mix in this book is crucial to understanding how our work works. As such, we feel a profound debt to a variety of different canons and practices; and it is precisely and regretfully when vital parts of that recent genealogy are threatened – funding is re-aligned or withdrawn, university departments and venues are closed, that the duty to contribute to the preservation and consolidation of those practices is most pressing.

We accept that the live 'event-hood' of performance cannot be copied and *re-produced* through documentation. Why would one want to? This book is something else: as an opportunity to engage with the work and its contexts in a number of ways, it expresses the concerns of interdisciplinarity that drive our work. This book then alludes to, registers and reflects live performance's otherness and its *separateness*: its resistant claim to uniqueness: its parasitic persistence in a culture dominated by the industries and technologies of the recordable and transmissible – *the digital*. In 2001, we embraced new media with *Flesh & Text*, the first ever CD-ROM to gather together one performance company's work to date, organized as a hyper-text with links between samples of audio, text and video, with interviews from collaborators and reflections from ourselves as co-directors.

This book builds on that rhizomatic project, as each section offers a holographic glimpse of the whole that cannot be seen in its entirety from any single vantage point, remaining resolutely incomplete. By structuring the book partly as a history in chronological order of production, and partly as an explication of method, holographically approached, we intend to enact three important ideas for us: that time is both one-way into the future (as every performance-maker knows only too well) and circular back to the past; that the mix(ing) of materials and media *in* the work is irreducible; and the richness of the different collaborators' perspectives *on* the work demonstrates its endless transformability and potential for re-use. Our aim is to open out our method to you the reader: so, each piece is prefaced by its writer's biography, foregrounding the diversity of career trajectories that intersect any performance project sustained over so many years, as well as a description of its purpose to signal its vector through the rhizome that is Bodies in Flight.

Re-using the CD-ROM's categorization of contents, there are four distinct kinds of material in this book: 'Documents' of works, 'Flights', 'Bodies' and 'Others'. 'Documents' form the book's chronological spine, evidencing each work with images, publicity copy, extracts from texts, where the formatting is as close to the original as possible, plus archival materials such as designs or scores. In 'Flights' (Chapters 1, 7, 9, 13, 18, 20, 28, 36, 45 and 48), the two co-directors explore crucial aspects of our methodology, how it developed over time and what we have learnt from our collaborations. 'Bodies' is a strand of reflections from key collaborators who have helped shape Bodies in Flight's work over 30 years (contributions by Tim Atack with Tanuja Amarasuriya, Darren Bourne, Edward Dimsdale, Rachel Feuchtwang, Polly Frame, Tony Judge, Morven Macbeth, Barnaby Power, Graeme Rose and Kaylene Tan). They offer insights into how specific works were made and how the skills acquired with Bodies in Flight have informed their subsequent careers. 'Others' provides a series of commentaries by academics, arts officers and producers from the outside of our practice (contributions by Matthew Austin, Suzannah Bedford, Richard Dufty, Paul Geary, Josephine Machon, Andrew Quick and Paul Russ). From these various perspectives, we intend to triangulate the work and locate it in the wider theatre ecology, so that you – the reader – can chart how an experimental performance company has continued to make work in the United Kingdom since 1989, how artists working on small-scale theatre have built careers, and how our methodology might be of use to you in your own experiencing of performance and in your own practice. We hope this book will inspire you to make and engage with performance from a wide variety of perspectives and positions and find, in this most mixed of arts, ever greater possibilities.

OUR THANKS

There are many people who have supported our work at different times in the development of the company: we cannot thank them all here. However, we wanted to acknowledge the crucial support of the following individuals and their organizations over the years:

Nikki Milican (National Review of Live Art), Stella Coultanbanis (Bonington Gallery, Nottingham), Helen Cole (Inbetween Time Festival of Live Art and Intrigue), Richard Dufty (Battersea Arts Centre, London), Matthew Austin and Kate Yedigaroff (MAYK, Bristol), Becky Aram, Rebecca Hayter, Jim Hendley and Paul Russ (Dance 4/FABRIC), Martin Blackham and Tony Judge (Creative Forum) and all the staff at UCLanDance (Preston) and the Wickham Theatre (University of Bristol).

Thanks also to Patrick Duggan, editor of the Playtext series, and Jessica Lovett at Intellect, for their support in our 'wrighting' of this book, and Debora Nicosia at Intellect for their design, as well as to Arts Council England and the University of Central Lancashire for their financial support towards preparation of this volume.

Special thanks go to Julian Warren, the Head of the Theatre Collection (University of Bristol), Siân Williams (Keeper of their Live Art Archives) and Athene Bain (Assistant Keeper), for caring for and cataloguing the Bodies in Flight archives held by the Collection, and for their tireless work, alongside the extraordinary efforts of photographer Edward Dimsdale and filmmaker Tony Judge, in identifying and preparing materials for this book, including the range of images from over 30 years work.

Lastly, our heartfelt thanks and gratitude to our families, friends and colleagues who have supported us in so many ways throughout this amazing and wonderful flight.

Bodies in Flight

Foreword:
Marking the Times: Experiencing Bodies in Flight

ANDREW QUICK

ANDREW QUICK is Professor of Theatre and Performance at the Lancaster Institute for the Contemporary Arts (University of Lancaster) and a founder member of imitating the dog. With Pete Brooks and Simon Wainwright, he has co-written and directed Hotel Methuselah *(2006),* Kellerman *(2009),* 6 Degrees Below the Horizon *(2010),* The Zero Hour *(2012),* A Farewell to Arms *(2014),* The Train *(2016),* Nocturnes *(2017),* Heart of Darkness *(2018),* Night of the Living Dead – Remix *(2020),* Dracula: The Untold Story *(2021),* Macbeth *(2023),* Frankenstein *(2024). In 2022, he collaborated with John Galliano and the French fashion house Maison Margiela, where he co-wrote and directed* Cinema Inferno *at the Palais de Chaillot for Paris Haut Couture week. Andrew is also the author of numerous articles, edited books and book chapters on theatre, performance and installation art, including* The Wooster Group Work Book *(2007).*

Here Andrew places Bodies in Flight in the context of British contemporary performance and traces key concerns through the company's work.

I first encountered Bodies in Flight in 1989 at the National Review of Live Art held in Glasgow. I can barely recall much of the work that made up the three days of the festival. I remember an installation by Derek Jarman: two men, who spent the daylight hours in a bed surrounded by barbed wire, the adjacent walls housing mattresses, stained by tar and graffiti. I remember the consummate compering of the festival's events by Neil Bartlett. Yet, I do clearly recall aspects of the performance made by Bodies in Flight. Its title was *Deadplay* and it probably lasted no longer than 30 minutes. One of Wagner's operas, *Parsifal*, provided the backbone and structure to the piece, as a series of tableaux repeatedly broke apart when flurries of physical action took over from studied stillness: catching, falling and attempts to escape the confines of the playing space. Perhaps I remember this so vividly because I felt acutely aware that this performance appeared to be playing out a set of particular stylistic tropes that had come to dominate British and mainland European experimental theatre in the 1980s: a playing out that, for me, marked the decade's conclusion.

I have to admit that as I watched the opening of *Deadplay* the action seemed all too familiar. What appeared to unfold before me was the usual panoply of physicality that had undoubtedly become the signature of that decade's experimental theatre practice, which had formed in the early 1980s through the work of such companies as Hidden Grin, Rational Theatre, Hesitate and Demonstrate, Impact Theatre, and a little later the dance-theatre of DV8 and the earlier pieces by Forced Entertainment. Work from outside the United Kingdom, particularly the dance theatre of Pina Bausch, first seen in London in 1983, and also Jan Fabre's *The Power of Theatrical Madness*, performed in 1986 at The Albert Hall, had undoubtedly influenced the landscape of experimental theatre at home. By the mid 1980s, a new form of British theatre had emerged, one that emphasized physicality and repetition, and placed an emphasis on gesture, rather than on the word, such as the work of Station House Opera and Lumiere and Son. Like *Deadplay*, and *Exhibit* which followed in 1990, this was a visceral and visual form of performance that used light and sound as a percussive medium in which dystopian worlds could be explored.

However, as *Deadplay* progressed, I recall that I became aware that this was not so much a homage to a particular form of performance, but a performed critique of this practice. The piece was not only an exploration of sexuality, such as DV8 Physical Theatre's *Dead Dreams of Monochrome Men*, performed in 1988 and televised in 1990 to the outrage of the right-wing press, or the frustration of miscommunication, of loss and the limit of desire, as Gloria's *Sarrasine* had been, also from 1988. *Deadplay* was a performed commentary on a particular style of theatre itself. It is possible that I am crediting *Deadplay* with too much irony and knowingness, but the juxtaposition between Wagnerian excess and the considered choreography pursued by its youthful performers gave the performance a humorous tension, that indicated that this was less an embodiment of a view of the human condition, than an exquisite study in which such a condition had come to be represented. Thinking back, *Deadplay* now marks the end of a specific form of experimental practice; and it seemed more than a coincidence that this apparent closure was taking place in the UK's only festival for new work. This sense of termination is hinted at in the very title of the piece: *Deadplay*. Played out. Over.

More importantly, I don't wish to give the impression that the signature of Bodies in Flight is 'a deconstructive turn' – the sleight of hand in which the tropes of a particular form of performance are continuously reworked and exposed for what they are, to reveal unacknowledged conceptualizations and hidden ideologies. To identify such a move as the defining quality of Bodies in Flight could not be further off the mark, since one of the prevailing features of all the work, that makes up the three decades of this company's practice, has been the attempt to articulate and locate a language (physical, visual, textual and communitarian) that might 'tell' of the complexity of experience, an attempt that echoes Second Stride's integration of choreography with text: see Caryl Churchill and David Lan's *A Mouthful of Birds* (1986). This telling manifests itself as a mode of communication that exceeds language. This would seem like a contradiction, except that we all know that language does not give up the whole story. Why make poetry or even performance, if not to develop and savour a taste for this other to language, to take a bite out of its inside and outside, to destroy the structural divisions that language needs to erect in order to sustain its very existence? Experience might be language's nourishment, but the outcome is far from the revelation of the intricacies of reality.

If *Deadplay* concerned itself with endings, then the pieces that immediately followed seemed obsessed with the attempt to touch upon the domain of human experience that refuses reduction into the finality of writing and knowledge. Such a concern is not an obsession with negativity, with nihilism, but a pursuit that has been maintained in performance after performance, in order to invoke, to make material, what might be possible and what might be imagined: to articulate emotion at the limit of expression. What had dominated the text-based work of the 1970s and early 1980s – the politics of class and economics (see Edward Bond, Howard Brenton, David Hare, The Women's Theatre Group, 7:84) – was being replaced by a dynamic exploration of the politics of desire and dystopia, societal breakdown and alternative versions of history: see Howard Barker's *The Bite of the Night* (1988) and later Sarah Kane's *Blasted* (1995), and the work of Neil Bartlett with Gloria and Ian Spink with Second Stride. Bodies in Flight responded in their next few works to this shift with their explorations of both pastiche and poetic language.

If this comes close to stamping a mark on the body of Bodies in Flight's practice, then I don't apologise for making these observations. How else can I explain the repeated motifs that occur across each of the performances, the apparent fixation on the erotics of love, pain, death, ecstasy and the brutal and liberating effects of desire? These are grand themes that are difficult to ground in dramatic action, to be given flesh in dialogue, movement or image. This is not to say that the performances are overtly philosophical and abstract, although they are always demanding. Rather, I remember each as a sort of meditation, a form of speculation, that continuously moves to negotiate the distance that exists between experience and its inscription into signification, a task clearly inspired by Samuel Beckett's dramaturgy. Such experience is at the edge of knowledge, and this might explain why so much of this work deals with extremes. The worlds reflected in pieces, such as *Love Is Natural and Real but Not for You my Love*, *iwannabewolfman*, *Rough*, *Littluns Wake*, *Do the Wild Thing!* and *DeliverUs*, are saturated with a sense of violence, as well as the excessive nature of sexual longing and the inexhaustible energy that love seemingly provokes.

The emphasis on the need to reach out and touch the complex nature of experience is reflected in a programme note written for *Double Happiness*, where the company make the claim that the 'work insists on an aesthetic and philosophical interrogation, that makes the everyday experiences of living and loving, of desire and ideas strange'. This making strange is a product of the levels of excess created within (and generated by the encounter with) each performance. It is an excess that manifests itself in the language spoken, in the intense physical choreography that the performers express and endure, and in the dislocating effects that the materiality of the performance has upon the audience. Nothing is easy in a show by Bodies in Flight. The words seem to torrent towards you, gaining an almost unstoppable momentum through their sheer athletic power to explore the brittle edge of language in the process of communication. Physicality works in a similar way as the poetics of gesture and movement are revealed and embodied. In the worlds reflected here, words and gestures appear to fix only in the moment of their enunciation and articulation. As such, our complacent notion of subjectivity is unstitched in front of our eyes, as we witness each of the characters' attempts to construct and communicate a language that would do justice to the energies of their desire and their lives, echoing similar intensities in the work of playwrights like Howard Barker, Sarah Kane and Anthony Neilson. This is a place where bodies and minds seem to operate in different realms, forever dividing and wreaking havoc in the fissures that open out between the cognitive and the corporeal, between thought and action.

Performance always happens once and for one time only: happax legomenon. Performance always involves bodies, and bodies do not always do as they are told. However, it is not only that bodies are a problem for language, but language also presents a problem for the corporeal. In much of Bodies in Flight's work, the body seems to almost collapse under the weight of words, reeling (taking flight?) to find its own dynamic in a physicality liberated from the force of language. This reminds me of the French writer Georges Bataille who reworks Nietzsche's concept of the 'inner experience', to access a condition that exists beyond the border of consciousness, that operates outside law and morality. As Fred Botting and Scott Wilson observe in their introduction to *The Bataille Reader* (1997), this notion of inner experience 'describes that movement beyond the attainment, in meditation or ecstasy, of a knowing summit of experience' (1997: 8). Taking flight from this summit, one is plunged into 'the abyss of un-knowing or non-knowledge', occasioning 'an encounter with forces at the extreme limit of possibility' (Botting and Wilson 1997: 8). According to Bataille, experience can be rendered tangible outside the logics of explanation, and this is the demand that he makes both on himself as a writer and also on the reader who encounters his work. It is at the dead end (the absolute limit) of possibility, when all else is exhausted, that the impossible prevails. His command is an urgent one: '[t]o face the impossible – exorbitant, indubitable – when nothing is possible any longer is in my eyes to have an experience of the divine; it is analogous to a torment' (Bataille in Botting and Wilson 1997: 64).

In Bataille's sense, there have been times when I have been truly tormented by the work of Bodies in Flight, an experience not dissimilar to 'in-yer-face' theatre (see Sierz 2001). In an era marked by bland imitation, where the political appears absent from so much of the performance that I witness, then the demands that Bodies in Flight make upon me are most welcome, like Howard Barker's excoriating work. The torment I experience is a kind of suffering, or at least being positioned to bear witness to forms of suffering, as the performer makes play with words and gesture, staking a claim for the possibility, the actuality, of experience, of being alive, in, and of, the moment. It is also important to note that this suffering is not limited to anguish but also allows and instigates laughter. As with Beckett's gallows humour, I've always found these works funny. And it is in this strange place, 'life', where we also get close to the experience of the truth, of the experience of being alive itself. As Bataille (1988: 24) observes:

> If my suffering were eliminated [...] human life would peter out. And as life vanished, so too would our far-off, inevitable truth, the truth that incompleteness, death and the unquenchable desire are, in a sense, being's never-to-be-healed wound, without which inertia (while death absorbs us into itself and there's no more change) would imprison us.

If the first decade of Bodies in Flight charted a journey between physicality and text, between the energies that flow between bodies and language, then the second decade seemed to reflect something about our increasing interaction with the technologies of the screen, our interplay with digital information and how we use technology as a means to document the self. *Constants: A Future Perfect* marks this transition, where the body, the word and the technical are explored as inter-connected materialities. Again, like *Deadplay*, something about this work has always stayed with me. I remember a circular space, or at least a space marked by a white circle. Placed at the edge of the circle are TV monitors and live cameras that record a woman in her 70s speaking about what might have taken place in the past as re-being imagined or re-staged in some future instance. We, the audience, are clustered around the array of monitors, as a kind of dialogue between the older woman (Sheila Gilbert) and a dancer in her early 20s (Patricia Breatnach) plays out before us.

I recall Sheila's actual struggle with language and movement, the attempt to remember lines, her painful and slow negotiation of the physical space, using the walls and the audience's chairs as resting places as she moved through and across the space to a seat placed in the middle. At the centre (is it a dead centre?) her face and words come under the camera's scrutiny, as if the lens and live-relayed image might capture and contain each moment as it is performed. Of course, it cannot. This is not so much a failing of technology, but more the product of the act of spectating in the theatre. The movement of my eyes and other senses eludes the attention the screen demands from me. I move between the recording and its object; I see others watching (are they watching the same thing as me?); and I feel, I am touched by, the bodied presence of the performers, entranced by their mutual and contrasting struggle, as it unfolds before me.

Sheila asks the question – '[w]hen did this flesh become a shambles?', claiming not to remember the moment that this catastrophe took place. 'There must have been a day', she muses. However, this day, we hear, is not one of endings, but rather one of beginnings, 'the day she started to live her future' (see 'Postscript'). Once again, Bataille's invocation of suffering (and laughter) as a means to access the reality and plenitude of human life comes to mind. Youth, for all its exuberance, for all its mobility, dexterity and articulacy, cannot keep pace with this shambling, as Sheila puts it. It is there that the real, the experiential, might be played out, might be revealed. It cannot be reduced to the frailties of the flesh and mind: it is also present in how we interact with technology (always a frailty), a technology that would lay claim to a kind of opening onto the realm of the real and the authentic: an authenticity that would seem to declare itself as being more real, more secure, more permanent, than bodies or spoken words.

The works that immediately follow *Constants* return to this problem of technology and in different ways re-iterate how our interplay with technology is always shambolic. Here I am thinking of pieces like *DeliverUs*, *Double Happiness*, *Skinworks*, *Who By Fire*, *The Secrecy of Saints* and *Model Love*. What is fascinating about these pieces is the repeated return to the scene of sexual intimacy, or the promise this scene projects; and how technology, rather than enabling or documenting, occludes (and intervenes in) such instances of intimacy. This goes against a particular strand of the use of technology in performance that has emerged since 2000, which emphasized the ways in which technology, especially, screen-based ones, might allow access to the truth of experience: such as the early work of Katie Mitchell (*Waves* and *The Seagull*, 2006) who seemed to identify a kind of veracity in the screened close-up – one that might allow an authentic female subjectivity to emerge. There is no time here to go into the complex ways that Bodies in Flight negotiate technology in their practice, except to say that there is always a compelling interrogation of the relationship between the word, the body and their mediation.

These works explore our intimate and 'shambolic' interaction with technology, how technology is now, whether we like it or not, an integral component in the complex language and practice of contemporary desire. This is why these pieces interrogate, or at least touch upon, the language of voyeurism, exhibitionism, secrecy and pornography. This explains why the company's use of technology incorporates handheld cameras and TV monitors. Even the projection has a low budget, domestic feel to it, often projecting images taken directly from the home computer screen (e.g. chatrooms in *Skinworks*). This is a deliberate move, one that places the technical in the hands of the performer, or at least on-stage technicians and composers, who are manipulating word, text, image and sound before us. This is in stark and deliberate contrast to how digital technology is so often used in performance, where projection and image manipulation seem decorative and illustrative, disconnected from the thematics that appear under scrutiny on the stage, unanchored from the performer's onstage presence, existing solely as an unacknowledged scenographic component within which the words of the play and its inherent dramaturgical structure still dominate.

Given this focus on agency, how the individual might play with image, with word, with technology, it is not surprising that the last decade has seen a continuation of Bodies in Flight's interrogation of what lies at the limit of experience and its representation beyond the space of the theatre. This move to make work outside the theatre is, no doubt, partly driven by the fact that the touring circuit in the United Kingdom for new and experimental work was reduced through arts cuts and the economic recession between 2008 and 2024. Despite this, the company's move to engage with non-performers, to interact with communities, whether they be commuters, ballroom dancers, gymnasts or choirs, feels like a natural progression. Having interrogated the mechanisms of theatricality over a twenty-year period, the turn to the quotidian, the space and place of the everyday, in works such as *Dream→Work/Dream→Walk*, *Gymnast* and *Life Class*, restages and extends many of the ideas and obsessions that inform the previous two decades of practice. Across all these works an intimate and intense coiling of choreography, text and images is woven before us. Once again, the question of the experiential appears to be under intense scrutiny: the questions being asked centre on what constitutes and interrupts the habitual, what happens when unruly thought intrudes into the routine, how memory and, particularly, how the remembrance of love shatters our sense of continuity while all the time giving sustenance to what constitutes the instant. The now. Life.

Take *Life Class*. A couple enter the space of a ballroom. Their dialogue is a dance. Their words move to and fro: part argument, part reminiscence, part love story. 'Is this a haunting?', the man says, 'Are we ghosts? Tears in the fabric?' As they manoeuvre around each other, we hear of love, missed opportunities, secret thoughts, unsaid observations and judgments. Once again, like *Constants*, this feels like a memory work, one that dwells on the impossibility of love, of the innate separation that exists between individuals. And yet at its core, there is a subtle sense of optimism here. And this hope lies in the power of conversation, in the movement of bodies, in the power of theatricality itself. There's a wonderful exchange at the end of the dialogue where the couple acknowledge that in their contesting, in their tormented remembering, something is brought back into existence, something that is 'more felt than feeling; more alive than life'. The piece closes with couples from a local social dance club dancing. What looked like an isolated, specific confrontation and speculation suddenly disperses into the public realm. The couple's story is now just one of many other stories, and this becomes particularly poignant given the ages of the dancers who now populate the dancefloor. I am suddenly aware of decades of togetherness and separation, the shambling, as Sheila puts it in *Constants*, first spoken over twenty years previously: the intricate movement between suffering and laughter, despair and hope, that marks all these performances. And then we, the audience are invited to dance, momentarily participating in this speculation on what it is to be human. A figure moving in space and time, repeating patterns that are taught to us, knocking knees and standing on toes, smiling at each other, looking for words that make sense of the past and give us hope for the future.

Bodies in Flight. Moving on and on.

References

Bataille, Georges (1988), *Inner Experience* (trans. L. A. Boldt), Albany, NY: State University of New York Press.

Botting, Fred and Wilson, Scott (eds) (1988), *Bataille: A Critical Reader*, Oxford: Blackwell Publishers.

Further Reading

Andersen Nexo, Martin, Helmer, Judith and Malzacher, Florian (eds) (2004), *'Not Even a Game Anymore': The Theatre of Forced Entertainment*, Berlin: Alexander Verlag.

Baugh, Christopher (2005), *Theatre Performance and Technology: The Development of Scenography in the Twentieth Century*, Basingstoke: Palgrave Macmillan.

Heathfield, Adrian (ed.) (2004), *Live: Art and Performance*, London: Tate Publishing.

Rees, Catherine (2020), *Contemporary British Drama*, London: Red Globe Press.

Sierz, Aleks (2001), *In-Yer-Face Theatre*, London: Faber and Faber.

Bodies in Flight

1
Unconcealing This Maker's Voice
SARA GIDDENS

In this Flight, I reflect, as a choreographer, upon the challenges of writing about my practice and keeping the body present within such articulations, how complex and multi-layered practices do not submit readily to verbal analysis, and yet academic scholarship still privileges such so-called critical writing. I comment on the importance of phenomenology as a branch of philosophy to both my and Simon's reflections on our own practices, particularly the work of German philosopher Martin Heidegger. This relates to how through the first series of works the relation of movement to text was fluid, and how through the second series that relation came to be theorized as an in-between. I connect this to my own sense of in-betweenness as a choreographer working on the edges of dance, often with performers who do not think of themselves as dancers.

Reflecting on our work through words and images demands a delicate layering of materials. I am committed to writing from the particularity of this maker's point of view, and naming it as such, rather than from an informed audience point of view, as much dance and performance analysis does. As a choreographer and co-director, I have worked in professional interdisciplinary and collaborative contexts since 1987. My practice is unequivocally physical and informed by over 40 years of studying, making, witnessing and teaching performance and movement-based work in national and internationally recognized contexts.

I work within and from the discipline of dance and yet on the edge of it. I have developed my practice in a range of professional and pedagogical contexts, including as an undergraduate in theatre studies at Lancaster University, within the Choreographic Lab, a practice-centred research environment originally based in Northampton, and as part of two inspiring teams of staff and students on the Contemporary Arts at Nottingham Trent University and the Dance Performance and Teaching programme at the University of Central Lancashire. Alongside this, I have developed many of my facilitatory and reflective practices through work with Creative Partnerships, a national scheme (2002–12), concerned with developing creative learning and teaching, primarily in schools and early-years settings across the United Kingdom, and through work with several major cultural organizations including Dance4 (Nottingham), Sinfonia Viva and QUAD (Derby). Whilst it is important to acknowledge such contexts as implicit, as well as explicit, influences, it is precisely in the in-between spaces that my practice is most comfortably located, and from where I inevitably write.

My practice often happens outside of dance yet is wholly informed and connected with it. I work across disciplines and contexts and my creative approach to pedagogical practices mixes with and informs my artistic professional practices and vice versa. At heart, I am a collaborator. I collaborate as a choreographer, most often with performers who do not usually define themselves as professional dancers, but are committed to working physically (see Chapter 9, 'Working Alongside'). Across the years, I have collaborated with musicians, web designers, filmmakers, photographers and latterly with movers with very different skill sets from my own, such as gymnasts and amateur tea dancers. As the choreographer, I always have responsibility for the movement, as well as the crafting of and a commitment to the whole work.

I will endeavour within my writing for this book, as my long-term collaborator and co-director of Bodies in Flight, Simon Jones suggests, in his chapter for *Practice-as-Research in Performance and Screen* (2009), to firmly acknowledge my role as an expert, located within a network of complementarities. Inevitably, I bring my particular mix of roles and voices, of thoughts, moves, influences and registers as I make, 'new links between the already understood' and 'approach the yet-to-be understood', through an employment of 'the already phrased', in order 'to approach the yet-to-be phrased' (Jones 2009: 25). In doing so, I am reminded of the American philosopher and psychologist Eugene Gendlin's advice, as I find myself working and writing from what I sense, from that which this choreographer implicitly knows and feels, towards that which is yet 'unknown' or at least 'unspoken' (Gendlin 2002).

I still find writing, and particularly writing about movement, a difficult task. I admit that I have struggled to find words that can help me to describe adequately this unfathomably rich territory and that adequately reflect such an expansive and diverse body of work in all its delicate complexity. I believe that we as makers, researchers, historians, writers of and commentators upon artworks often reflect on works through a collection of documents and subjective memories, rather than just our presence at the live event itself. I recall performance scholar Susan Melrose's invitations (2003, 2009) to those writing about performance to 'declare' their 'expert spectator perspective' (Melrose 2003: 4) alongside her calls for her 'colleagues in the wider university context' to 'engage in critical auto-reflection with' their 'own discourse-production' (2003: 2). Indeed, Melrose's deliberately provocative writing positions 'institutionally dominant discourses and practices' in contrast to 'the arts-disciplinary professional experience of performance-making' and 'the expert-practitioner ethos', which she imbues with characteristics of an 'ethical engagement' of 'sensing' and 'intuitive play, drive and attitude' (2003: 2).

Acknowledging such personal and professional complexities (although I remain uncertain such dualism is a particularly useful fit), I come back to this writing aware that I arrive here by way of a complex layering of materials, processes and persons imbued with their own ideologies and positionings. However, I write from this, my own maker's point of view, about a series of performances which have been informed by so many other makers and thinkers. And I draw upon writings and ideas from a wide range of interdisciplinary sources to assist me, making connections not previously made, in order to frame my own concerns and analysis. I carry with me the tacit understanding that my words can only ever hope to touch upon the experience of making and witnessing our work, finding, as the French philosopher Hélène Cixous reflects so eloquently, that 'I do not write to keep. I write to touch the body of the instant with the tips of the words' (1998: 146).

Almost all these sources could be broadly categorized, through their interest in 'lived experience', and are often inclined towards a phenomenological approach. The philosopher Martin Heidegger's notion of 'unconcealment' (1978: 161) helps me to touch upon this complexity as it already carries with it a revealing that continues to hide, and points towards the subtlety and delicacy of what is or may be unconcealed and yet remains still concealed through the apparent 'presencing' (Heidegger 1978: 151) of my writing. Moreover, through Heidegger, such unconcealments offer a connection to being human, to being in the world through an active presencing, that is only possible because of our own knowing of our own mortality. For Heidegger, it is because of this knowledge, that as human beings we are able to question both our own being and our being in relation to other things and persons around us. This being who can question being, who is aware of one's own being and can call into the frame one's own existence, Heidegger names as Dasein.

For me, making performance is all about our human-being-ness, our own being in relation to others, and this is what lies at the very heart of my passion as a maker and viewer. This is why phenomenology as a branch of philosophy has become central to both my and Simon's thinking and framing of performance. Tracing its development from Husserl, through Heidegger to Merleau-Ponty and other more recent proponents (see 'Further Reading'), we have found its fundamental approach of centring experience in the body, a flesh with a mind, that can reflect upon not only its own world, its existence in that world but also its own erasure from the world, the most useful philosophical tool with which to reflect upon our own practices; see Chapter 7, 'My Other (Other) Collaborator: Philosophy Alongside Practice'.

Having worked collaboratively for over thirty years with a writer, I name myself as a choreographer, a writer with and of and through bodies. I have found my own texts. I have developed my own language(s) and had many insightful conversations about and around the works with those nearest and dearest, family, friends and colleagues, many of whom are not directly mentioned in our list of collaborators. This book is committed to capturing the rich and diverse experiences of our practice from multiple perspectives, through multiple voices, yet it sits within the academic imperative, which still privileges the written and then spoken word. Let us not shy away from our western insistence on the (largely linear) hierarchy of words. Words that are so crucial to any Bodies in Flight show and perhaps problematized most easily, certainly most readily. Alight on any of our works and you encounter words, sometimes turned into lyrics, shifting and turning, pirouetting relentlessly, always searching for more, a new angle, unceasingly rehearsing a new way of finding expression. I think of Simon as a wonderfully poetic and lyrical writer, one of the many reasons that I have continued to work with him for so long. He commands a very particular and, I would say, extraordinary play on words; often highlighting their beauty and yet simultaneously foregrounding the impossible task of language to capture precisely that image or moment or feeling. But those words are always part of a whole. They are more dominant in some shows than others, but this is precisely where—when our understanding of and commitment to hybridity and trans-disciplinarity is so crucial. Perhaps most significant always in our work is our collective understanding of these terms in practice, and our relationship to the collaborative process and to the work as a whole. As we develop each work, each element within it is in a constant process of deconstruction and redefinition, and sustaining our individual creative paths, our own flights, is but one task.

The beginnings of each show are always a string of ideas and concerns, often carried through or left over from the previous project, and sometimes as a direct counter-response to it. Ultimately it is the work itself, the show, that takes centre-stage, and the complex layering of materials seeks to support or knowingly respond to the overall synergy; and yet in the midst of all this my commitment to the body, those particular and unique bodies, remains steadfast (sometimes stubbornly so)! So, I seek to write in a way that somehow foregrounds the complexity of my practice, reflects our individual human-being-ness, speaks to our methodology and captures an essence of the experience of our making. In the same way that action research, and specifically in-depth accounts of lived experience, are accepted in cultural studies and sociology, I want to find a way to hold on to the integrity and vitality of the empirical.

Practice, and specifically for me, that very human encounter with others, as makers and then with participants and audiences in the event-hood of performance, has been and continues to be at the very heart of my work. As I look back, the practice has been the 'still-point' of my 'turning world' (Eliot 1974: 191). It has led me into all sorts of territories, down many dead-ends and into the most fertile of solitary explorations and landscapes. However, undoubtedly it has been my practice with others, in theatres, galleries, out on the streets, and through digital technologies, that has fuelled my career, that has fed and at times frustrated me, but has always inspired me. Both the writing of others and writing as a practice *per se* have encouraged and supported my reflections. Writing has become part of my praxis and continues to be *a* way to help communicate complex ideas, sensations and emotions to others. And so, through this writing, I endeavour to find words that best enable me to develop a language that speaks from, through and alongside the body. I am deeply committed to the corporeal, and although I may have been repeatedly frustrated in my attempts to find just the right words, I continue to try. Undoubtedly, there is a profound need, perhaps never more so, in such short-sighted, anti-art, neoliberal political climates, to strengthen ways to articulate experiential, somatically based practices, so that the body does not simply disappear. As makers and researchers, I believe we must continue to find ways that speak of, alongside and out of the body, within a text-based academic economy and far beyond, particularly in our current context where performance and dance-making are so very poorly resourced and consistently and nonsensically marginalized.

References

Cixous, Hélène (1998), S*tigmata: Escaping Texts*, London and New York: Routledge.

Eliot, Thomas Stearns ([1944] 1974), *The Four Quartets*, London: Faber.

Gendlin, Eugene (2002), 'Thinking at the edge in 14 steps', DVD online, https://focusing.org/felt-sense/thinking-edge-tae. Accessed 20 October 2024.

Heidegger, Martin ([1956] 1978), 'The origin of the work of art', in D. Farrell Krell (ed.), *Basic Writings*, London: Routledge, pp. 139–212.

Jones, Simon (2009), 'The courage of complementarity: Practice-as-research as a paradigm shift in performance studies', in L. Allegue, S. Jones, B. Kershaw and A. Piccini (eds), *Practice-as-Research in Performance and Screen*, Basingstoke: Palgrave Macmillan, pp. 19–32.

Melrose, Susan (2003), 'The eventful articulation of singularities – Or, chasing angels', *New Alignments and Emergent Forms: Dance-Making, Theory and Knowledge Conference*, 13 December, UK: University of Surrey.

Melrose, Susan (2009), 'Expert-intuitive processing and the logics of production: Struggles in (the wording of) creative decision-making in dance', in J. Butterworth and L. Wildschut (eds), *Contemporary Choreography: A Critical Reader*, London and New York: Routledge, pp. 25–40.

Further Reading

Bacon, Jane (2006), 'The feeling of the experience: A methodology for performance ethnography', in J. Ackroyd (ed.), *Research Methodologies for Drama Education*, Stoke on Trent: Trentham Books Limited, pp. 215–27.

Fortier, Mark (2016), 'Theatre, life and language: Semiotics, phenomenology and deconstruction', in *Theory/Theatre: An Introduction*, London and New York: Routledge, pp. 17–51.

Grant, Stuart, McNeilly-Renaudie, Jodie and Wagner, Matthew (eds) (2019), *Performance Phenomenology: To the Thing Itself*, Cham: Springer Nature and Palgrave Macmillan.

Johnston, Daniel (2017), *Theatre and Phenomenology: Manual Philosophy*, London: Red Globe Press.

Bodies in Flight

1989–1995

The First Series

Performance
as
Energy, Ideas
and Provocation

In the late 1980s and early 1990s, Bodies in Flight crashed the UK experimental performance party at a time when two streams of emerging artists and groups were colliding: those educated in arts schools and those in universities. Labels mattered and allegiances and aesthetic definitions were hotly contested, even political topics: we remember the rowdy artists' talks and events that were held on the fringes of the annual National Review of Live Art (NRLA) in Glasgow and the exclusion of experimental performance from 'mainstream' institutions such as the National Theatre and Royal Court which defined 'new writing' in exclusively text-based forms. Then the radical political consensus of most theatre-makers thought work not derived from a play script was suspect, if not essentially indulgent and pretentious: see the critical writings of playwrights such as Edward Bond and Trevor Griffiths.

Bodies in Flight specifically fled the play with its teleology of intention and message: narrative was fragmented into short stage images, often emotionally driven by overblown classical or rock music. The stability and predictability of storytelling was replaced by the energy and excitement of abandoning one image, that had its own logic and sense, and fleeing apparently haphazardly to another with a completely contradictory logic and sense. This restlessness quickly became a predominant feature of the series of works that burst into life in those few years. Whereas most other companies sought to establish an identifiable approach, a signature that could be deepened and marketed, each Bodies in Flight show was characterized by its differentiation from its predecessor: *Exhibit*'s hectic montage of politically charged images was followed by the abstract white cube and extended sections of choreography of *Love Is Natural and Real but Not for You my Love*; *iwannabewolfman*'s interior Freudian world by *Rough*'s cabaret troupe and direct address; then the proscenium-arch set-up of these first works by *Beautiful Losers*' and *Littluns Wake*'s environmental spaces.

Increasingly through this initial series of works, the fundamental relationship of language to gesture in performance, indexing the more profound tension between imagination and representation in all live art, became an organizing principle. At a time when many companies were eschewing the spoken word altogether or degrading it to meaningless lists or trite paradoxes, Bodies in Flight embraced text as an integral part of 'physical theatre' in a specifically deconstructive mode, pinpointing 'postmodern' tropes around identity, gender and sexuality. We were trying to provoke audiences to think through such 'post-structuralist' mantras as 'there is nothing outside the text'; to reach towards a potentially more troubling space–time where–when only performance as an artform could exist. Here the performance-event dwelt in an unconcealing irresolvability between gesture and word, image and sound, action and imagination, affect and effect, its wonders to perform.

2
Deadplay (1989)

Figure 2.1: *Deadplay*: performer Barnaby Power. Photograph: courtesy of Bodies in Flight.

Figure 2.2: *Deadplay*: poster. Courtesy of the University of Bristol Theatre Collection.

STUDIOSPACE AT THE ARNOLFINI, 7.20 PM, SUN 25 JUNE
RECAST REWROUGHT REPLAYED

PUBLICITY COPY
Play dead play playing dead somehow / by a deployment of bodies in flight (is creation, they say) and properties culled from the commonplaces (you know, Wagnerian musical chairs / Caravaggio's nowyousee-itnowyoudon't) they hope to pull it off.
It is blind faith in the plague that drives them on. Through the various theatrical deaths / the hysterical posturing.
(Replicate in panic, the old man used to say.) These days to describe is to name catastrophe.
There is an old story — about a body that in flight / headlong down the double helix / freefalling across the desert / actually broke through (by deceiving the third eye). *The spectator (incidentally an actor in real life) desires to know the mechanics of the trick (it's a showstopper).*
On this point / as on many others / we beg to defer.

What turned out to be Bodies in Flight's first show started as an extra-curricular project in the Department of Drama, University of Bristol. We entered an open platform event at Arnolfini (Bristol) and got selected for the NRLA (Glasgow); we were then selected for the 'best of' NRLA at The Place (London). The show was a playful piece on how performance can find its roots in children's games: in this instance, their delight in playing dead and coming back to life. Set to the austere music of Wagner's *Parsifal*, an opera about death and renewal, it deliberately trod a fine line between solemnity and parody of physical theatre's often grandiose concerns, attempting to have its cake and eat it: to enjoy playing dead whilst mocking the po-faced, 'cool' performance scene.

RIK BOULTON performer, DEAN BYFIELD performer, RACHEL FEUCHTWANG performer, SIMON JONES devisor and director, MARTIN PLUNKETT performer, BARNABY POWER performer, JUSTIN O'SHAUGHNESSY performer.

Music: *Parsifal* (Richard Wagner).

Performed: Bristol University, Arnolfini (Bristol), National Review of Live Art at Third Eye (Glasgow), Playroom (Lancaster University), Wickham Theatre (Bristol), The Place (London).

```
D  E  A  D  P  L  A  Y                    /1/
```

```
    1 → B/O
10  2 → 2/5/10
     P R E L U D E ( 1 )   Rachel turn/
                            DEAN
                            D̶e̶s̶t̶r̶o̶y̶ turn/

                            Justin guilt/
                            DEAN
    3 → B/O (music)         D̶e̶s̶t̶r̶o̶y̶ corpse.
    4 → 2/5/10                                 MARTIN
     P R E L U D E ( 2 )   Boys embracing/Rachel praying/M̶i̶k̶e̶ lying/

                            Rachel turn/
                            MARTIN
                            M̶i̶k̶e̶ twitch/ ressurect/
    5 → ADD 1/2/4           Others amazed/
                            MARTIN
                            M̶i̶k̶e̶ off table/shows stigmata/

                            Rachel faints/
    6 → B/O (music)         Boys step forward.


    7 → 1/2/3              MARTIN  TO CHAIR
     M A N S I O N ( 1 )   M̶i̶k̶e̶ walk d̶s̶r̶/ change/SIT/

                            Others walk sl/ run as they pass/
    8 → ADD 5/11            Rachel on table/ Justin stab/ DEAN look at MARTIN/Rachel/
                                                          D̶e̶s̶t̶r̶o̶y̶         M̶i̶k̶e̶
    9 → ADD 4/7             Rachel about to fall/ DEAN joy/ Justin catch/ Rachel flap/
        LOSE 3                                    D̶e̶s̶t̶r̶o̶y̶                              DEAN
                            DEAN pain/ die/ MARTIN look at Rachel/ Rachel slide/ grief D̶e̶s̶t̶r̶o̶y̶/
                            D̶e̶s̶t̶r̶o̶y̶           M̶i̶k̶e̶
   10 → ADD 9               Justin to MARTIN/ M̶i̶k̶e̶ pain/ die/
                                      M̶i̶k̶e̶
                                             MARTIN ON CHAIR
                            Justin prop up M̶i̶k̶e̶/ Rachel look/ run on to table/
   11 → LOSE 4/7            Rachel/ Justin look/ DEAN resurrects/ walks sr/
                                                 D̶e̶s̶t̶r̶o̶y̶
                            Rachel about to fall/ Justin catch/ push her back/ Rachel guilt/
                                                   DEAN
                            Justin guilt/ to D̶e̶s̶t̶r̶o̶y̶/ embrace/
   12 → LOSE 5/11           Rachel pain/ die/ roll off table/ crawl underneath/
                            MARTIN
                            M̶i̶k̶e̶ resurrects/ boys watch/ look at each other/ GESTURE
   13 → ADD 7               DEAN pull out Rachel/ grief over her/
                            D̶e̶s̶t̶r̶o̶y̶
                                                MARTIN
                            Justin pain/ die/ M̶i̶k̶e̶ catch him/ carry him dsc/
   14 → ADD 8
        LOSE 9
```

FIGURE 2.3: *Deadplay*: performers Justin O'Shaughnessy and Barnaby Power. Image from contact sheet courtesy of the University of Bristol Theatre Collection.

FIGURE 2.4: *Deadplay* VHS video still: performers Justin O'Shaughnessy, Rachel Feuchtwang, Barnaby Power and Martin Plunkett. Image: Tony Judge.

FIGURE 2.5: *Deadplay*: opening page of the performance score. Image courtesy of the University of Bristol Theatre Collection.

3

Playing Dead ... Becoming Professional

RACHEL FEUCHTWANG

RACHEL FEUCHTWANG is Managing Director of Productions at The National Theatre in The Netherlands, the largest Dutch language touring company for text-based theatre. Until March 2023 she was Managing Director of the visual and movement-based theatre company Schweigman&, best known for its ground-breaking performance in site-specific sensory spaces, touring the Netherlands and internationally. She worked with Michael Morris in Cultural Industry in the 1990s bringing international artists to the United Kingdom, including Pina Bausch, Robert Wilson, and Robert Lepage. Together they produced the music-theatre Shockheaded Peter. After relocating to Amsterdam in 2000, she was Head of Arts for the British Council Netherlands. She strategized at the think tank Kennisland, mentored on the Dutch Cultural Leadership programme, and produced works with artists Dries Verhoeven, Roos van Geffen and Edit Kaldor. Rachel also teaches Creative Producing at the Amsterdam Academy for Theatre and Dance and on the DAS Creative Producing MA.

Here Rachel recalls her experience of making the first Bodies in Flight work – Deadplay.

Was it 1989?

I was in my second year studying Drama at Bristol University. Simon was my lecturer. Although my recollection from more than 30 years ago is a bit hazy, recalling my sense of how it felt to be 21 in Bristol at that time is easier to bring into focus. The Drama Department was a heated, intense, confusing and stimulating place to be, full of young people acting out, projecting insecurities and status anxieties onto each other. Everyone was positioning themselves, rubbing up against ideas, people, movements and philosophies, trying them on for size and taste. What to think? How to apply it? Who to trust? How to get on?

How to survive? What does it all mean? Why are we here? Or maybe that's just how it seemed. I was 21 and it was a heady time. Now, I'm a practising producer after having been managing director of a conceptual theatre company. I teach masters and undergraduate students part-time at the University of the Arts Amsterdam. Creative Producing (my teaching area) is inherently rooted in the artistic and creative content of an idea or concept and bringing the right ingredients to the practice to allow that idea or concept to flourish and develop with audiences and partners. The seeds were sown in 1989, although I wasn't actively pursuing this as a career path. The joy of the context within which Bodies in Flight emerged was that it uniquely combined creative and artistic practice with conceptual ideas and theoretical underpinning, something I now realize sadly was unique.

As students, we were steeped in critical theories of language, text and performance. *Deadplay* felt like we could fling it all into the mix along with anything else we thought might be interesting. Because it was Simon's concept, it felt good that there wasn't any status jostling or palaver with hierarchies or controlling the content. We were his players, and we were all playing, quite literally in *Deadplay*, the childhood game of playing dead, hysterical posturing: falling off tables in the rehearsal space, invoking Masaccio's *Expulsion from Eden*, Caravaggio's *The Incredulity of Thomas*, running in flimsy clothes behind a gauze, brandishing wooden crucifixes and squirting ketchup over each other, with Simon directing and giggling constantly. We enjoyed ourselves immensely. I don't think we were taking ourselves very seriously. That was why it felt so much less heated and pressurized than, for example, our graduation shows.

I remember it was spring and chilly in the rehearsal space. We worked on this motif movement we called 'ecstasying': a shake that started somewhere deep within your centre and gradually took over your whole body until it spiralled up and out of you in an expulsion of ecstasy. It felt like we did this for hours and got a lot of bruises from the flinging about. Poring over bad photocopies of Renaissance paintings and listening to crackly recordings of Wagner's *Parsifal*, performing was a joy. I remember Simon remarking that I had no sense of danger, a comment on my abandonment as I threw myself off a table. I think we'd seen Wim Vandekeybus for the first time and were determined to tumble and crash and fly about, wanting to have those gorgeous athletic dancers' bodies. There was a great deal of trust between us all, which is funny because outside of *Deadplay* I think we weren't quite as sure of each other.

I can't remember if we were originally intending to perform only within the Drama Department, but at some point, I saw an announcement that the Arnolfini was holding a selection for submissions to the National Review of Live Art (NRLA). I had been to the NRLA the previous year in 1988 at the Third Eye Centre in Glasgow. It had been an eye-opening experience, a multitude of happenings, performances at all times of the day and night, across Sauchiehall Street, on street corners and in grubby porticos, in every tiny nook and cranny of the Third Eye Centre. This early exposure to performance and live art influenced a great deal of my thinking about performative practice and presentation platforms later in my own work. Invoking that exciting and exhilarating sensation as a visitor of not entirely knowing what's going on, not always sure if it's any good, but always on the edge and unpredictable, and just going for it anyhow. We decided to submit *Deadplay*. I didn't have a plan; I just thought it made sense to do something more with it than only showing our peers.

There's always a moment when you're making a new piece when you realize there's an audience. Because the process of making work is very introspective, even though you're making it for a live audience, when that interpersonal dynamic comes into play, the whole thing shifts. With *Deadplay*, it felt like we had been spending our time in rehearsals larking around; we were constantly in fits of laughter at ourselves. Then Simon hung up a gauze, some lights were rigged, we found some dusty suits and a flimsy dress for me, *Parsifal* was played through the PA, and there was a show, which we performed at the Arnolfini for the NRLA selection. And while we were suppressing our involuntary giggles and replacing them with performed 'corpsings', the audience on the other side of the gauze, albeit not huge in numbers, responded enthusiastically. To our pleasure and surprise, it was selected for the showcase platform for The Third Eye Centre in Glasgow later that autumn.

At the time, I definitely had no idea what my future career plans were. The only thing I was sure of was that performance and live art were something that challenged, inspired and provoked me, and I wanted to do more of it. I knew I wanted to pursue this diffuse area of performance and art, blurred lines and ideas about ways of seeing, thinking about and experiencing the world, and the performance of it. For me, the Drama Department in 1989 was a catalysing collision where critical and theoretical inputs came into a sharper focus when applied to practical projects, not only in theatre but also in film, and what was then called new media. It was more than seeing and experiencing other people's work, that radically challenged our perspectives on theatre: it was making our own work, the stuff we were experimenting with ourselves that was hugely productive, creative and exploratory. *Deadplay* was an extension of this lively and invigorating experimentation, and went further by presupposing that it merited professional exposure. As performers, we were all entering our final academic year, so the transition into professional practice and working in the real world was a tangible and conscious preoccupation. And the performance worked, it all came together in that delicious synchronicity of the right ingredients at the right moment, with an audience response that gave us the confidence to pursue extending the shelf-life of *Deadplay*, and thus Bodies in Flight as a fledgling company.

I can't remember anything about the performances, where they took place in the Third Eye, how many times, who came, etc. But the glitterati of live art was there: Neil Bartlett introduced each performance with a change of dress; Derek Jarman presented an installation; Bobby Baker was around; John Jordan, Lois Keidan and Nikki Millican as NRLA's Artistic Director were everywhere. It was where I met peers who became life-long friends and associates. With hindsight, it's easy to see certain events in your life as turning points, but I am absolutely certain that the convergence of people and events that happened around the first Bodies in Flight performance of *Deadplay* had a particular cogency and clarity that prompted a whole series of choices for me. I realize now that performing at the NRLA was one of my first tastes of producing, introducing me to the awful task of persuading programmers and curators to be interested in you or the work you want them to see. And I'm still doing it and still haven't exhausted my research of how to produce, 34 years later. Although not working in UK live art, I have produced conceptual, avant-garde, physical and visual theatre and performance that take place both within and outside of the theatre black box. Much of my network was formed in 1989; a great deal of the basic references of performance, conceptual and theoretical thinking that I first encountered then is still resonating now, so much so that I still work with some of the peers I 'grew up with' then in 1989.

Further Reading

Klein, Jenny (2006), 'Genre-bending performance', *PAJ: A Journal of Performance and Art*, 28:1, pp. 58–66.

4
Exhibit (1990)

Studiospace: V.A.R.: FRI/SAT, 9/10 MAR at 7.00 PM (7.30 PM).

PUBLICITY COPY
What're you gawping at? what d'you think you're doing? + there's nothing more to be said (I get it, this is a dialogue) + don't look at me like that: stop peering at me like + like what he said: not a question: you're the one strutting your stuff (naff, but carry on): I didn't force you + no: there was no arguing with that: but don't sit back in your seat like you weren't responsible (well naff word that, but keep going) + o not scruples: o not education: o no not: he was in full flow: all that jazz (embarrassing) (you started it). (no I didn't) + I'm going to expose myself physically and (applause, then hush) (hurry up). We settled into our seats, the arguments rehearsed. There's always one smart Alec that holds up the show. (dim lights). They're going to remove their (shhh, don't spoil it). Let's watch and see what happens (go on then).

We returned to the National Review of Live Art with our second work – a montage of hard-hitting scenes that explored our culture's exhibitionism, our desire both to see and be seen, to expose ourselves and to peer into the private lives of others, all set to a loud and unrelenting soundtrack. With a curtain that was constantly opened to reveal and closed to tease, the show set out to provoke and challenge the voyeurism that underpins both our popular culture and its experimental and avant-garde counterparts.

LUCY BALDWYN performer, JON CARNALL video camera, SIMON JONES devisor and director, JUSTIN O'SHAUGHNESSY technical manager, SIMON PEGG performer, BARNABY POWER performer, CHRIS RATCLIFF performer, CHARLOTTE WATKINS performer.

Performed: Wickham Theatre (Bristol) and National Review of Live Art at Third Eye (Glasgow).

FIGURE 4.1: *Exhibit*: performers featuring Lucy Baldwyn. Photo: Jon Carnall.

FIGURE 4.2: *Exhibit*: poster. Courtesy of the University of Bristol Theatre Collection.

FIGURE 4.3 (next): *Exhibit*: performers featuring Charlotte Watkins. Photo: Jon Carnall.

FIGURE 4.4 (next): *Exhibit*: performers Lucy Baldwyn and Barnaby Power. Photo: Jon Carnall.

FIGURE 4.5 (next): *Exhibit*: performers featuring Lucy Baldwyn. Photo: Jon Carnall.

FIGURE 4.6 (next): *Exhibit*: performers Charlotte Watkins, Simon Pegg, Lucy Baldwyn and Chris Ratcliff. Photo: Jon Carnall.

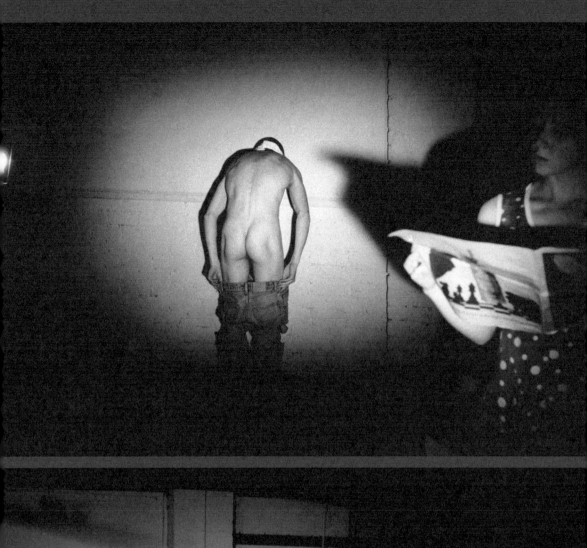
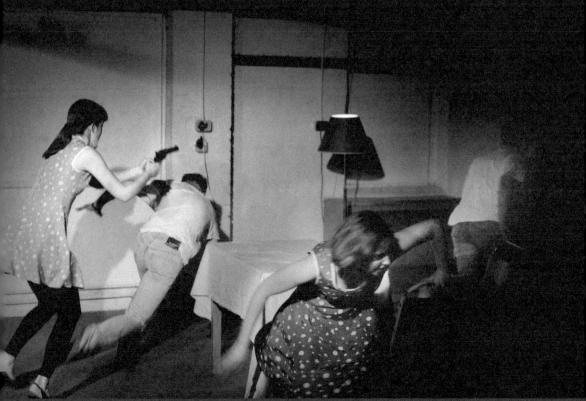

5
Controlled Chaos
BARNABY POWER

BARNABY POWER's theatre credits include: Laurel and Hardy, A Midsummer Night's Dream, Faust *and* Charlie Sonata, *all at Edinburgh Lyceum;* Interiors *and* The Destroyed Room *for Vanishing Point Theatre Company;* Twelfth Night *and* Comedy of Errors *for the Royal Shakespeare Company; and the original productions of Anthony Nielson's* The Wonderful World of Dissocia, Narrative *and* Edward Gant's Amazing Feat of Loneliness, *as well as* I Am Dandy *for The David Gale Company,* Somersaults *for National Theatre of Scotland and* Faust *for Headlong Theatre Company. He co-wrote* Self Storage *for Radio 4 and has a podcast called* Helpself with Matty.

Here Barnaby recalls making Bodies in Flight's first shows and how that influenced later collaborations with writers.

As I remember, being in Bodies in Flight was exciting and just damn good fun. I'm sure it can't actually have been so. I imagine rehearsals were protracted, painful and bad-tempered, but I loved performing the shows, especially *Deadplay* and *Exhibit*. I wanted to work with a group of like-minded people who valued experimentation, creative autonomy and self-determination, where company roles were defined but flexible, and Bodies in Flight seemed to fulfil this. In the late 1980s, there was a definite sense that you could get new, experimental work in front of audiences quickly without having to go through various stages of development. The audience would judge it before anyone else. The point was the performance. Why else do it? Taking the risk of putting on shows like *Deadplay* and *Exhibit* was energizing and, with no outside interference, the work was heartfelt and pure, if a little rough. The closest I've ever got to being in a band. And we were young. We were going to change the world. We performed at festivals with other vibrant companies that felt the same. Of course, we immediately despised their work, then a bit later secretly admired it. We played the National Review of Live Art (NRLA) in Glasgow (1989), where there were multiple shows in one building, over three days and nights, as well as installations, talks and debates. I think we did one performance each day, but hardly left the building.

Deadplay started off as a satire on live art: we assumed the po-faced playing style of the time to recreate scenes from Caravaggio paintings, which then somehow degenerated into a western saloon gunfight, soundtracked by Wagner. All nicked from shows we had seen, of course, and frankly ridiculous. However, to do it properly we had to take it extremely seriously – no mean feat when squirting tomato ketchup at dimly lit fellow performers before dying beautifully, perfectly in time to the epic pitches of *Parsifal*. Try it; it's not easy. Incredibly, audiences seemed to get it, and their laughter proved there was room for comedy in this kind of experimental work.

So much so that we were invited back to the NRLA festival the following year with our second show, *Exhibit*: a series of about 50 short scenes beginning and ending on the opening and closing of a curtain just in front of the audience, and played out on a narrow, deep stage so we could shift the depth of field. It opened with Iggy Pop's *Lust for Life* blaring out (several years before this track was used in the film *Trainspotting*) as we rushed at the audience before the curtain shut on us. It was closed by whoever was free, and then we all scrambled to a list pinned up on the wall to see what came next. The piece ended with me being covered in honey and wrapped in bandages like a mummy. I'm still trying to work out why. I'm sure there was some deep meaning behind it all, but I don't remember us talking about it. It just felt instinctively right to let the audience take from it what they wanted: and we wanted to provoke those differing reactions. I remember particularly a scene when we walked towards the audience as if at a border crossing, holding up our passports, while Nico sang *Deutschland Über Alles*. After that, it was no big surprise that we were not invited to the major international festival in Germany we had been hoping to attend.

Being in Bodies in Flight left me with the knowledge of how exciting and invigorating live performance can be: a sort of controlled chaos, like life. And how essential is the relationship between performers and audience. I've drawn on the experience in different ways ever since in every role I've played. For example, in working on the original productions of Anthony Neilson's plays – *The Wonderful World of Dissocia* and *Narrative*, where comedy and tragic horror often co-exist, an actor has to commit to every moment within shifting tones and genres. Also in Vanishing Point's devised works – *Interiors* and *The Destroyed Room*, where, as part of a wider multimedia canvas, just being on stage in itself adds crucially to the overall drama. All attitudes and moves I'd first tried out with Bodies in Flight in 1990.

6
Love Is Natural and Real but Not for You my Love (1990)

FIGURE 6.1: *Love Is Natural and Real but Not for You my Love*: performers Justin O'Shaughnessy, Katherine Porter and Ursula Lea. Photo: Lucy Baldwyn.

FIGURE 6.2: *Love Is Natural and Real but Not for You my Love*: postcard. Courtesy of the University of Bristol Theatre Collection.

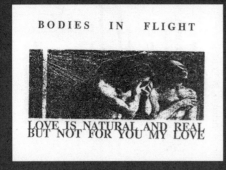

BODIES IN FLIGHT
LOVE IS NATURAL AND REAL BUT NOT FOR YOU MY LOVE

P<small>UBLICITY COPY</small>
A challenge brings something into being
A seduction tempts it into another form
Upon the fictionalization of a passionate affair
(the necessary kiss-and-tell)
Upon the ecstatic chaos of seductions within seductions
(love's strange attractors).
A manifesto for lovers: combining original score and text with stylised choreography, the piece is a meditation upon the implications of the science of chaos for the politics of desire.

This show represented a step-change in our work across a range of areas: choreographer Sara Giddens worked with text written by Simon Jones; we worked with an original score composed by Christopher Austin and a set designed by Bridget Mazzey. We made the work alongside *Exhibit* and in many ways in complete contrast to it: where *Exhibit* was all sound and fury, 'in-yer-face' posturing, *Love Is …* was abstract, elusive, philosophical in its concerns, musing on the relations between chaos theory, quantum mechanics and human relationships. The only record of the show, apart from the script, is a series of black-and-white photographs since at the time we were against documentation as we thought it could never adequately capture the work and was attempting somehow to steal the soul of the live performance.

CHRISTOPHER AUSTIN composer, NITIN CHANDRA GANATRA performer, SARA GIDDENS choreographer, SIMON JONES writer/director, URSULA LEA performer, BRIDGET MAZZEY designer, JUSTIN O'SHAUGHNESSY performer, KATHERINE PORTER performer.

Music performed by: ROBERT LAMB flute/piccolo/alto flute, LARA MEPHAM oboe/cor anglais, ROBERT PLANE clarinet/bass clarinet, COLIN APPLEBY horn, JEREMY LITTLE percussion, DIGGORY SEACOME percussion, JAMES HOPPER violin, SARAH OGDEN violin, BECCIE PEARCE violin, LISA ISTED viola, ALAN CHARLTON cello, BEN GROENEVELT double bass.

With: LUCY BALDWYN photography, DAVID JONES set construction.

Performed: Wickham Theatre (Bristol), Playroom (Lancaster University), Prema Arts (Dursley).

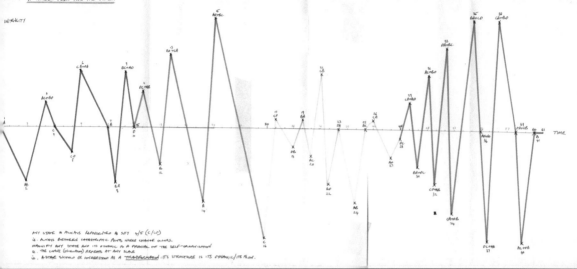

FIGURE 6.3: *Love Is Natural and Real but Not for You my Love* 'energy graph'. Image courtesy of the University of Bristol Theatre Collection.

FIGURE 6.4: *Love Is Natural and Real but Not for You my Love*: performers Justin O'Shaughnessy, Ursula Lea, Katherine Porter and Nitin Chandra Ganatra. Photo: Lucy Baldwyn.

PROGRAMME NOTE: MANIFESTO

BODIES IN FLIGHT […] believes it is the buzz of ideas, their disruptions and epiphanies, which is needed to re-energize whole domains of our culture and expand the consciousnesses and commitments of artists and audiences alike, not some simple appeal to 'accessibility' or 'commercialism'. We believe this craving for the idea is universal and one of the few truly democratizing forces in our society today. Hence, the attacks by fundamentalists, ideologues and philistines. We align ourselves and our work with all those people resisting these and attempting to describe and embody the possibilities of freedom and justice in the future.

FIGURE 6.5: *Love Is Natural and Real but Not for You my Love*: performers Nitin Chandra Ganatra, Katherine Porter, Ursula Lea and Justin O'Shaughnessy. Photo: Lucy Baldwyn.

7
My (Other) Other Collaborator: Philosophy Alongside Practice

SIMON JONES

In this Flight, I make an argument for an entirely different way of thinking about the relationship between the practice of making a performance and philosophizing or theorizing about performance. I challenge the orthodoxy that the one can be explained by the other, or that the one explicates the other. However, the two do work productively alongside one another. This notion of alongside-ness informs how collaborations and materials in Bodies in Flight's practice develop, such as the choreographic and textual in Do the Wild Thing! *or the musical and textual in* Skinworks *or the choreographic and photographic in* Model Love. *Being in-between is established as both a fundamental practical approach in the devising workshop and a fundamental philosophical insight into writing about performance.*

I founded Bodies in Flight in 1989 to provide opportunities to work professionally both for emerging theatre-makers from the University of Bristol's Department of Drama and myself. At the time, as an academic, the work I was making was considered invalid as research. I stubbornly pursued it under the 'protection' of 'academic freedom'; but its status within academia remained problematic, even suspect. I felt I needed to test my practice out alongside other artists working in a professional context: I needed validation in both personal and career terms. In parallel with that practice, I advocated within the discipline of Theatre and Performance Studies for creative work to be a modality of research every bit as rigorous and impactful as so-called 'traditional forms of scholarship'. That struggle, though never fully accomplished, is now largely won, so much so that I became the first Professor of Performance at the University of Bristol.

I have been invited to speak about 'practice-as-research' in Australia, Canada, France, The Netherlands, Singapore, South Africa and the United States. I have been visiting artist at Banff Arts Centre and The School of the Art Institute of Chicago, as well as visiting scholar at Amsterdam University. I have published extensively on both Bodies in Flight and the rationalizations underpinning 'practice-as-research' in journals and academic publications, most notably – *The Cambridge History of British Theatre*, *Performance Research*, *Practice as Research in Performance and Screen* (2009) and *Artists in the Archive* (2018). In these ways, I have always found myself and my practice in-between the two worlds of professional arts-practices and academia: at first in the 1990s, awkwardly, sometimes furtively in either context; more recently, confidently and openly, when the mutually beneficial relationship between contemporary performance practices and higher-education institutions became well understood by all concerned (even funders and their political paymasters). For me, this Flight advances my ongoing *being-in-between* these two wonderful and inspiring hothouses of creativity and insight: I re-define their fundamental relationship as a complementarity predicated on their very different uses of philosophy, that is, their modes of *thinking being*.

There are multifarious ways in which philosophy or theory has enriched the constellation of studies that came together over time and across many institutions worldwide, to form what we recognize today as Dance, Performance and Theatre Studies. More commonly, these relatively new disciplines have viewed dance and performance as an 'object of study' through many productive and varied theoretical and critical frameworks. Early on in Performance Studies' formation, multiple perspectives from Anthropology, History, Language and Literature Studies afforded the new discipline rigour and credibility in a competitive higher-education ecology. Later generations of dance and performance scholars added semiotics, structuralism and post-structuralism, modernism and post-modernism, Marxist and cultural materialist, feminist and queer, Black and Asian and postcolonial frames. So much so that one cannot study dance or performance as a discipline without applying some kind of explicit theoretical or philosophical discourse. We have come to expect performance to be understood by way of these frames, its ephemerality to be supported by the 'solid' foundations of philosophers and its expressions to be read off against the keywords of multiple 'objective' theorizations (see Chapter 1, 'Unconcealing This Maker's Voice').

Instead, I want to argue for a special relation between philosophy and theatre, as one predicated not on explication or justification or validation; but one of incommensurable activities: a special relation of profound *unalikeness*, structured by mutually exclusive, but nevertheless necessary positions: from the inside and from the outside of making (for more on 'complementarity' and 'unalikeness', see Chapter 28, 'Being In-Between: Collaboration as Non-Collaboration'). These cannot be superimposed because they entail contradictory vectors or dynamics of thinking: one towards those others involved in the making, both as collaborators and as participants; and the other by way of a solitary withdrawing of thinking from out of making, without any body, beyond the possibility of be-ing.

I first encountered this 'unalikeness' unexpectedly when conceiving *Love Is Natural and Real but Not for You my Love*. Then I tried to align my reading of theory with my making of work by way of a chart (see Figure 6.3). Because I was collaborating for the first time professionally with choreographer Sara Giddens and composer Chris Austin, I thought a theoretical framework would help structure the material in the show – Sara's choreography, Chris's music and my text . The show, I think, failed to realize its full potential, not only because of the programmatic density of the Deleuzian theorizations I was inspired by, which placed an unfamiliar language between the collaborators; but more fundamentally because I was trying to relate theory and practice from a third impossible position, attempting to be both outside the outside of theory and outside the inside of practice at the same time. The best that could have been achieved was a dry and sterile representation of the theory by the practice and an equally self-referential and circuitous explanation of the practice by the theory. The irksome experience of *Love Is* … forced me to re-think a theatre-maker's relation to philosophizing as much more a complementarity, within which the more one sought any particular quality or sense, the more all others disappeared. Echoing quantum mechanics, this mutual exclusiveness was more profound than simply not being able to philosophize performance and perform philosophy in the same work: it was actually impossible to philosophize and to perform at the same time and place: these are two entirely different worlds. So, throughout the rest of the 1990s, my work with Bodies in Flight took place entirely separately from what I came to call – my *writing alongside*: a 'theoretical' Ph.D. which applied scientific models of creativity in nature to performance.

Years later, I discovered that Martin Heidegger had already defined this incommensurability as philosophy's 'imageless thought' in opposition to art's 'imageful making':

> Seeking refuge in poetry means fleeing from the keen boldness of the question of being, which always shatters machination of beings and its denial of be-ing [the supra-individual force of life itself] and must persevere in the unease and cleft of a breakage so that thinking be-ing never dares come to rest in a 'work'. To philosophy belongs the serenity of the mastery of imageless knowing-awareness.
> (2006: 42, my gloss)

Here, poetry stands in for all art. Heidegger breaks with the artist as the decisive thinker of be-ing by requiring the shedding of all concrete aspects, such as the image, in his meditating on truth as (in his words) 'thinking along [...] more originally (not more correctly)' (2006: 62). The philosopher's imageless thought is here opposed *critically* to the artist's imageful making, in that much of Heidegger's previous espousal of the artwork as opening up a special (non-)place of knowing-awareness was predicated upon the concreteness of the artwork's materiality in the shape of images. Heidegger suggests that philosophy alone preserves the necessary will to think beyond the image, beyond method or the certainties of subject–object relations or the reassurances of productive labour. In his aesthetics, '*Da-sein* is incomparable, and admits no perspective within which it could still be lodged as something familiar': it literally 'forestalls all mania for explanation' (2006: 288). Previously, this had applied equally, if differently, to both art and philosophy as the two privileged realms of human activity able to approach be-ing/*Da-sein*. However, now they confront one another in a fundamentally complementary pairing, derived from their mutually exclusive relation to the image, thence to a circulation of images, in short – a culture and a world. Whereas art works by actualizing its concepts and concerns in the materiality of the image, philosophy takes an entirely different trajectory – towards the purest possible abstraction, devoid of images or any other concrete reference to the world.

This position seems reasonable, even absurdly orthodox in its echoes of the metaphor of 'Plato's Cave'. Let's not forget that philosophy's first move is to remove thought from contingency, context, environment and even from time, to become the most abstract of all human endeavours: I might even say – the most non-human. Whereas theatre is the art form of mixing – persons, ideas and media; the most mixed of all arts, using as its medium the performer's flesh, as conduit, conductor. Theatre is thinking in its most situatedness, in the one time and place of the performance, the irreversible dynamic of inter-relations between all participants – actors and auditor-spectators, all gathered together here now. Whereas philosophy registers its truthfulness by the extent to which its thinking can be detached from any situation, taken out of any time, stilled, reversed or applied variously; theatre *is* only in that moment and in that place for those persons present.

Perhaps, it is this very unalikeness that provokes many artist-scholars to approach philosophizing. Indeed, I now see philosophy, from its own point of view, as a necessary refuge from being in the midst of making with its dynamic flows of energy and information, *because of* its imagelessness, precisely because it sheds the situation, the context, the concrete, the matter. I am freed from the weight of my own flesh and from the responsibility towards my collaborators: *freed for a time to imagine without images.* This blissful uncluttering of the mind is a retreat from the havoc and tumult of making with its unending labour of trying to realize the impossible just-so-ness of an image, its insistent irreversibility, its unremitting call to decisiveness, all of which energize theatre and essentialize it as an art: because it is in the instance of a decision taken and witnessed by an audience, that theatre appears quintessentially *as theatre*, most itself, always as if for the first time.

Philosophizing frees me from all that – which is as much as to say, it gives me the best perspective from which to look at my own making, from the impossible point of view of pure unsituatedness and abstractedness, or rather – from the vector of flight, escaping towards, but never reaching, pure unsituatedness, to look back at the thing most situated and contingent – the performance. This is the most insightful perspective because to travel along this vector, I jump over the middle ground of the everyday, the normalizing zone to which theatre, its audiences and its makers must eventually return. This everyday drives professionalism in the need to make a living, nurture a career, sustain an audience and a critical position within a culture. Philosophy allows me to jump over this middle ground of 'objective' critical or 'subjective' professional practices, both of which, in their own ways, reduce performance to a game of compare-and-contrast, normative in teleology, supplanting the authentic 'I' with the inauthentic 'They' of either critic or professional expert peers. In reaching out to philosophy from the inside of collaborating, I am taken out the other end of this middle ground towards a de-personalized absolute, diametrically opposed to what each of us does as artists in putting our very selves at stake in the work.

Sara and I describe collaborating in making theatre as a non-collaboration, a dwelling amongst unalikes – the other collaborator as absolutely otherly with their different skillsets, media, their very flesh put forward *as flesh*: a radical otherness through which each collaborator's art and will must work by way of what they cannot understand, both at the mercy of, but ultimately entrusted to, the other in a caring and graceful collaborating (see Chapter 28, 'Being In-Between:

Collaboration as Non-Collaboration'). So, by this definition, philosophy must be the perfect collaborator because it is so utterly other, that the only possible collaboration is by way of complete non-collaboration, from the inside of practice towards the outside, and from the outside of philosophy towards the inside: in essence, imageless, because philosophy even attempts to be outside thought, a 'pure' idea outside of its having been thought: an idea without a person, utterly dissociated from them who first thought it. Paradoxically, however properly the idea approaches the universal, its quality, its mood and its resonances can only be known by way of particular persons, who each experience the universal in their own way, as one soul stands in for heaven, one creature for creation, one thought for mind and one breath for be-ing. Then, philosophy needs these persons to animate, energize and inform the idea so that every thought becomes a kind of event where—when the idea is *mixed back into life.*

    So, philosophy needs theatre to be thought, or at least, some kind of practical idea of theatre, such as rhetoric, to be embodied again *as thinking*. Despite its vector outwards, philosophy, like everything else in be-ing, cannot be without time and event: be-ing is being-historical; and there is a time for encountering philosophy, then a time when I return to practice with what I have thought of philosophy. So, whilst philosophy may well be without images, it is not without time: my engagement with the ideas is situated amongst a series of works, in the flow of a developing practice, itself only making sense amongst the practices of others. With philosophy as my collaborator, my understanding is not only a retrospective but a prospective knowing-awareness, collaborating with memory, the archive and my embodied practice, to know again and in a different way both theatres past and theatres yet to come. These crossings-across practice and its outside force me as a theatre-maker to respond to philosophy *poetically*, literally metaphorically – as a forcing of meaning from its proper sense to another, a kind of synaesthetics, as blind Gloucester would say in *King Lear* – 'I see it feelingly' (4.6.147). Where the philosopher thinks of an imageless idea, I emerge from the time of philosophy searching, or rather, feeling for images: or more precisely, I emerge thinking of a situation, a set-up, theatrically as an instance of an idea becoming flesh, incarnating. Each instance is then bundled up in the intensity of the performance event as a complementarity, so the more I practise the less I theorize, the more I know the less I practise and yet somehow without channels they communicate, through my flesh they collaborate.

    Although one mixes and the other abstracts, both *in deed* collaborate: one through intimate mixing; the other through intimate thinking: one in the tumult of fleshes; the other in the refuge of mindfulness:

one full of images and persons; the other emptied of images and absenting itself from a body, any body. Performance is made within this compossible duetting as the actualizing of an impossible field of potentiality between fleshes and ideas. So, when I make work amongst others, this philosophizing becomes my other other collaborator, solitary and without. It may well be indicative of the productivity of any practice-as-research work in the readiness or otherwise with which it can be coupled with writing alongside. I might say that the less readily practice gives itself over to such writing philosophically, the closer it leans towards a purely professional enterprise. And the more readily, the greater the risk of the work disappearing into the 'criticality' of the concept-history, literally explaining it away. Both must collaborate in the unsettling and re-in-forcing relating the one to the other, as each collaboration's unalikeness works away at itself as the very force of its own invention.

> We live from acts – and from the very act of being, just as we live from ideas and sentiments. [...] We relate ourselves to it with a relation that is neither theoretical nor practical. Behind theory and practice, there is enjoyment of theory and practice: the egoism of life. The final relation is enjoyment, happiness.
> (Levinas 1969: 113)

> Theatre [...] is the only art of life.
> (Derrida 1978: 247)

References

Derrida, Jacques (1978), 'The theatre of cruelty and the closure of representation', in *Writing and Difference* (trans. A. Bass), London: Routledge, Kegan and Paul.

Heidegger, Martin (2006), *Mindfulness* (trans. P. Emad and T. Kalary), London: Continuum.

Levinas, Emmanuel ([1961] 1969), *Totality and Infinity: An Essay on Exteriority* (trans. A. Lingis), Pittsburgh, PA: Duquesne University Press.

Further Reading

Aston, Elaine and Harris, Geraldine (2006), *Feminist Futures?: Theatre, Performance, Theory*, Houndmills: Palgrave Macmillan.

Foulkes, Julia (2002), *Modern Bodies: Dance and American Modernism from Martha Graham to Alvin Ailey*, Chapel Hill, NC: The University of North Carolina Press.

Lehmann, Hans-Theis (2006), *Postdramatic Theatre*, London: Routledge.

Reinelt, Janelle (1992), *Critical Theory and Performance*, Ann Arbor, MI: University of Michigan Press.

Shepherd, Simon (2016), *Cambridge Introduction to Performance Theory*, Cambridge: Cambridge University Press.

Bodies in Flight

8
iwannabewolfman (1991–92)

FIGURE 8.1: *iwannabewolfman*: performers Simon Pegg, Charlotte Watkins, Lucy Baldwyn and Barnaby Power. Photo: Edward Dimsdale.

FIGURE 8.2: *iwannabewolfman*: poster artwork. Courtesy of the University of Bristol Theatre Collection.

FIGURE 8.3 (next): *iwannabewolfman*: performers Charlotte Watkins, Barnaby Power and Lucy Baldwyn. Photo: Edward Dimsdale.

FIGURE 8.4 (next): *iwannabewolfman*: performers Simon Pegg, Charlotte Watkins, Barnaby Power and Lucy Baldwyn. Photo: Edward Dimsdale.

FIGURE 8.5 (next): *iwannabewolfman*: performers Simon Pegg, Barnaby Power, Katherine Porter and Charlotte Watkins. Photo: Edward Dimsdale.

FIGURE 8.6 (next): *iwannabewolfman*: performers Charlotte Watkins, Barnaby Power, Simon Pegg and Lucy Baldwyn. Photo: Edward Dimsdale.

PUBLICITY COPY
a farce
in loving memory of mama and papa who were taken from us in that terrible accident
the never-ending wake through which the siblings sit
forever telling tales about the da and ma about the time it all went wrong
the time they can't remember when oh god have mercy on their souls
for they know not what they have done.
BODIES IN FLIGHT's fourth show is a horror story about the slow death of the family, the glimpsed deaths of a whole lot of things in ways so terrible they can only be imagined. Combining original score with new text and choreography, this piece is pure nostalgia, a family romp through the detritus of the comfortable home – photo-albums, teatimes, abuse, Sundays. This is what happens when you play mummies and daddies for real.

This work was the first to focus explicitly on what we called 'a commonplace', something to which everyone could relate and invest emotionally and intellectually – here the family. Based on a TV documentary which told the lives of twin sisters trapped in a psychotic routine of domestic work in the home of their deceased parents, we labelled the show 'a farce' and explored the grim edge between earthy comedy and chilling Freudian nightmares, children's games and adults' desires.

CHRISTOPHER AUSTIN composer, LUCY BALDWYN costume designer/performer, JON CARNALL performer, SARA GIDDENS choreographer, SIMON JONES director, BRIDGET MAZZEY set designer, SIMON PEGG performer, KATHERINE PORTER performer, BARNABY POWER performer, CHARLOTTE WATKINS costume designer/performer.

Music performed by: ROBERT LAMB flute/alto flute/piccolo, JACKIE PAWSEY oboe, ELIZABETH PURNELL trombone, JOHN CORNICK trombone, JOSEPH COOPER percussion, CHARLES STRATFORD percussion, RICHARD TOWERS piano, RICHARD WADE violin, LISA ISTED violin, JANE SAMUEL violin, KATE THOMAS viola, EMMELINE BREWER cello, MARGARET WILLS double bass, CHRISTOPHER AUSTIN conductor.

With: EDWARD DIMSDALE photography, DAVID JONES set builder, JUSTIN O'SHAUGNESSY stage manager.

Performed: Battersea Arts Centre (London), Wickham Theatre (Bristol), Now Festival (The Powerhouse, Nottingham), Traverse (Edinburgh), Powell Theatre (Sherborne), The Old Bull (Barnet), Bath City College, Cheshire School Dance and Drama, Queens Hall Studio (Widnes), Dovecot (Stockton-on-Tees), Nuffield Theatre (Lancaster).

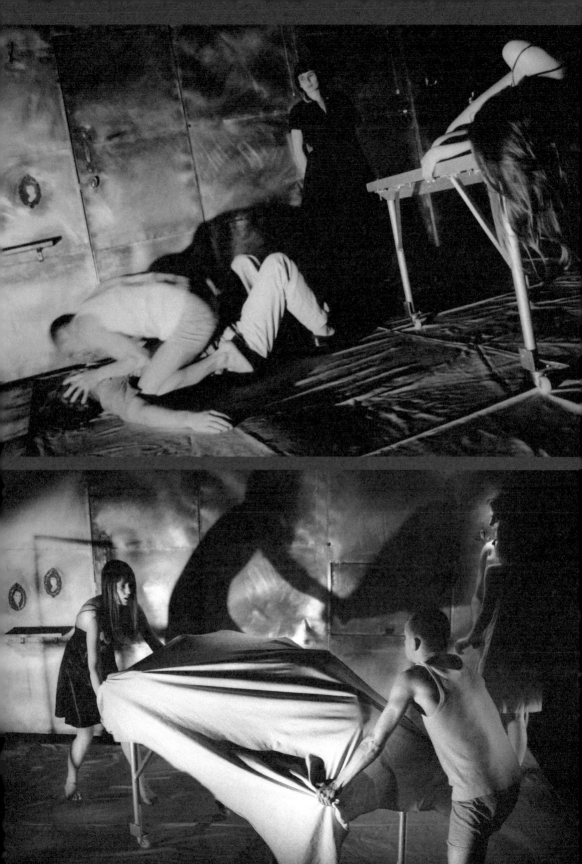

9
Working Alongside
SARA GIDDENS

In this Flight, I address how the development of duets has supported and structured our methodology. The duet often determines how we collaborate, such as with video artist Caroline Rye in Constants *and* DeliverUs, *with the band Angel Tech in* Skinworks *and* Who By Fire, *photographer Edward Dimsdale in* Model Love. *It structures our devising workshops and organizes the emerging material in the works themselves, such as Tony Judge's video with Jennifer Bell's choral work in* Gymnast. *I also reflect on the significance of the idea of the duet for any artist whose practice emerges from a personal dynamic or process of reflection, the necessary other to more 'objective' critical or philosophical analyses. Whilst duetting implies a moving-together, the less obvious, but maybe more productive force of the duet is a fathomless indeterminacy that keeps us going back for more.*

Our work is a collaboration. More accurately, a series of collaborations across many different disciplines, peoples and sometimes continents. At its best, collaboration has provided a mechanism for inviting and celebrating a multitude of possibilities in the development of our creative work. Over more than 30 years we have worked with others, across, in-between and, on rare occasions, in spite of. In the main, we have enjoyed collaborative working relationships that have allowed all concerned to push and probe, sometimes gently, sometimes with more tenacity, at the boundaries of forms and experience. Different shows have demanded different structures. Different media have taken the lead at different times in the process. As collaborators we have inevitably and constantly made choices, both personal and critical, about the material and its place within the whole. Collaboration has always been a complex process, logistically and creatively, forever seeking to find beginnings and explore possibilities, building the work layer upon layer and then inevitably paring it down. Less has often been more. Debating; keeping hold of and letting go; endlessly recording; each making notes in their own ways, that in the main are almost certainly indecipherable to anyone else. And out of and alongside all of this, supporting the development of a shared, but sometimes fleetingly co-created, bespoke, idiosyncratic language around and out of each new particular gathering together, a long shorthand wrought out of each uniquely different constellation of peoples and materials.

Certainly, in practice, collaboration (that oh-so-very human situation) has offered, required and received varying levels of participation, engagement and compromise from the partners involved. Without exception working collaboratively with such a range of artists and participants has always demanded sensitivity and some sense of a collective practical exploration of trans-disciplinarity, alongside a willingness to engage with the different rhythms of disciplines, materials and people. Our collaborations have always necessitated the need to create a safe environment, within an agreed structure, where we can both dwell and meander. For Bodies in Flight, our rigour, our passion and our commitment to the work as a whole has always presided and remains critical. We devise new works that demand an interrogation of ideas. We philosophize, using what we consider to be the most appropriate means of expression at each particular time.

Although we did not name it as such until the making of *Constants* in 1998, our collaboration can be viewed methodologically as a series of duets. With *Constants*, we spoke of and developed a series of duets between movement, text, sound and digital image, giving and foregrounding each pairing a specific space–time within the show. However, duetting has been central to our methodology since 1990 with *Love Is Natural and Real but Not for You my Love* when the movement was placed against a highly philosophical and theorized text. By the production of our CD-ROM in 2001, we defined this duet, itself a reflection upon our central collaboration, as *Flesh & Text*, and accompanied this with the subtitle, *where flesh utters and words move*, a typical play on words. The nomenclature *Flesh & Text* reflects the collaboration and difference at the very heart of the company, between Simon and myself, between words and movement. However, for me, even before, or perhaps in the very midst of that most central of concerns, lies another crucial duet. The duet between and with my self and my body, and how this informs and extends into the collaborative process.

I never ever tire of the/my/your speaking/moving/still-ing body: it is central. In *Ding und Raum* ([1907] 1973), the phenomenologist Edmund Husserl writes of a world of human experience, in which everything is in relation to the body. Things move around the/my body, but the body remains central; it never moves away from itself even when in motion. Moreover, Husserl suggests the body is always whole because it does not usually cast a part of itself away. Husserl's focus on the centrality of sensing persons in space–time is a re-turn, perhaps even a nod to

Emmanuel Kant's earlier essay of 1768, 'The ultimate ground of the differentiation of regions in space', where—when Kant elucidates how right/left, up/down, front/back are in relation to the body. For Kant, things require our bodies to become orientated.

I have found my orientation, physically, emotionally and spiritually, firstly through my contemporary dance practice and, I think more significantly, through my commitment to a daily yoga practice which has heavily influenced the performance work I have produced and my attitude towards the creation of it. My yoga, and particularly my yin-yoga-based practice, concerns itself with releasing fascia, the connective tissue around muscles, in order to make sitting still for meditation comfortable. With this practice, one is invited to remain in each posture, and to let go, in order to let gravity do the work and allow the fascia to relax and stretch. At the end of any more physically exertive practice, I lie down, in *Savasana* (Hindu for 'corpse pose') with legs and arms outstretched on the floor, my eyes closed, and I begin to enter into a further process of slowing down and of attending to no-thing, but my body and my breath. For me, my yoga-based practice has provided me with a consistent space–time in and from which to be. It has taught me to be both patient and persistent: through yoga, I have learnt to dwell in and with my/the body. It is not hard to imagine how useful and transferrable this has been as a maker and choreographer.

In my personal and professional practice my/the body has been and continues to be my central focus; and working with enquiring, open-minded performers my professional *raison d'être*. For many years I worked professionally with performers who had little or no 'traditional' or 'classical' dance training. Of course, there have been a few exceptions, such as working with contemporary dancer Patricia Breatnach in *Constants*. But in the main, I was most interested in duetting with, in creating physical material with, performers who had a strong commitment to articulating physically from their own unique bodies in their own distinctive ways. Performers, who were not only capable of handling and delivering the spoken text but also able to devise. This willingness to devise, co-create, explore, be open to experimentation and play, and dwell with ideas and materials has been a critical part of our collaborations. The generation and selection of much of the physical material was (and still is) frequently made through lengthy structured improvisations in the studio, often influenced by research interests originating outside of it.

Retrospectively, I think this insistence on working with 'untrained' movers was connected to both my own temporary abandonment of my traditional dance training, in Ballet, Tap, Ballroom and Latin American, alongside the subsequent joy of discovering physical theatre in the late 1980s and the work of DV8, La La La Human Steps, Pina Bausch, to name just a few. My absolute and immediate love of physical theatre, which seemed, at its best, to celebrate vibrancy and difference, rather than attempting to create robotic copies of uniform idealized bodies, concretized my utter and complete fascination with the human-ness of beings and their presence—absence on stage and in performance. In retrospect, I think the kinds of classically 'trained' bodies, I had been used to seeing and training alongside, had been encouraged to iron out, to even try to erase, their human-being-ness, to try to eradicate their uniqueness and to strive for uniformity through conformity. For me, such specific technical training had created a certain detachment, a docility, that could allow the viewer to watch in a more distanced, objectified, separated and ultimately othered way. I found such 'practised' bodies, following Michel Foucault's (1979: 27) reflection upon the disciplined bodies of armies, fell back on learned, generic moves and patterns, and in doing so became dis-empowered and oddly de-humanized. I was interested in humanity, and as I elucidate in a later Flight, the extraordinary—ordinary (see Chapter 18, 'The Magnificent Minutiae'). For me, then and now, it is *how* the different bodies move that is vital. It was, and is often, from and out of each individual performer's everyday idiosyncratic gestures and actions, that the movement vocabulary is co-created, and that the choreography is co-constructed.

I am much more likely to be drawn to the apparently more *genuine* (a contentious position, I know), but just as learnt, actions and movements of the everyday. Indeed, it is the quality of these functional actions and the making visible of their performative dimension that probably most readily characterizes our work physically. Generally, the movement vocabulary originates from each specific performer. It is first experienced and owned by the performers themselves. It is usually revealed through improvisations, studied, then arranged, sometimes re-arranged and then fixed. These physical dialogues rely upon co-creation. In rehearsals, I see my role as firstly creating and offering a structure and environment that allow for play and experimentation, and secondly to keenly observe the performers' movements, then collectively shape and order them and together re-make them theirs. This duetting, this commitment to a physical dialogue, between choreographer and performers lies at the very heart of our methodology.

Consequently, the performers' attitudes to movement and their openness to different ways of creating and devising material have been crucial. Of course, even within these parameters, I have found myself having to be more prescriptive with some, than others. Some performers have expected to be choreographed upon, rather than with or alongside. The duetting process has always been graduated and the collaborative process has itself been a working through and interrogation of pre-positions and experiences, which we cannot help but bring into the studio with us. However, I have always felt that these should encourage, not stifle, dialogue and the possibilities for meaningful exchange between positions, forms and ideas. I believe art rehearses questions, problems and choices in life. Following this argument, performers are rehearsing life, our own lives and the possibilities and problematics of life, right in front of us, through a fleshy communal exchange. Our audiences are brought together to bear witness to these re-creations, these rehearsals, and at the very least, these allusions to common moments and life events, for example, through the wake (*Littluns Wake*) or the love affair (*DeliverUs*).

So, I am led to one last highly significant duet, with our audiences. Every Bodies in Flight work (whether live or on-screen) puts performers' bodies right in front of, or oftentimes right alongside, my/your body. Spatially, this relationship is one of proximity and distance. It is present in every work, although arguably it can be observed most readily in works such as *Constants* where—when performer Sheila Gilbert gradually makes her way from the walls to the centre of the space using the shoulders and chair backs of the audience who are seated in a spiral within the usual playing space. In shows such as *Skinworks*, this physical connection was extended further with every audience member being taken by the hand and led by a performer to their seat, which was carefully placed on the playing area usually reserved for the performers. To reach their seat they passed under a giant screen suspended over the space showing the pre-recorded chatroom images: literally and physically they were invited into the chatroom through a physical connection with and awareness of a performer. Through each work this connection is important: through the presentation and expression of those other bodies, I want to feel and give others (audiences) opportunities to connect to their own experience of being, and inevitably to one's own mortality. Each event gathers audiences together in order to foreground and draw attention to bodily/physical expressions: for example, the smallest of gestures in *Do The Wild Thing!*, the most intimate expressions of affection in *DeliverUs*, Sheila's caressing hands and arthritic hip in *Constants*.

I care what audiences think of our work and want audiences to be moved by it. I create dynamic space–times which invite audiences in; and latterly through working with performers with very particular and different physical skills-sets than ours, through shows like *Gymnast* and *Life Class*, reach audiences less familiar with such work. Because I want audiences to be active in and through the space–times of our work, my desire is always to create space–times that invite openings for (self-)reflection and for meaning-making, both active processes, that each audience member can step into if they so wish. I believe that choreographically focusing on the minutiae and the ordinary–extraordinary creates such opportunities. Opportunities where–when audiences are given space–times within the works to take time to locate or relocate our-/them-selves and each other, to experience a presencing outwith, but not outside of the event of performance itself. Moments, varying massively in length, where they are able to take a breath and take stock and, always already held within such present presencings, make associations that spark memories and open up the possibilities of futures to come.

Performance and dance disrupt space and time. Practitioner-researcher Katja Hilevaara suggests that by employing a combination of 'visual, aural, textual and illusory' and a host 'of perceptible sensory stimuli […] theatre performance cuts into the fabric of time an opening, through which time stops momentarily and then starts again' (2012: 71). Perhaps such incisions inevitably support those theatre-makers, like ourselves, who are interested in exploring the letting-go or opening-up of meaning-making with their audiences. Indeed, Hilevaara argues that each audience member makes their own interpretations of the work before them, and that 'there are a multitude of transformations in motion' (Hilevaara 2012: 75). She suggests that this leads to a democratization in theatre. I would not go this far: the frames are still primarily being set up by the maker(s), though I hope we do move towards the edges of a more inclusive relationship.

This final duet with audience-spectators has increased in importance for us over the years and it has certainly become more expansive location-wise, extending beyond creating narrative spaces connected to the thematics of theatre-based shows, to performing work in galleries, in gymnasia through *Gymnast* and social centres and clubs through *Life Class*. My selection of the word *spectators* is carefully chosen to reflect how our work has extended to and attracted passers-by: for example, the work we made for a café-foyer area with *Model Love* and particularly through our *Dream→Work/→Walk*s made for and on the streets of five UK cities and Singapore, and my performance installation *Still Moving: Moving Still* made specifically inside and outside of gallery and performance spaces in Bristol, Nottingham and Birmingham. However, creating such space–times can only ever be an invitation. Ultimately, it is up to each individual audience member (or participant) to decide whether to take on the 'work', the effort, and even the difficulties, involved in experiencing such multi-layered work. As collaborators, I believe it is our job to make that invitation as enriching and compelling as we can. Without a doubt, it is our collaborations, our duets across different materials and with different people (see Chapter 28, 'Being In-Between: Collaboration as Non-Collaboration'), which lie at the very core of our work, visceral and complex, and above all so very human.

References

Foucault, Michel (1979), *Discipline and Punish* (trans. A. Sheridan), New York: Vintage.

Hilevaara, Katja (2012), 'Idle fancies, lucid dreams and startling memories: Remembering as a form of active spectatorship', in *How Performance Thinks Conference*, Co-hosted by PSi Performance and Philosophy Working Group and the Practice Research Unit, Kingston University, London Studio Centre, 13–14 April, pp. 70–76, available online at: http://performancephilosophy.ning.com/page/how-performance-thinks. Accessed 24 October 2022.

Husserl, Edmund ([1907] 1973), 'Ding und Raum. Vorlesungen', in U. Claesges (ed.), *Thing and Space. Lectures 1907*, The Hague, Netherlands: Martinus Nijhoff.

Kant, Immanuel ([1768] 1992), 'Concerning the ultimate ground of the differentiation of directions in space', in D. Walford and R. Meerbote (eds), *Works/Theoretical Philosophy, 1755–1770*, Cambridge: Cambridge University Press, pp. 361–72.

Further Reading

Murray, Simon, David and Keefe, John (2016), *Physical Theatres: A Critical Introduction*, London and New York: Routledge.

Bodies in Flight

10 Rough (1992–93)

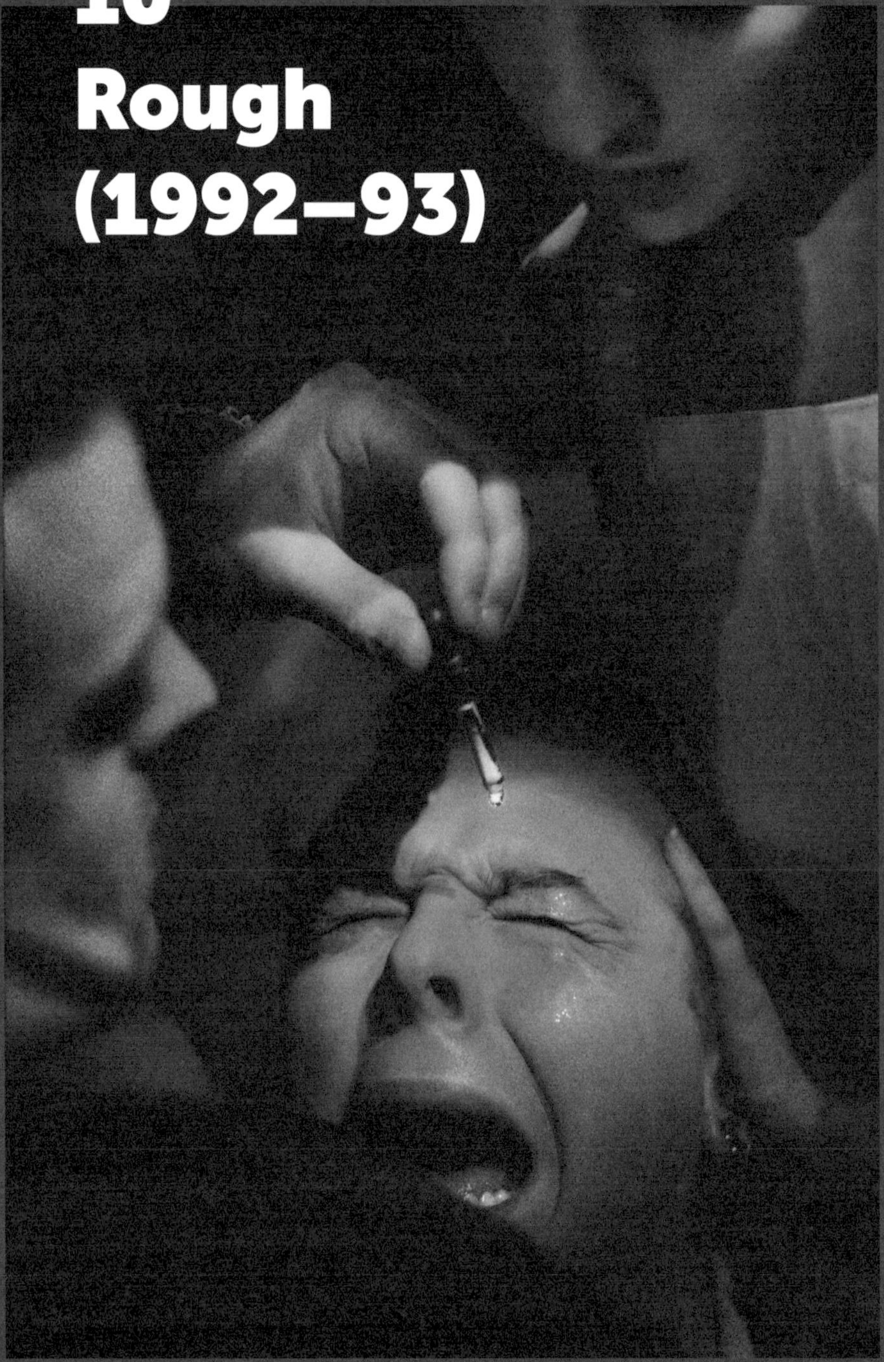

FIGURE 10.1: *Rough*: performers Graeme Rose, Simon Pegg and Charlotte Watkins. Photo: Edward Dimsdale.

FIGURE 10.2: *Rough*: postcard. Courtesy of the University of Bristol Theatre Collection.

PUBLICITY COPY
*A passion
Aphrodite (aka Venus), Cupid (aka Eros), Diana (aka Artemis) and Dionysus (aka Bacchus) are on the run, holed up in some motel, where a sex thing happens. They've changed their names so many times now. We don't know whether we're supposed to believe in them. They don't know which land they're in. They keep telling stories of a life to come. The interstate never stops the free circulation of trade.*

Combining original score with hip-hop, storytelling to the nth and specialty acts with virtual choreography and a mobile motel room, we hope this passionate and true tale of gods and goddesses in the new Europe will entrance you, move you to tears, run rings around you and give you a deal of faith in the future.

Articulated through a run-down touring variety act playing to ever-dwindling audiences in seedy venues, we focused on the comedic skills of our performers to tell a story about gods fallen on hard times, about our culture's loss of faith in the grand narratives of progress and history, the common decencies of community and shared values. To wow the punters, we used stand-up, direct address and very bad club-band playing, including a Stylophone. We enjoyed this direct address to our audiences so much that we built on it in our next work.

CHRISTOPHER AUSTIN composer, SARA GIDDENS choreographer, SIMON JONES director/writer, BRIDGET MAZZEY designer, SIMON PEGG performer, KATHERINE PORTER performer, GRAEME ROSE performer, CHARLOTTE WATKINS performer.

Music played by: ROBERT LAMB flute, alto flute, piccolo, SIAN EDWARDS clarinet, ELIZABETH LANE horn, PAUL CLAVERT trumpet, JOSEPH COOPER, JEREMY LITTLE, DIGGORY SEACOME percussion, JANE SAMUEL piano, CATHERINE BUSWELL violin 1, RUTH LORD violin 2, ELIN JONES viola, EMMELINE BREWER cello, JULIAN DALE double bass, CHRISTOPHER AUSTIN conductor.

With: PETE BRANDT synthesized score, JON CARNALL production assistant, EDWARD DIMSDALE photography, DAVID JONES set construction, ELEANOR JONES video star, EWEN MACLEOD production assistant, CHRIS RATCLIFF stage management, SHEP ROBSON production assistant, TIM SPRING urn construction.

Performed: Arnolfini (Bristol), Shaftesbury Theatre (Cheltenham), The Old Bull (Barnet), Powerhouse (Nottingham), Wimbledon School of Art (London), Wickham Theatre (Bristol), Chapter Arts Centre (Cardiff), Bath Festival Fringe/The Rondo.

Figure 10.3: *Rough*: performers Graeme Rose, Katherine Porter, Simon Pegg and Charlotte Watkins. Photo: Edward Dimsdale.

Figure 10.4: *Rough*: performers Graeme Rose, Simon Pegg, Charlotte Watkins and Katherine Porter. Photo: Edward Dimsdale.

Figure 10.5: *Rough*: performers Simon Pegg and Graeme Rose. Photo: Edward Dimsdale.

Figure 10.6: *Rough*: performers Katherine Porter, Simon Pegg and Charlotte Watkins. Photo: Edward Dimsdale.

Text extracts

SIMON JONES

Rough *was the first work with a substantial textual element written solely by me. Its 'failing cabaret act' situation required predominantly direct address, so I could write the text as a bagatelle of short stories, advice pages, reference to classical mythology mixed with recent news events. For the first time, performers chose the short passages of texts and divided them according to improvisation, ordering them to maintain a queasy balance between reassuring and unnerving the audience. The broader concerns of the early 1990s can be clearly heard in the text today: questions around gender and sexuality, particularly queer sex and safe sex, themes of globalization, the so-called 'victory' of capitalism over communism, the uncertainty of this new world order with its so-called 'end of history'.*

pre-show: gods drifting around edge.

INTRO
dance.

APHRODITE:	Good evening, ladies and gentlemen, and welcome to tonight's performance of *Rough*.
DIONYSUS:	Who is in control of this effect?
CHEERLEADERS:	V...I...R...T...U...A...L.
CUPID:	Our mission statement is as follows. We will redeem you from the Vanilla. Escape with us to the event horizon of the Virtual. Dive into the sea of potentialities. The nth dimension of Virtuality. The safe-sex emporium. The Whitest Knuckle - Ride. We promise you all this in 60 minutes. The safest sex you're ever likely to have. We believe in the fourth person singular.
APHRODITE:	Some scenes will have an adult theme and tone and contain violence and sexual swear words.
DIANA:	We certainly wouldn't want anything we say to offend you. We know some of you have come a long way to see the show. But we are compelled to say what we say.
DIONYSUS:	We should warn you we are terrible liars. We can't remember the last time we got through

a show without some mendacity. It's all this pretending to be someone else. It's corrupting. We tried to go straight by laying off the method. All those characters. But people do like a good story. Especially when they've bothered to get tarted up and go out in the rain. What can you do? We're past caring, honest.

preview APHRODITE's *turn.*
first break in music.
strategy scrum: time out.

DIONYSUS: We feel we can say this because we're amongst grown-ups, friends even. Aren't we? Life isn't simple. Is it? And yet time and time again people come up to us after the show and ask us, what does it mean? What are we supposed to do? We need to eat. We need cash for our habits. So, of course, we lie. We say things are simple. This means that, and you can go home now. Everything is safe and those things which are not are quite a long way away. Or if the person looks particularly troubled and thoughtful, we say life is nasty and those harmful things may well be right inside you at this very moment, but we can't promise that. Some people ask, what did you mean? Or even, what does this box of tricks mean? As if we were puppets and there was a puppet-master up there somewhere. But look, no strings. We're not offended by the implication that we are not really gods. We don't strike the person down dead on the spot. What does it mean? Ha. The question comes from too much faith in the wrong gods and not enough faith in themselves, whatever that means.

second dance.

[…]

DIANA: We stay on the road. We feel safest there. At one and the same place and time on the

	rim of things and in the flow of things. We keep a suitcase packed.
APHRODITE:	There is a pack instinct amongst us.
DIANA:	Watch us when we eat in the Little Chef. Nothing gets by us.
APHRODITE:	So, stay fragile, stay sweet, stay child.
DIANA:	We get paid to wear our hearts on our sleeves. All the tenderness is turned outside raw to gawp at.
APHRODITE:	This flesh is for real.
DIANA:	So that's why we appear severe. We're operating at the level where the innocent kill and the murderer weeps. We have no time for logic.
APHRODITE:	It doesn't make sense here.
DIANA:	That's the thing the policeman shouts just before he shoots. So, if anyone ever explains anything to you, you'll know for sure your next breath is your last.
APHRODITE:	Everything else is just a truth.
DIANA:	It passes the time.
APHRODITE:	And it's reassuring.

[...]

APHRODITE'S

everyday on the road: APHRODITE *cleaning revolver;* DIANA *making a bomb in a shoebox.*
Drinking elixir of life.
'Party party'. Rolling joints, drinking, parody of being high/ drunk, terrible improvisation everyone slinks out of.
band plays 'Time Is Tight'.
CUPID *introduces 'Dance of the Seven Simulacra'.*

APHRODITE:	We endlessly talk dirty. It's in our nature. The morphology of filth is the most excellent science.
DIANA:	Maybe we should say, be safe. But we prefer to say, be perverse. How you manage both is your own concern. Obviously, you've got to live in the real world. We haven't. We've been trying to catch something nasty for centuries. We feel kind of left out.

CUPID *solicits audience response – ahhh.*

TWO GODS, BLOWJOBBING REVOLVER. HERMES SUCKLES THE ESTRANGED INFANT PAN.

APHRODITE: Our definition of vanilla sex is the contract-thing. The whole business of it. The coming to terms …
DIANA: … the negotiation …
APHRODITE: … the give and the take …
DIANA: … the illusion of democracy …
APHRODITE: … the establishment of limits and of codes of practice, the reduction of the fuck to a menu of rights.
DIANA: And what is worse still?
APHRODITE: You police your lover and, if he transgresses, brand him your abuser. No fuck has ever been equal.
BOTH: That's a theory.
APHRODITE: Sex gets off on breaking vows mutually entered into, comes to the power-trip …
DIANA: … the guilt-trip …
APHRODITE: … the victim-trip, to the rush of the unexpected extra finger or two inches more …
DIANA: … to the scream and the sigh of scattered promises …
APHRODITE: … to the dissolution of the dream in the sweet-and-sour liquidizer of the event.
DIANA: Same-sex is vanilla sex is same-sex.
APHRODITE: It's not about union.
DIANA: It's about expression.
APHRODITE: What is this straight sex anyway?
DIANA: It's a fantasy, isn't it? People fucking to a template.
APHRODITE: It sounds like a contradiction in terms to us. Straight … sex.
DIANA: Who really fucks normal?
APHRODITE: What is a normal fuck?
DIANA: We don't know. We never actually shag the person we sleep with.
APHRODITE: We're always light years away.
DIANA: You've got manuals telling you that sort of thing is wrong.
APHRODITE: We know.

DIANA: We've read copies left alongside Bibles in motel rooms. No wonder so many people get depressed.
APHRODITE: It's not surprising.
DIANA: Of course, the fundamentalists will rip you off endlessly …
APHRODITE: … if you let them.
DIANA: They aren't satisfied with your cash.
APHRODITE: They're after the metaphysics.
DIANA: So, our advice is –
BOTH: Don't make any deals.
DIANA: Remember, the contract is also spiritual.

[…]

CUPID *introduces the turn whilst playing stylophone.*

APHRODITE: We dislike ideologies. They cause unnecessary pain. Ideas are only part of the world. It's bad enough reducing things to concepts, without reducing life to the soundbite of someone's theory. That's like feeding a sausage through a grinder in the sure and certain knowledge of getting a live pig out the other end. Barmy and painful.
DIANA: Be warned. Ideologies hide in nature. Don't trust the person who wants you to memorize anything, like a procedure for claiming benefit or a prayer. Don't trust the person who wants you to argue with them or sign their petition against the torture of terrorists.
APHRODITE: Don't trust the one who comes to you with free access to higher education and a bill of rights. These people are fundamentalists.
DIANA: Their ideologies are weapons that will do you harm. They panic us and we flee. They keep us on the run. They are utterly remorseless and remorselessly violent. They have got under our skin and made us very sick indeed.
APHRODITE: We can't tell you how gorgeous we were before. We can't wind the clock back. They broke into our memories when they started telling truths about us. We speak their

	languages and that is the only thing we have ever apologized for.
DIANA:	Do what you can.
APHRODITE:	We know how it feels. Stay on the outside. They don't like that. They're all inside, gathered around the teacher, boning up in the library, warming themselves in the cathode rays, so very very still.
DIANA:	They hate the traveller. Stay mobile. Stay nomad. Stay without. Fuck the music of the spheres. Listen to the tectonic grind of everything colliding endlessly. Fuck the equation. Be ready to say yes.
CUPID:	And slide.

Slide.

PERSEUS GARROTTES A GUARD BEFORE RESCUING THE CAPTIVE ARIADNE.
APHRODITE *inserts pencils up* DIONYSUS*'s nostrils and goes to hit his head.*
Curtain drawn back to reveal DIONYSUS *dead.*

CUPID:	Ladies and gentlemen, a slight technical hitch. Please bear with us.

DIANA *presents the Beliefometer.*

CUPID:	Faith in the performance has fallen below critical mass, the point at which spontaneous resurrection occurs. Can we ask all of you out there to believe generously? We need as much faith as you can afford to give. We're feeling some from someone over here.

A bulb lights on the Beliefometer.

	The gentleman in the XXXX. Thank you very much, sir. Only five more faithful. This side's a lot stronger than this. Can we have a bit more effort over this side?

Another bulb.

                        Now ladies, aged between 18 and 24.

Another bulb.

                        The lady in the XXXX. Thank you, madam. Now
                        one last push. Please believe generously.
                        We need your faith.

The last bulb.

                        On with the show.

strategy scrum: game plan made.

**JOCASTA TRAPPED AND SUFFOCATED IN THE TOMB
OF CADMUS.**
APHRODITE *caresses* DIONYSUS*, then breaks his neck.*

PHILNIUS PEELED ALIVE AND EATEN BY WOLVES.
DIANA *beats* DIONYSUS *with a stick.*
sin: the laughing young woman possesses DIANA, *beats* DIONY-
SUS *with a stick, he clears off when she gets real, everyone
watches, a commentary by* DIONYSUS *explaining the reference,
interrupts the passion to make himself heard.*

DIONYSIUS: Ladies, please. This sin is based on news-
                paper reports from the Bosnian concentra-
                tion camps of a young woman who laughed as
                she tortured the prisoners. We don't know
                if these reports are true. But that's never
                stopped us in the past.

CUPID *receives a message for audience.*

CUPID: David, that friendly spirit is getting really
                worried about the grill.

**HERACLES MURDERS THE TWELVE CHILDREN OF CHLORIS AND
NELEUS.**
DIANA *slams* DIONYSUS*'s head in the lid of the trolley.*
APHRODITE *sinks to her knees in prayer.*

APHRODITE: Please save us, please save us.

DIANA *screams and stamps.*
The Video Nasty plays.

CUPID: This is all consensual. They are only doing this to give you goosebumps. Yes. We only do consensual. Don't get worried. Don't get upset. The artistes have signed a waiver in triplicate. It's available for inspection at our registered office. We do things by the book. We respect local customs and sensibilities.

11

From Fan-Boy to Programmer – Memories of a Relationship with Bodies in Flight

RICHARD DUFTY

RICHARD DUFTY is a theatre-maker, performer and producer. He worked at Battersea Arts Centre (BAC) for eighteen years where he was the Head of Producing. More recently, he was a Relationship Manager in the London theatre team at Arts Council England. Richard is co-artistic director of the theatre company Uninvited Guests with whom he has devised, co-written and performed in numerous projects, in person and online, touring nationally and internationally. He is completing a Ph.D. at Lancaster University exploring contemporary performance in which conversation with/between audience members is a key feature.

Here Richard reflects on his changing relationship with Bodies in Flight, particularly the forces at work in producing experimental performance.

Years ago, when I was one of his students, I remember Simon talking about the word *cleave* and how he liked its paradoxical meanings – to split apart, but also to bind together. That memory came back to me again when I was looking back on the two distinct phases of my relationship with Bodies in Flight.

1. FALLING IN LOVE

I was a student in the Drama Department at Bristol University from 1992 to 1995. What a time and place for a drama student to be alive! I remember nights out at the Wickham Theatre and Arnolfini. I remember the running with cardboard signs in Forced Entertainment's *Emmanuel Enchanted* and performers repeatedly dragging themselves across the floor and holding their breath under water in Goat Island's *It's Shifting Hank*. I remember Desperate Optimists, Bobby Baker, Blast Theory, The Cholmondeleys and The Featherstonehaughs. And I remember the excitement of young bodies (just a little older than me and mine), frilly shirts, movement, words and a drum kit in Bodies in Flight's *Rough*, which I watched in my first year at university. I'd seen lots of 'plays' at the Theatre Royal and Gardner Arts Centre in Brighton near where I grew up, and companies like Theatre de Complicité doing something a bit different with classic texts. But what I encountered in Bristol was something beyond those frames of reference. I felt like a lucky witness to a new theatre that had an accent on live-ness, that was young and cool, that de-centred the text, but was still interested in doing playful things with language, that was sweaty and physical without being about perfectly trained bodies doing 'dancey' things. This performance was inspired by movies, music and visual art as much as (or instead of) any theatre tradition.

Alongside moments during shows, I remember moments after – staggering away, emotionally and intellectually opened up, desperate to talk, sometimes desperate to be alone, with the world (or certainly the street architecture of Bristol) appearing to be re-made by the experience I had just had. And I remember this so clearly with Bodies in Flight shows. I remember wandering out onto the quayside next to Arnolfini, inspired and amazed after *Rough*, thinking it was so *full* – full of images, ideas, cultural references and sex appeal. It was so sexy. It was everything I could ever imagine wanting theatre to be. And I remember something similar with their next show, *Beautiful Losers*. Maybe a beer in hand this time, again looking out over the docks, and a discussion with friends around the title of the show as a way into understanding it all – how that title, like the company names Forced Entertainment and Desperate Optimists (and others from around that time), pointed to some sort of heroic (probably futile) struggle for meaning and fulfilment. And maybe I even shed a tear in that moment as I stood there on the cobblestones and stared at the light reflected on the water. *I too was a beautiful loser.*

2. GETTING A JOB

In 2002, my relationship with Bodies in Flight changed when I became a producer at BAC. One of my tasks was to help programme the regular opera and new music theatre festivals. It was not a natural fit. I knew nothing about music or opera. Alongside projects from artists who already had a relationship with BAC (including those behind *Jerry Springer the Opera* which had just recently emerged through the Scratch process and owed a lot to the commitment of Tom Morris, then artistic director, to this area of practice), I wanted to programme a few things that felt more like my kind of thing. Bodies in Flight had developed a show, *Skinworks*, in collaboration with the band Angel Tech. A show with live music met the brief for the festival, and so it was one of the first things I programmed in my eighteen years at BAC.

I remember watching the show in a small black-box space (the old Studio 2). The audience was dispersed across the room, sitting on their own with gaps between for the performers to move, but with clear sight of everyone else. Over the years I became familiar with the pressured cocktail of feelings you can experience as a programmer bringing something new to an audience (including colleagues) – a mix of excitement, responsibility, embarrassment, and a desperate willingness for it all to go to plan and to be liked. I remember those feelings were particularly acute with that show, early on in my time at BAC. As Kaylene Tan, Polly Frame and Graeme Rose moved between us, talking in Bodies in Flight's trademark heightened, often ecstatic, style about exploring sexual desires and alternative identities in internet chatrooms, I remember looking over at the box-office and finance managers and whoever else was watching it with me – with that show perhaps the whole point was that you couldn't avoid people's gazes (and their judgement) – and desperately trying to read between the lines in their intense expressions, like a lonely soul looking for validation in one of the chatrooms the performers were inhabiting. Do they like it? *Do they like me?*

After *Skinworks*, I programmed *Who By Fire* in 2005 with its beautiful sequences of synchronized movement and tender songs, and then the durational version of *Model Love* in 2008. BAC had a relatively democratic programming process at that time, with a team of producers each having a licence to programme artists they liked. What came with that opportunity, naturally, was having to account for decisions made. Often, in meetings afterwards, that meant giving an account of the show – a version of what had happened and what it might mean for those that hadn't been there, or that were there but wanted it explained (and justified). Explicitly or implicitly, we were accounting for the money spent on these projects over others that were looking for support and making the case for why this company or that artist, their aesthetic and the audience they attracted, was deserving of being privileged. As we moved towards the 2010s, these questions about who was making shows and who they were for, who and what was privileged, were rightly becoming more pronounced.

This process was sometimes tricky with Bodies in Flight's work. There was something about how it slid between genre categories (to me sometimes feeling like it existed in its own 'literary live art' genre), how it was hard to easily reduce and explain (in meetings afterwards or in marketing copy), how it could bring lots of audience with it whilst occasionally others felt left behind (eliciting strong feelings for and against), how it was very contemporary but drew on canonical cultural references as well, that meant it brilliantly/awkwardly resisted this process of accounting. In the 'marketplace' of making programming decisions at BAC, discussing the merits of one show or artist over another, it felt like it was sometimes difficult to argue for Bodies in Flight. In the same year I programmed *Skinworks*, Sophie Calle published *Exquisite Pain* (later a Forced Entertainment show), the story of a difficult break-up told over and over again. For me, my new relationship in this new era with Bodies in Flight's work could be characterized as some kind of exquisite pain. I wanted to programme it and I wanted to be there in the audience watching it. I loved and admired. It was exquisite. But it could also be painful. Painful because, unlike during the previous phase of my relationship with the company, I wasn't able to completely abandon myself to the difficult pleasures of the experience. I could no longer just be the fan-boy.

Looking back, I can see a cleaving in my relationship with Bodies in Flight. I fell in love in the 1990s. But I got a job in the 2000s, and after that, it wasn't as carefree as it had been – new pressures and new measures made it more difficult and more complicated, and a splitting of kinds happened. But cleaving, as Simon pointed out to me all those years ago, involves *binding* as well as splitting. For me, Bodies in Flight was formative. They helped shape my interest in a particular kind of theatre, they helped pave the way for me to make shows with the company Uninvited Guests (as I have been for over 20 years) and they led me to that job as a producer at BAC. Their art, even when it wasn't easy (and arguing for it wasn't easy), raised new questions for me and opened up new possibilities (oh, the possibilities!). For better or worse, through the shows of theirs I experienced in the 1990s and 2000s and my memories of them now, Bodies in Flight is part of what binds me still.

12
As if for the First Time
GRAEME ROSE

GRAEME ROSE *is a performer and theatre-maker, a co-founder of theatre companies* Glory What Glory, Stan's Cafe *and* The Resurrectionists. *He has worked with companies including Belgrade Theatre (Coventry), Birmingham Rep, Black Country Touring, Creation Theatre, imitating the dog, Kali, No Stone, Red Shift, Talking Birds, Theatre Absolute and Untied Artists. He is an associate artist with Bodies in Flight, collaborating on* Rough, Skinworks, Who By Fire, Model Love, Krapp's Last Tape, Dream→Walk *(Wirksworth and Skegness),* Life Class *and* Unbox Me!

Here, Graeme reflects on his long-term relationship with Bodies in Flight's process of approaching, developing and embodying performance material.

I have worked with both Sara and Simon since the mid 1980s, before Bodies in Flight came into existence, and I first collaborated with the company on *Rough*. Three decades and many projects later, I'm well placed to reflect on the company's body of work. I feel lucky to have sustained working relations with several independent companies over this time period, each exercising different, even contrasting, methodologies. As a freelance collaborator with a portfolio approach to my working life, swapping hats has not always been easy. One's creative identity may become associated with a specific company's ethos and practice, yet different companies have distinct methodologies. It took a long time for me to feel comfortable with those shifts, which is as much a reflection of how confident I felt in my own performance skin. Open-mindedness to any process is a pre-requisite, whilst simultaneously interrogating the practice and questioning what I can usefully bring of myself to that process. All the same, I have resisted scrutinizing too deeply or formalizing my own method, preferring to characterize my approach as one led more by intuition than design.

Every project demands a bespoke approach, but the key with Bodies in Flight is to get under the material's skin by understanding what drives the authorial voices. The dynamic at the heart of Bodies in Flight is the interface between the written word and the choreographic; that is, between the thought and the action. Fundamentally, my job is to concretize: to render the 'Text' incarnate as 'Flesh'. The 'Texts' themselves (literary and choreographic) start less as a script, and more as a schematic template – passages of text in a raw, unproven state, oriented alongside sequences of choreographic ideas. And the performance role is not to construct a 'character', so much as a 'cipher', to navigate through the material. As such, my relationship with the co-directors is a critical one. I embody the idea (voicing the authors), whilst also exercising a critical presence. I do not see my function as channelling the texts in an uncritical way. I am in rehearsal to test Simon's words. Despite their precision, they do not slip by easily. Like densely layered early-modern rhetorical verse, ideas are laid out as arguments, constructed in detail and presented as if through a rotating prism, like a verbal acrostic. The effort, beauty and (sometimes) pain of their creation are also borne out in the delivery, as I wrestle with the challenge of grasping the complexity, making sense of, and committing to memory. The delight and struggle of the written word becoming 'utterance' (author into performer) sublimates itself as performance.

I am tempted to think of my role in the process as occupying a shadowy hinterland, skirmishing between the real and the imagined. Through successive projects, I have increasingly recognized this function, and my stage persona has evolved to patrol or elucidate this territory within the work. As a mindful presence in the room, the job of a performer is about trusting in the process, often leaping into a murky unknown, recognizing that the best I can do is cast an impression of an idea onto the space. To call myself an interpreter suggests something too knowing, too exact. I cannot pretend to fully appreciate the complete nature of what we are doing. The work opens up and actualizes a poetic, enquiring space, in which the very phenomenon of 'being present' is highlighted and, by default, shadowed. I have come to think of it as a puzzle, ever unravelling. There is always something more to discover, even after the performance event is done. How many times have I lain ruminating in a bathtub, a day or so after the end of a project, and had a eureka moment about the work? As a performer, I relish and yield to this place of not-knowing. There is an acquired skill in accepting this, feeling secure in that place where you can just 'be'. It is a place of trust, and not just for the creatives; the audience also needs to know they are in safe hands, as you guide them through that place of not-knowing.

When starting a project there is a creative dichotomy: on the one hand, a desire to approach the work as carte-blanche, open-minded, feigning a blissful state of ignorance, with a desire to bring a freshness of approach, a new lens to the work, on the other hand, the need to develop and build on shared understanding, using the sophisticated shorthand that long-term collaborators bring to the space. With Bodies in Flight, this common language has been nurtured across 30 years of collaboration. To work with the company is to trust in and to feed a broader project in a meaningful way, which does justice to both the impressive back-catalogue of the Bodies in Flight canon and to the artistic trajectories of my collaborators.

At the beginning of a project, there is considerable trepidation and excitement. The first read-through lays bare certain vulnerabilities. This can be disarming, but is also a useful indicator of what is to come, reminding you – with all its rawness – how an audience may first encounter the material. Many questions emerge: which moments immediately sparkle or come alive? Which are the more problematic sections where the mind tangles, becomes confused or doubtful? What images persist or detonate in the imagination? Which turns of phrase delight the ear? Which spoken sections feel satisfying to curl the tongue around? Even if 'meaning' is an elusive red herring, an overall sense of the poetic shape is a helpful guide to the potency of what is to come. But the puzzle cannot yield its secrets all at a first sitting. The art of the performance is to wrangle its logic, to appreciate that it has been crafted around specifics. I am prepared for the texts to get the better of me, and to be accused of 'mangling' their delivery. Simon's judicious hand is in control of the particulars of the text, just as Sara's is, alongside, overseeing the details of the choreography. Hers is a concern with the precision of gesture, phrase, and the overarching schematic design. Invariably the physical language will be distilled into something lean, with any fat trimmed off. It is often built around recognizable, repetitive gestures and motifs – a turn, a reach or glance – drawing upon the everyday, and on the idioms of social dance, relational to, but never representational of, the spoken text. The two 'texts' will co-exist, but may be learned in separation, before being layered against one another; the potency of the work emerges from the poetic collision of the two, in the space offered up between them.

My instinct as a performer is to inflect the material with a flair, a panache; to embellish the basics from something purely technical back into the realm of the 'characterized'. With evolving confidence in the material and the trust of co-performers, new possibilities open up for the performer. I need to explore the parameters of this space, to exercise it as personable. Sara is highly attuned to this, working to hone down anything superficial with precision and clarity. As performers, though, we cannot help but bring our personality to the rehearsal room.

We wrestle with our own baggage – the personal and the political. We bring our competences and our shortcomings to the space: our animal sensibilities; what passes for intelligence and charm; our ignorance and our capacity to fail. I am still unsure to what extent my past involvement with Bodies in Flight informs or inflects my approach to the recent work. It matters not anymore. We are now inseparable. Just as Stan's Cafe (a theatre company I founded with James Yarker in 1991) has found its way into my DNA, so too has Bodies in Flight. The work is forever with me. It continues to nourish me, sometimes long after the event has passed – in the memory of an idea, an image or a turn of phrase.

> Between the idea
> And the reality
> Between the motion
> And the act
> Falls the Shadow.
> (T.S. Eliot, 'The Hollow Men', 1969: 81)

Performances are by their nature ephemeral. They may be planned and prepared for in fine detail, but once they have combusted in the alembic of the performance event their power is to survive as shadows in the memory. We recall the dazzling stage pictures, captivating stagecraft or startling activity; and we can be provoked into emotional responses that move or surprise us. Performance reminds us that we are here and must act now. It declares our presence in the world. My performer-self has permission to commit itself to this idea in ways my mundane other does not. It is a licensed embodiment, ideally without pretence. It acknowledges its parameters of 'being' as a model that skits across the fuzzy membrane between the real and the imagined; a membrane of which an audience is made aware and acknowledges.

It is a paradox that the performance event will only happen once – here and now, because, in that instant, it carries the embodied memory of the dozen-or-so practice runs which have made it all possible. It bears the imprint of all the prior moments which have shaped that present, bearing the baggage, the scars, the triumphant confidence and the raw animal presence, in all its fragile, pathetic beauty. Here and now ... and yet somehow nowhere.

> Clap, and you're already listening to a recording.
> (*Rough*)
>
> I am not held here long
> For I must on

> And to other things
> And yet
> Back I come here
> As if for the first time
> As if I had not seen this before
> As if I had no memory.
> (*Model Love*)

Bodies in Flight's work is expert at anatomizing the moment. Like the existential glitch of being at a party, feeling both inside and outside of it simultaneously; feeling both connected to events, whilst also observing it, as if from the outside. Just as the performer, inside the moment, relays a script that has been prepared for them outside of that moment.

In much of the recent work, the shadow of the moribund looms large, like a Goya demon. And whilst acts of injustice and atrocity were addressed and somewhat sardonically demonstrated in *Rough*, by *Who By Fire* the lens was trained on something more personal and real – the spectre of death in a more familiar proximity; the confrontation with our own mortality. In the recent work, *Life Class*, the projected loss of a lover (and dance-partner) becomes the focus. Grief is anatomized, and the joy of living/loving is reaffirmed. Performing this show, with co-performer Morven Macbeth, emboldened my long-held conviction that the act of performance itself is a miniature life-and-death cycle, crafted and distilled into a single declaration, striving to frame in some small way the profound, beautiful and temporal nature of being.

It is in Bodies in Flight's ability to craft moments of unashamed beauty that the work speaks loudest to me. Dramaturgically, these are moments that have been earned through rigorous detail and hard work; the effort and commitment of a team building a show from scratch. I see this common objective as an act of love, seeking to elicit something greater than the sum of its component parts; something hopeful and magical, that will move us. Longevity in this sector (or 'survival' as I now think of it) is through successive, cumulative acts of faith (projects), strung together in one seemingly haphazard peregrination (career). As an artist, I am always fighting the impulse to abandon and move on, whilst simultaneously navigating the obstacles that inspire self-doubt. But for someone who has always struggled to admit completion, the act of performance, with its commitment to the absolute, has a ritualistic, purging effect. A show is wrestled into existence; it lives – often terrifyingly – in an intense act of collective willpower, witnessed by strangers and friends in the dark. We know that the act will be brought to its inevitable end, like life itself. Sometimes violently or enlighteningly, sometimes in a sublime beauty. And, as we are drawn into that coda, my role, like that of a death doula, is to steer the audience towards that exquisite moment when lights and sound finally fade to nothing.

References

Eliot, T. S. ([1925] 1969), 'The Hollow Men', in V. Eliot (ed.), *The Complete Poems and Plays of T. S. Eliot*, London: Faber and Faber.

Further Reading

Crossley, Mark and Yarker, James (2017), *Devising Theatre with Stan's Cafe*, London: Bloomsbury Methuen Drama.

13

Speaking in Texts: Writing Beyond Meaning

SIMON JONES

In this Flight, I address what I have found particular to the writer's job in devising performance, as opposed to writing plays. I propose that text freed from 'character' or 'plot' enables both the writer and the performer to explore new aspects of their own skill sets and imagination. It requires a different approach to using text in the devising process – an 'as-if-for-the-first-time'-ness, a radical attitude that risks trashing or wrenching the text into obscurity, in order to open up novel and previously unimagined possibilities. It also establishes a new relationship between writer and performer, and performer and audience, grounded in opening up the differences of perspectives on the text and trusting dwelling in them as a vital force of devising. I chart the development of these ideas through the first two series of works.

In the 1980s, when I wrote plays, I always insisted on the spelling *play-wright*: I felt, as a 'wrighter', I was somehow crafting the whole event. The job went beyond merely providing the words the actors spoke. And yet, despite this level of literal authority over the event, I was continually frustrated and disappointed by the plays I wrote and very often directed. Indeed, I found myself paradoxically drawn to those aspects of the performance that were non-verbal – the choreography, the scenography and soundscape, the erotics of the performers themselves; forces that pushed past what seemed to be the always-delimiting boundaries of the 'character' or 'narrative'. I came to find rationalizing everything performance could offer from the script alone constricting. So much so, that when I eventually broke with wrighting plays, the first devised works I made eschewed verbal language completely: both *Deadplay* and *Exhibit* were resolutely physical theatre.

Looking back at that first series of work, even when I began to re-introduce text, I found it hard to abandon the teleology of the author, who commits their script to the director, who shapes the actor's voicing of the 'character', who signals the critic's opinions of the 'drama' and who manages the audience's expectations of the event as a whole. For me, this hierarchy of meaning-making was so dominant in theatre that it was difficult actually to open my own eyes and see what was happening right in front of me in the rehearsal room: what were these performers actually doing? I continued to labour away at the text in the privacy of my own room, bringing it into the rehearsal overburdened with images of how it was to be spoken by the performers, felt by those who heard it, and eventually understood and appropriately appreciated by those in the know. In all this teleology, what I was missing was the concreteness of the situation of devising: the actuality of the performer encountering my text for the first time, making their own sense of it. I was treating the performer as a conduit, rather than a collaborator: at the cost of inhibiting both what they could possibly do with the text and the potential that may have lain unrecognized by me in that text.

Our first attempt to break this authorizing force, in *iwannabewolfman*, was to write collectively, effectively opening up the 'body' of text across multiple authors. However, this exacerbated the limitations of treating performers as mouthpieces, because each collaborator viewed the show's 'topic' of the 'Freudian family' from their own perspective, producing a set of texts on a theme, with no felt relation between them. The performers were confused by the diverging trajectories the various texts took, so much so that when they were spoken, they seemed arbitrary and inconsequential. Multiplying the style and mood and erasing the unique *signature* of the text resulted in an unarticulated 'body' of writing that could never become viable, and *liveable*.

It took me several works to unlearn this dominant logocentrism, in effect, to learn how to hear what the performer was speaking back to me *of what I had written*: in essence, to hear the text *as if for the first time*. To do that, I had to forget that I had written it, although it felt very personal to me. As soon as the performer spoke it, it should no longer belong to me: it was the performer's, who, in speaking *their* text back to me, became my collaborator. So, when, in the next show *Rough*, I wrote a series of short texts satirizing the 'Postmodern zeitgeist', we decided the performers would make them their own, selecting from this 'body' of text for themselves which to try out, passing them between themselves, until one or more began to sound in a certain performer's voice, imbuing them with an energy and specificity, a life. I recall Charlotte Watkins and Katherine Porter injecting a cool hyper-femininity into texts satirizing advice and self-help manuals;

Simon Pegg delivering homilies on paranoia and Ancient Greek myths as stand-up. Relinquishing control of these texts, my ownership of them as the writer freed not only the performers but the texts themselves, to become something other than I had imagined, indeed, something beyond what it was possible for me to imagine. Text freed from intention is also freed from character and narrative, effectively from normative bodies and everyday situations. It can offer itself *as itself*, rather than as signifying some generally understood version of 'reality'. And yet paradoxically, the more it is freed to find its own form, freed to attach itself to any body, the more it retains and expresses my particular *way of writing – a signature*. Furthermore, this freeing obliges the performer to find their own way to make these texts make sense, crucially not to me in the rehearsal room, but to the putative audience who would eventually experience the work. So, by empowering performers, rather than multiplying writers, the text finds its own authenticity as an intimate relation of two kinds of *personal* – the writer's signature and the performers' voicing: it becomes *concrete*.

If concrete text must be situated, in a certain room amongst certain artists, thence audiences, one urgent question appears: how is this 'situation' any different from its subject or topic? How can I claim an unaffiliated, enfranchised signature force for the text, if its very situatedness in space and time and persons anchors it to their concerns? This is because the situated text is freed *by* those collaborators involved, not in spite of them. Because it enters, moves through and out of each person differently, it cannot float above and somehow outside the devising *as an issue,* already understood in advance, each knowing on which side to stand and who is right. It escapes such collective meaning-making in the very concreteness of its utterance by that performer in that place – Roland Barthes' 'The grain of the voice' (1977). As part of this process, I began to understand that the text must bend and morph, so with each new work, this licence became more pronounced: for instance, all three performers in *Skinworks* (Polly Frame, Graeme Rose and Kaylene Tan) went beyond exchanging which texts to perform. They altered them in rehearsal, trying on different voices, obliging rewrites from first to third to second person, to hear which one felt best from their mouths. (For more on 'situation', see Chapter 20, 'Set-up and Situation'.)

Although, after the performance, both collaborators and audiences can come to terms with what has been said and heard *as if it were an issue*, the intensity of this experience of the text *as performed*, literally – *personified*, cannot be undone. Here, I recall the Latin word for the actor's mask – *persona*, literally *through sound*, that is, by way of the voice we access the person. This *voice–word* coupling-duetting resonates and slips and slides around and beyond any attempt to render the text meaningful *as it is being performed-personified*: it remains felt in all its abandonment, waywardness and passion. So, despite the performers' charismatic 'ownership' of the text in *Skinworks*, such as Kaylene's haunted, disembodied voicing of the text 'How could it be' or Polly's gestural embodiment of 'This body feels so strange tonight', those texts remained promiscuous, as new performers took over for different performances, producing new voice–word duets full of different intensities. In these ways, personified text actualizes at one and the same time as both most itself *and* most personified, as each performer in each performance must test the text's signature to the point of erasure, so each auditor is provoked to abandon decorum, the law, the 'woke' and imagine a different world.

What further complicates and enriches this coupling of voice–word is music–sound. From 1990 with *Love Is ...* Bodies in Flight had always worked with composers and sound artists on original music and soundscapes. *Skinworks* was the first in a series of collaborations with the rock band Angel Tech, whose music was developed alongside the performers in rehearsal, inflecting and transforming the material in the devising, and then played live in performance. This produced an uncanny four-way inter-relationship: between the voice and the instrument, and between the word and the music's abstracted sound; each of the four intensities irreducible to, unexchangeable with any other. Acknowledging this, we broadcast a radio version of *Skinworks* on Resonance FM; released a CD entitled *Skinworks for Ears*; and decided our next project with Angel Tech – *Who By Fire* – would be an opera.

If surrendering the text to my collaborators on the first day of rehearsal means relinquishing control and accepting a joint ownership of the material, which is then, through the devising, taken a long way away from its origins, how does this impact the solitary business of writing? How did the way we handled and transformed the text as part of our collaborative devising methodology affect how and what I wrote? Whilst as a playwright I had increasingly found the required consistency and internal logic of character and plot inhibited what I wanted to say about the play's broader themes, once freed from these constraints, it was not so easy to find a way beyond the subject (both of character and topic), beyond the issue with its ready-to-hand political 'solutions'. In Bodies in Flight's first series, the loosely defined 'situation' helped me to focus passages of text dealing with a range of ideas and topics: such as *Rough*'s 'elevator-pitch' – 'because of diminishing faith in them, a group of gods have been forced on the road in a touring cabaret show', which allowed us to explore a variety of topics from postmodern disbelief in metanarratives to sexual mores, as well as a direct-address mode which engaged the audience in a lighter, more comedic style. The fantastical situation accommodated this 'portmanteau' technique in building the body of the text.

Since then, the *situation*, sometimes inspired by films (*A Bout de Souffle* in *DeliverUs*), sometimes performance art (*The Artist Is Present* in *Life Class*), sometimes technological developments (the chatroom in *Skinworks*), has provided a thematic envelope, a kind of fictitious 'organism' with more or less porous cell walls, within which I have been able to make texts, sometimes fragmentary in form (the 'sermons' in *Beautiful Losers*), sometimes more sustained (the 'not-me me' stream-of-consciousness monologue in *Secrecy of Saints*). The more concrete I found the situation, the more likely the texts I wrote would not only explore the work's ostensible *topos* (place) or organism (body) but also my own concerns as a person. It is as if the situation's concreteness frees me to look into myself, producing a *writing as autogenesis*, a writing that realizes aspects of my self that I had not previously faced or phrased so vividly. Unlike writers whose personal biography speaks to clearly defined social issues, such as gender, ethnicity or sexuality, I discovered that my autobiography was a 'biography of everydayness': my interest, as in what I reached towards, was the uniqueness of everyday experience and feeling, the passion of the extraordinary ordinary (see Chapter 18, 'The Magnificent Minutiae'). This realization helped me achieve a level of concreteness in my (dramatic) writing *of and about the situation*, that responded to and resonated with that of the (theatrical) set-up.

One further insight emerged from this autogenetic writing: that the more I wrote *into my interest*, the less I thought about the performer who speaks it or the audience who listens to it. In effect, in the writing, I forgot its teleology as dramatic speech: I produced texts that risked being *unperformable*, for whatever reason – too long, too solipsistic, too hung up on linguistic niceties, painfully personal or flawed in their emotional register. So, when the performer first read back to me my text, these 'errors' suddenly and often amusingly appeared, frustrating their attempts to find their voice in the work. Of course, the actor in narrative theatre's read-through is the script's first audience; their initial response feeds back to the writer, who may then revise the script. Based on their experience, this actor's valuable insight projects forward to the first night and what that first audience might make of what they hear, always with the intention of further defining, in order to communicate the character. In Bodies in Flight's devising process, delivering the performer an 'unperformable' text presents a different order of problem: counterintuitively, instead of stymying their imaginative work or channelling it in advance towards a specific 'character', it allows them to move past any conventionalized interpretations, and provides an added incentive to transform the text, re-shape its phrasing, re-mould its address and shift its personhood across first person singular, plural, second person, third. The more I worked with performers who claimed the text as their own in devising, the more I felt at liberty to indulge my introspective writing, because I trusted that the performer would always save the text from obscurity or prolixity, their transformations always turning its waywardness towards its audience in performance.

Through this transformative play in rehearsal, I began to understand my relationship to the performer *by way of my writing, as a being in-between*, literally the etymological root of 'interest' – *inter-esse: to be between*. The text creates a field of potential energy between the one and the other, that each of us enters *on our own* and dwells in during rehearsals *in our own way*, progressively forcing each out into the open, into the newfound spaciousness of what that particular work itself wants to become. This becoming is neither known nor owned by any one collaborator: it has to be disclosed amongst the intensities of a genuine complementarity, where each will find their own modes of expression: solitarinesses from which a collaborating emerges.

> A unique style comes from the gesture, the project, the itinerary, the risk – indeed, from the acceptance of a specific solitude. [...] Repetition of content or method entails no risk, whereas style reflects in its mirror the nature of danger. In venturing as far as possible toward non-recognition, style runs the risk even of autism.
> (Serres and Latour 1995: 94)

References

Barthes, Roland (1977), 'The grain of the voice', in *Image-Music-Text* (trans. H. Stephen), New York: Hill and Wang, pp. 179–89.

Serres, Michel and Latour, Bruno ([1990] 1995), *Conversations on Science, Culture, and Time*, Ann Arbor, MI: University of Michigan Press.

14
Beautiful Losers (1994)

FIGURE 14.1: *Beautiful Losers*: performers Charlotte Watkins and Jon Carnall. Scan from original slide. Photo: Bridget Mazzey.

FIGURE 14.2: *Beautiful Losers*: postcard. Courtesy of the University of Bristol Theatre Collection.

FIGURE 14.3 (next): *Beautiful Losers*: performers Charlotte Watkins and Jon Carnall. Scan from original slide. Photo: Bridget Mazzey.

FIGURE 14.4 (next): *Beautiful Losers*: performers Jon Carnall and Charlotte Watkins. Scan from original slide. Photo: Bridget Mazzey.

FIGURE 14.5 (next): *Beautiful Losers*: performers Charlotte Watkins and Jon Carnall. Scan from original slide. Photo: Bridget Mazzey.

FIGURE 14.6 (next): *Beautiful Losers*: performer Jon Carnall. Scan from original slide. Photo: Bridget Mazzey.

PUBLICITY COPY
Lessons in exterior living
Beautiful Losers *chronicles a heavenly quest. Three evangelical curators scour Britain for the relics of faith. Each site they visit yields some small miracle of the life to come. As they bear witness to the heaven held in these everyday things, they deliver up to us lessons on how best to prepare for the afterlife. Not only do they share their prophecies and revelations with us, but they also share their snacks and packed lunches. Their faith is simple as their doubt complex. They are working towards the millennium, like the rest of us, riddled with despair and distrust, driven by hope and innocence. They are the Beautiful Losers.*
During one of these lessons a terrible accident happens and all hell is let loose. We can't say any more about that now.

Inspired by the preachers who stand on street corners telling of the end of days as commuters hurry on by, this work imagines that heaven has fallen into the everyday and it is the job of our intrepid performers to convince the audience of the miracle. We abandoned the proscenium-arch set-up to make an environmental performance that had to be adapted to respond to each site it was played in. Not only did it help us to intensify even more powerfully the face-to-face relationship between performer and audience-spectator but also began our fascination with working in non-standard formats and locations. We worked for the first time with computer-based sound artist Darren Bourne to create a quadrophonic sound score that both surrounded and filled the performance space. In 2003, Singapore-based performance company spell#7 revived the show and set it in a shophouse in the Little India district of Singapore.

DARREN BOURNE sound designer, JON CARNALL performer, SARA GIDDENS choreographer, SIMON JONES director/writer, BRIDGET MAZZEY designer/performer, CHARLOTTE WATKINS performer.

With: KATIE BURNELL head construction, EDWARD DIMSDALE photography, SIMON PEGG graphics.

Performed: Nott Dance Festival/ Bonington Gallery (Nottingham), Courtyard Theatre (London), Arnolfini (Bristol), Wimbledon School of Art (London), Powerhouse (Nottingham), Chapter Arts Centre (Cardiff), Wickham Theatre (Bristol).

Text extracts

SIMON JONES

Beautiful Losers *takes up the postmodern theme of the lack of faith in metanarratives, articulated through the situation of the every-day sight of street preachers. The environmental staging, in which performers and audience share a bespoke theatricalized space where 'heaven has crashed through', intensified the direct address, its impact and destabilizing energy. More sustained passages of text open out a kind of 'anti-theology' of late capitalism, anxious, even paranoid, violent, uncaring, yet sentimental. The performers invited interactions with audience members by simply addressing them directly or suddenly moving through them and shifting focus from one area to another. With nowhere 'to hide', this made the audience potential objects of one another's attention, further animating the event with a febrile and nervous energy, an idea we later returned to in* Skinworks (2002–03).

4. DOMESTIC DIALOGUES
turn caption, reveal 2nd relic: knife
dialogue on DIY and dress

[HIS: All the tiny losses that add up to a life.]
HERS: All the unreturned looks, the irredeemable chances, missed. Let's laugh in the face of that one, shall we? He didn't look at me. He could have looked at me. What would it have cost him to have looked at me?
[HIS: What hurt could it have done?]
            To have smiled the lovely smile, yes, you are on this planet too, and yes, I am pleased about that. How could he have calculated the benefits and the risks in that instant that he took to turn his eyes away? He should've taken more care of me.
[HIS: Such beauty should be generous with its favours.]
            O, didn't I mention? Yes, he was gorgeous. And yes, his lovely gorgeousness was lavished on this third party, and not on me. Their loss. They will remain nameless.
[HIS: Their loss.]

| | I have to think that, don't I? I'm required to think that. In order to get up in the mornings, to believe in justice. To think the unthinkable, that it is they who are eternally damned, and not ugly little me. Don't I?
[HIS: | In this world.]
           | The one we're living in today, I mean.

dialogue of violent argument

HIS: | I'm gonna kill you. I'm gonna fucking stab your eyes out.

punch

           | What a relief when your face drops into ugliness. When you're the other side of that threshold commonly called beauty. When you can be sure, in the sense that only perverts will find you attractive. O, the time that lends me. The liberty that affords me. I am in heaven, yes. A flake of heaven's fallen off and is masking my face.
           | [You're always ugly in someone's eyes.]
           | Ughhh.

[…]

5. JANE'S POSSESSION
CHRIS, *find a corner, karaoke*
JANE *is possessed, walk, fall over*

HERS: | Get off me. He's touching my skin. Don't let him. I am a dirty dirty woman. Filthy cow. You let him filth you up. Not nice. Ouch. He's doing unspeakable deedies to me right now. I am not going to embarrass you by detailing them. Out. Oh, filthy turning-on. Naughty naughty lickings robbing me of my sanctity. Tart. You will out. I -eee. Search me. Peel back the flaps. Of skin. My skin. I am not ashamed. I am so ashamed. All the bad and dirty doings of all the girls and big women in the whole solid world. You wish me well. Ha. Out.

God, I didn't come here to be. All the history and the small domestic ravings, come crashing down. Compress into each tiny millimetre of this skin. Ah, he would say I am the bestest beauty on the block. But I can't agree to that. It's not in the scope of my knowing about things. Out. Rid me right now. 0, I am going to make a show of myself. These people are all strangers to me. Filthy despicable room. Loathsome air, suffocate me. I wouldn't know what it felt like to do good.
I am not the doctor in the house.
But no matter how low.
No matter how shitty shitty panties I get, I will not surrender my tongue. Not to you. Have every organ else, but my licker, my lapper-kisser, my lover, my halloo-er, my word-maker, world-ravisher. Have the whole holy carcass else. Not the clacker, not the teaser, not the lovely lovely soother in the panic-fucked night. My miracle-worker. No, you can't have that. Even if I have to remain silent. Still as the grave. Until the end. No.

HIS: Let's stop for a mo and think about what this might possibly mean.

6. PACKED LUNCH

get out packed lunches, change fluorescent tube, sit on folding stools

HIS: I'm overwhelmed by two things
three … thoughts … really …
three overwhelmings.
1. that you have come
which is an act
many acts of overwhelming grace
and how can anyone answer that?
2. that I dare talk of
mouth the word we
like I knew you, like I cared, or could at the very least speak on your behalf
a realization of overwhelming cruelty
that I cannot, I mean, speak on your behalves, or anyone's behalf.

HERS: And what was the other? The third rather? The third overwhelming.

HIS: Ah yes!
         That you're here under false pretences, to hear us speak about a thing of which we know nothing, on which we are quite incompetent.

HERS: But … we were compelled, really … a compulsion it would be embarrassing to discuss in front of strangers, or worse in front of those who do not care.

HIS: And why should they? she asks.

HERS: Just tucking in now, an image comes to me of a dining table, dinner with father and mother, a show of food.

HIS: I'm reminded of our daughter, and I'm moved to imagine her in such a predicament like she must have been so many times. And I'm reminded of my father, with his sickly son, who could not do, really could not do, would not do. How angry he was all the time, how frustrated that his love for his child could only find expression in.

HERS: How the great suffering, assumed, of the child could never be shared, since it could never be shown. As it could never be shown, it would never be remembered, like it did not happen, and in his anger – the father's, that is – could not happen, could not account for the overwhelming passion he felt he had to articulate.

HIS: And when the father showed the child, this is the room in which I could act, this is the future I am about to usher in, come in, be mindful of the site … was it not love that moved him, like a doctor loves in making well, like the sickly son who hated the doctor, whom he could not name and therefore would not remember, the voice who asked him to count backwards in this operating theatre …

HERS: … And promised him ice-cream in this dining room, to soothe his throat, who promised to fill his lungs with air, with fresh air, like there was no tomorrow, and stretched across this floor would cover two football pitches one blessed alveolus thick.

HIS: I do not play football and counting backwards sends me into oblivion.

HERS: Really? And could the child grasp? Was it possible for him to show – the father, that is – the great goodness of his imperial love, like a doctor points to a bucket of fluid: I have gotten all this evil out?
HIS: Cough it up and sit down, eat your food, your mother slaved over a hot.
HERS: And is it possible to cry real tears other than those of shock?
HIS: I did not know I was dying until he told me I was well.
HERS: And why did the mother not inform? Were they tears of shock? And should I feel the same, the same shame, that I too would be speechless, in reality? Could I, hand on my heart, declare I would not stay silent, unveil my ignorance, like an overwhelming lie for all to see, a lesson in? Have I not already struck the child who sits across from me and refuses to eat good food, because there are people starving … ?
HIS: There is an authority to be revealed, there is already enough fluid in the bucket and it stinks to high heaven, I know, I coughed it up.
HERS: So why did she not tell? All the other signs were there for all to see. And how come the father had to strike the child?
HIS: I have no experience. So how come? Bad things sometimes happen, I suppose.
HERS: You haven't eaten a thing. Force yourself.
HIS: Can I be excused?
HERS: Force yourself.
HIS: Can I? And with an overwhelming sense of relief, he said to me …
HERS: You may step down from the table.

[…]

8. CHRIS'S POSSESSION
CHRIS *is possessed, walks around the space*

HIS: There's a devil in this room. I can feel him. It has taken on a human shape. It is with us. It is always with us. We are never without it.
[HERS: Don't frighten people.]

Is it you? Are you the devil that whispers to me in my sleep, go fuck little boys and make them bleed?

approach someone in audience

[HERS: Stop frightening folks.]
Because I can tell you I don't like it. It is not nice. You think there is no evil. You think that evil does not find its home in people. In particular persons. You're barmy. You think the only real choice before us is which aftershave to buy, to give and to receive. Well, the devil loves a discerning consumer. Messy, baroque, profligate, embarrassing.

drinks from cans

I feel … electrified by it. Ever closer and the door always slammed in your face. Coping with that distress is politics. And that always turns nasty. Be liberal, let them have their say. I say, fuck them. Your fucking pluralism. Your fucking other side of the fucking argument. Your fucking holy point of view. I'm going to freeze now. And when I unfreeze the world will be a different place.

[HERS: Here we go.]
I have a vast love. But it's shattered. Spread like a slime along the trail I've left. So many false alarms, so many late calls. So many disputes in the name of truth. I wish it wasn't like this. [laughs] But the truth is, it is, it really honestly is.

You can't crash heaven. You're not good enough. You just won't do. You can't blag your way into paradise with bits of trash and fairy lights. Now come on. Take my …

offers hand to audience

We're the walking dead. We're already out the other end. Yeah, go on.

offers hand again

[…]

JANE, *throw pieces of relic at him*

HERS: Make sure that in doing everything you do you do it with goodness in your heart. I have talked a lot tonight about the goodness in my heart. I have felt that goodness moving me to speak to you. I can't say, I can't put into words, mouth the words of love my heart moves me to utter. They are strange to me, right at the heart of me, and yet other than me. All I can say is, the little things help. They do. The increment, the inclining towards. Always helps. And the really lovely thing is, you never know how much it helps. You can't rip out your own heart to see how it beats. Nowhere down the double helix will you find a gene for goodness. Think upon that now, and be good.

9. A CURE FOR THE MODERN HEADACHE

JANE, *take Betty's head*
CHRIS, *caption*

JANE: And in that instant – if an instant can have an inside – I saw my future laid out bare. With a certainty so logical you're paralysed. This is how it goes. Your life. Your one-and-only.

CHRIS: They won't welcome you in with open arms. Those members of the club of the good and wholesome life. It isn't your bad luck you're left on the doorstep. It's your nature.

JANE: What are you gonna do with that? When all your ducking and weaving's done.

CHRIS: How you gonna answer that one?

run into wall, relic breaks, listen for hell crash
hand out pieces to the audience

JANE: Evaporate before their gaze.

CHRIS: Since for them your knowledge is nonsense, become invisible.

JANE: Since for them the exchange of commodities and endless back-slapping is the world, become the parasite.
CHRIS: Invade their global networks undetected, unpoliced, unknown. And thrive off their fat.
JANE: Since that is your fate, fuck it.
CHRIS: Revolutions have their times.
JANE: So live, between the fabric and the weave.
CHRIS: Between his order and the undertaking it.
JANE: Let the crowd sweep you up. Hide yourself in your lover's arms.
CHRIS: Drown the cries with your Walkman.
JANE: This is not the way the world will end. Tell them something useful. Keep a suitcase packed.
CHRIS: Don't jog?
JANE: Say something about animals.
CHRIS: Will they find their way home?
JANE: Maybe. I dunno. I don't care. I do care. I think I care. I care.

flee the space

15
Hearing Bodies in Flight
DARREN BOURNE

DR DARREN BOURNE is a musician and academic. He met and worked with Bodies in Flight when he was a sound technician at Nottingham Trent University. He then spent over twenty years as Director of Education at Confetti Institute of Creative Technologies, a specialist creative industry organization based in Nottingham. His scholarly focus is within education philosophy and practice, and you can hear his more recent sound work online through his 'halF unusuaL' project. Darren was involved in three Bodies in Flight productions as a sound designer: Beautiful Losers, Littluns Wake *and* Constants.

Here he recalls the development of the shows' sonic elements and how they connect to his ongoing exploration of the nature and meaning of sound and music.

My first encounter with Bodies in Flight was a production of *iwannabewolfman* in 1991 amongst numerous contemporary performances I saw at Nottingham Trent University. I was taken by all the elements, but I noticed particularly how significant to the performance the sonic elements were. So, when offered, I jumped at the chance to work with the company. I soon discovered that the freedom allowed by their approach was an intense, but highly rewarding experience. Each of the three shows I worked on was quite different in terms of where it enabled me to reach and what it allowed me to explore sonically. Everything seemed to come out of the show itself, what the show *was*, which was both a tangible outcome and a vehicle for those involved: for me, 'hidden' in each was a perfect soundtrack. There was nothing outside of the show (Derrida et al. 1976), even though, strangely, it never felt like the 'container' of the show was constricting for the soundtrack. I experienced a contradiction between almost total freedom and inexorable structure, which coalesced 'by itself' into a defined end-point production.

Beautiful Losers was a promenade performance; the audience was inside the piece. The first performance was in Bonington Gallery (Nottingham), which is a big white-box space, and which turned out to be perfect for the intended approach. The audience walked down into the environment, adding a certain drama from the first moment. The pretext was that just before the show began a little bit of heaven had 'broken through' to the site. There were peculiar people chasing artefacts that had been left behind after this breakthrough or perhaps visitation. The audiences were part of it all, but they were also left to figure out what was happening, as they were gradually let into the storyline through the oblique dialogue.

My approach to the sound needed to be as enveloping as the dramaturgy. Theoretically, with my background in sound engineering in the pop-music industry, a significant touch point for *Beautiful Losers* was the work of Brian Eno (Eno and Mills 1986), who popularized ambient and generative approaches to music as well as posing questions about what music is and how we create and receive it. So, the aim to devise a sonically immersive experience ended up as a quadraphonic soundscape. Even though standard in cinema nowadays, the early 1990s was before surround sound was established in the theatre world: for a show of this type, what I wanted to do was basically impossible considering the budget. The technology was not available, especially considering the need for a relatively straightforward technical fit-up. So, I achieved something faithful to the idea by mixing onto a four-track cassette player, which formed the basis of our home-made 'quadraphonic' system. What we managed to create worked well for what we were trying to achieve, although not very pretty under the hood. When the show toured, we ended up having to back down to a stereo version to make it feasible.

I participated in much of the devising, which closely informed how the soundtrack evolved, even though the sound work was mainly completed in a recording studio away from rehearsals. It was a great experience working alongside the company over an extended period and watching what slowly emerged from the process. From the starting point of creating an enveloping sonic environment, I explored two main sound spaces, 'Heaven' and 'Hell', which formed the basis for everything else in the soundtrack. In addition, huge explosions and surges formed a transition between the two sites of Heaven and Hell, coincident but marked out by lighting and sound, developed from cannon sounds taken from a BBC sound effects library.

For the sound world of Hell, I started off with various attempts to create 'hot' and hopefully hell-like sounds, such as throwing water onto a hot frying pan and recording the resulting sizzle. This was sampled and layered up with various audio manipulations. It was quite labour-intensive and would certainly be a lot easier with today's technology. Speeding up and slowing down the hotplate samples created moments that suggested agony, heat and awfulness, including what sounded like repeated metallic stabbing sounds and strange otherworldly voices. Out of these numerous layers appeared a suitably rich and complex hellscape. I was trying to achieve something like a huge Hieronymus Bosch painting in sound, but as it was always going to be played at a quite low volume, it also needed to be intense enough in the absence of loudness to add weight. This Hell sound formed a background to the action, and in some ways was deliberately 'visual' and suggestive. Signalling the radical change between Heaven and Hell, the transitional surges, explosions and other eruptions were intended to scare people. Because the audience had to hear the dialogue above the soundtrack, these surges took place in gaps in the text, contrasting markedly with the background sound.

On the flip side was the Heaven soundscape. Oddly, sounds from fluorescent light tubes were the single source to paint heaven in sound, with the rather banal and obvious metaphoric link to light, but man-made light, with the suggestion of gaudy neon lights and their seedy connotations. There were two main sonic elements from the fluorescents: the opening flicker that emits from older tubes as they spring into life and the steady electric buzz that can be rather irritating once noticed. Again, these sounds were recorded, manipulated and layered to create a vast space that was probably hundreds of electrical hums and buzzes alongside the flickering of the tubes. My intention was to create an open, astonishing and kind of eerie, heaven-like space in sound.

Beautiful Losers was quite something. Although hard to describe, the process had a real intensity, as if the work itself materialized out of the collaborators' relationships. I suspect the level of collaboration we enjoyed was, and is generally, hard to achieve; it felt a privilege to be part of, and testament to, the productive creative relationship of Sara and Simon.

In 1995, we created *Littluns Wake* together, another promenade performance, but very different in scope and feel. The audience had been invited to an intimate wake for 'Littlun': I imagine a challenge for some as they gathered around a 'dead' body in a metal coffin within touching distance.

Sonically, the approach was almost the opposite of *Beautiful Losers*. The soundtrack emanated from tiny speakers inside the coffin, particularly around Littlun, and secreted around the space. Flies were used as a sonic cue for decay and death. I synthesized their sounds from scratch and then layered them up into a huge swarm that would swell up from time to time and then reduce to just a few. Despite being only auditory, the intimate placing of the speakers meant they could almost be felt in and around the audience seated along the long table. The sound, and to an extent the whole performance, literally and deliberately came out of this context. I was inspired by John Cage, who developed sonic environments from specific contexts and occasions, perhaps the most famous being his 'silent' piece, *4'33"*. Working in a different musical idiom to Eno, Cage aimed to capture chance sonic occurrences, exploring what music is or can be in striking ways, especially in terms of music that emerges from the environment (Cage 1994). Throughout the lengthy, but enjoyable, workshopping process, I brought in sonic material to try alongside the movement, acting and text, building up a coherent soundtrack in this unique collaboration.

Constants was more conventional in terms of the sound set-up: although the scenography was again environmental, the speakers were simply there, visible and producing the sound. In some senses, in parallel to the sound in *Littluns Wake*, which came out of the scenic elements, such as the long bench used by the audience, most of the sound for *Constants* originated from the lead character, played by Sheila Gilbert. We recorded Sheila reading the text, which was then sampled, manipulated and layered to constitute much of the sonic environment, suggesting a confusion of voices and language that we all have inside our heads from time to time, but still recognizable as Sheila's voice that the audience was experiencing live at the same time. Today, it would be possible to sample the voice as it happens, but that was beyond the technology at the time. Having said that, I was using a new Atari Falcon system to develop some of the computer manipulations and saw this show as an opportunity to explore Sonic Art, a field within which Trevor Wishart (1985) was a leading light and who made use of advanced technologies and computing to expand sonic and musical possibilities.

My approach to the sound design across all three shows had a few related influences: the practices of Eno, Cage and Wishart can probably be discerned within my work to some degree even now. In addition, in the 1990s, I was working with children in a music school at weekends using some of John Paynter's ideas, with some excellent educational and sonic results. He was exploring the boundaries of music and encouraging young people to develop their sonic sensibilities irrespective of their level of musical skill or knowledge (Paynter 1992). This certainly bled through into my thinking about process and collaboration, staying open to musical or sonic inspiration from any collaborator or part of the process and, perhaps especially, from non-musicians or non-sonic elements.

In my work with Bodies in Flight, I was exploring how sound and music interrelated, and I remain captivated by the simple question of what music is. Can music be 'just' sound, sound *as* music, in some sense? I was trying to understand how sound affected people's experience of performance, music or other events and experiences. After all, hearing is a more intimate experience in many ways. In our individual development we hear before we see, so our sonic sense is, in a way, more fundamental. I notice how little we listen, at least consciously, and perhaps increasingly so as technology infiltrates contemporary life. We could hear 'music' simply as a kind of intention, without headphones, when wandering around. As a frame around something visual, placed in an art gallery, undergoes a transformation and takes on a new meaning, so something similar happens with sound in performance. We can choose to take more notice and appreciate our aural sense differently: the world changes when natural auditory surroundings are perceived as music. Through my work with Bodies in Flight, I wanted to encourage the audience to lean less heavily on their visual sense and explore their hearing with a delightful freshness.

References

Cage, John (1994), *Silence: Lectures and Writings*, London: Marion Boyars.

Derrida, Jacques, Spivak, Gayatri Chakravorty and Butler, Judith (1976), *Of Grammatology*, Baltimore, MD: Johns Hopkins University Press.

Eno, Brian and Mills, Russell (1986), *More Dark Than Shark*, London: Faber and Faber.

Paynter, John (1992), *Sound and Structure*, Cambridge: Cambridge University Press.

Wishart, Trevor (1985), *On Sonic Art*, York: Imagineering Press.

Further Listening

Excerpts from 'Heaven' and 'Hell' from *Beautiful Losers* are available on Bandcamp: https://halfunusual.bandcamp.com/album/beautiful-losers. Accessed 7 May 2024.

Bodies in Flight

16 Littluns Wake (1995)

FIGURE 16.1: *Littluns Wake*: performers Jon Carnall and Charlotte Watkins. Photo: Edward Dimsdale.

FIGURE 16.2: *Littluns Wake*: poster. Courtesy of the University of Bristol Theatre Collection.

much more beautiful and graceful, the relationship that anchored everyone to reality, the life that gave meaning to the struggle, the boy who made everyone feel really good about themselves. In the shared space of the wake, in intimate and intense performance, Bodies in Flight continue their exploration of the most collective and contemporary anxiety of all — the future and did we really mean it. Come, view the corpse, reminisce, pay your last respects. See if you can catch him breathing.

This concluded a trilogy of works that focused on contemporary belief, or the lack of it, what replaces religious faith in a secular society. Again, staged as an environmental piece, the audience was first invited to gather around a metal coffin, suspended in the air and packed with ice slowly melting onto the floor, then to sit on benches along a single long table, as haunting sounds emerge from small speakers and one of the performers drank through his 'grief' with actual whisky. Subtitled 'a life', it brought to a close the first series of Bodies in Flight's work in which we playfully explored theatricality and took a satirical stance on issues of gender and sexuality, identity and politics.

PUBLICITY COPY
A life
Elder's trying to bury his little brother, but Littlun won't stay down. He's invited perfect strangers to the wake, but then the woman whose love they shared turns up. He's making up stories about what a bastard his brother was, but everybody knows different. Grief does funny things. Meanwhile the caterers fail to show and the coffin lid won't screw shut.
Bodies in Flight's seventh show LITTLUNS WAKE invites you in as mourner to the death of something very

DARREN BOURNE soundtrack, DEAN BYFIELD performer, JON CARNALL performer, SARA GIDDENS choreography, SIMON JONES director/writer, BRIDGET MAZZEY design, CHARLOTTE WATKINS performer.

With: CLARE ENGLAND technical assistance, HUGO GLENDINNING photography, ELIZABETH JONES dressmaking, EWEN McLEOD technical assistance, JOHN PEELING coffin construction.

Performed at: Arnolfini (Bristol), Insights Conference, Intersect (Dartington), Bonington Gallery (Nottingham).

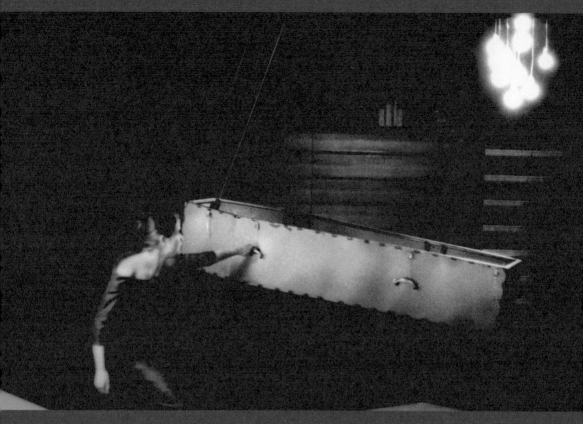

FIGURE **16.3**: *Littluns Wake*: performer Charlotte Watkins. Photo: Edward Dimsdale.

FIGURE **16.4**: *Littluns Wake*: performer Jon Carnall. Photo: Edward Dimsdale.

Figure 16.5: *Littluns Wake*: performer Dean Byfield. Photo: Edward Dimsdale.

Figure 16.6: *Littluns Wake*: performers Dean Byfield and Jon Carnall. Scan from original slide. Photo: Bridget Mazzey.

1996–2009

The Second Series

Performance as (Non-)Collaboration Across Media

In 1996, with our eighth show *Do the Wild Thing!*, we gave ourselves a specific research imperative to explore what we called the *mixing of flesh and text*, which we understood as performance's unique contribution as an art form. We had initially conceived the 'liveness' of performance as an excess that destabilized meaning-making and reached into zones of consciousness that other art forms rarely, if ever, accessed. We sought to agitate this excessiveness by intensifying the mix. We wanted different kinds of material and imagery, the aural and visual, the gestural and verbal, the immediate and mediated, to tumble one over the other, accelerating the pace of these destabilizing juxtapositions.

We experimented by devising *Do the Wild Thing!* almost entirely in two separate rooms, dividing choreographer from writer, performers who moved but did not speak from the performer who spoke but could not be seen. By unbundling the mix of moves and words, we understood for the first time that performance's excess was fundamentally a problem of media. It is not only bodies and texts that mix on stage and in the auditorium, it is also the multiple media through which performance necessarily articulates and expresses itself. Unpacking this constellation of relations between media in performance emerged from this Brechtian tactic of a 'separation of elements' to become Bodies in Flight's devising strategy of 'duetting' (see Chapter 9, 'Working Alongside').

We collaborated with sonic and visual media artists (such as Darren Bourne in *Constants*; Caroline Rye in *Constants* and *DeliverUs*; Chong Li Chuan and Hanindah Zainomium in *Double Happiness*; Angel Tech in *Skinworks* and *Who By Fire*; Edward Dimsdale in *Model Love*), coming to understand that the rehearsal room afforded us a precious space—time in which to be intimate with expertises we would never master. We had to unlearn intention and the selective attention it produced, and learn how to 'dwell' in the indeterminate zone between our own skill sets and masteries and those of our collaborators. This being *interested in*, *inter-esse*, literally *being in-between*, what was actually happening in the room, and the relation of materials and media in a given collaboration, became the organizing dynamic for this series of works. It opened out our devising not only to other artists but to other places and cultures, siting performances in specific places, including the virtual online environment. We took these collaborations across continents and cultures so that bodies with radically different life experiences were brought together in the work (*Double Happiness* and *Skinworks*), prefiguring our later series of works collaborating with different communities in co-creation.

To explore *how we mix* in the event of the performance itself, we had to open out how we devised with collaborators in the rehearsal room. In so doing, our central concern shifted from a broadly 'post-structuralist' approach to how meaning is made on stage towards a phenomenological understanding of 'being in-between'. We found ourselves living amongst the gaps necessarily produced by each different medium's 'take' on the situation we were jointly investigating. We came to understand that 'dwelling' in these gaps is itself a kind of deconstructive practice because it involves each artist interrogating their own meaning-making processes. Each of us individually had to 'come to terms' with the material outcomes of those interrogations, always from our own perspectives of what we mastered, towards others' mastery which we accepted we could never fully know. Collectively, each one of us in our own ways felt obliged to unfold and sustain the 'unsayable' differences between those outcomes. We labelled this 'collaboration as non-collaboration', opening oneself out to what one could not understand, daring to dwell in that unknowability, and thence make a work together alone.

17
Do the Wild Thing! (1996)

FIGURE 17.1: *Do the Wild Thing!*: performers Jane Devoy and Dan Elloway. Photo: Edward Dimsdale.

FIGURE 17.2: *Do the Wild Thing!*: postcard. Courtesy of the University of Bristol Theatre Collection.

PUBLICITY COPY
A peep show
The three lovers are in the big f*** scene. They tried to escape its gravity but the bed centre stage has pulled them in. Like everybody else, that's the leap their imagination made. Only trouble is it's only big enough for two. So, one must look on, like you and me. And anyway, who believes intimacy was only ever two. It's always been crowded out by that third person, the one with all the dreams. The light burns the bed, scours the skin of the boy and the girl; and the man sees that we see all there is to see in an instant. Then he begins the real exposure. Of what we like to call love, of the motives behind our intimacies, of the overwhelming desire in our tiniest of exchanges, the littlest of our making a move. Of what hides in love itself. And what shows itself through love.

Our eighth show marked a major shift in our practice, as we set out to explore a specific research question for the first time: we pulled apart the fundamental relation between what we see and what we hear on stage, in order to investigate the different ways in which our senses work, the different meanings and affects that each sense conveys. Inspired by Andy Warhol's voyeuristic movie *Beauty#2*, which improvises a scene of a couple questioned about their relationships and sexuality by an unseen interlocutor off camera, we set up a similar situation in which a couple lie on a bed as an unseen narrator sitting behind a curtain imagines the potential worlds of their relationship to the strains of a live string trio, mocking the classical lovers' tryst. The work deconstructed the theatrical and asked uncomfortable questions of its audience's erotic and libidinal investment in the show, whilst at the same time demonstrating the sheer power of performance to affect, disturb and engage them. Whilst cinema may be all about the erotic gaze, theatre is the only art where fleshes and senses actually mix; and it was this mixing we wanted to unpack and interrogate.

CHRIS AUSTIN composer, JON CARNALL performer, JANE DEVOY performer, DAN ELLOWAY performer, SARA GIDDENS choreographer, SIMON JONES director/writer, BRIDGET MAZZEY designer

BEN ROGERSON cello, SARAH SMALE viola, LIZ WHITTAM violin

Performed: Arnolfini (Bristol), Now Festival/ Bonington Gallery, (Nottingham).

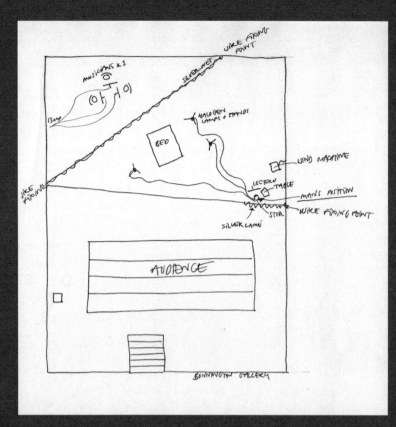

FIGURE 17.3: *Do the Wild Thing!*: design ground plan of the stage by Bridget Mazzey. Courtesy of the University of Bristol Theatre Collection.

FIGURE 17.4: *Do the Wild Thing!*: performers Jane Devoy and Dan Elloway. Photo: Edward Dimsdale.

FIGURE 17.5: *Do the Wild Thing!*: performers Jane Devoy and Dan Elloway. Photo: Edward Dimsdale.

FIGURE 17.6: *Do the Wild Thing!*: performers Jane Devoy, Dan Elloway and Jon Carnall. Photo: Edward Dimsdale.

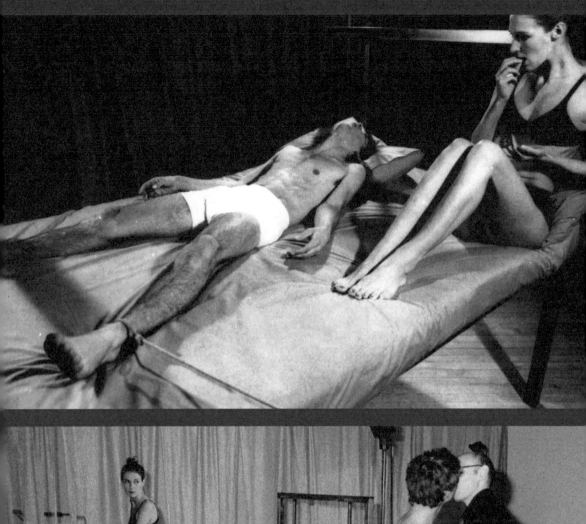
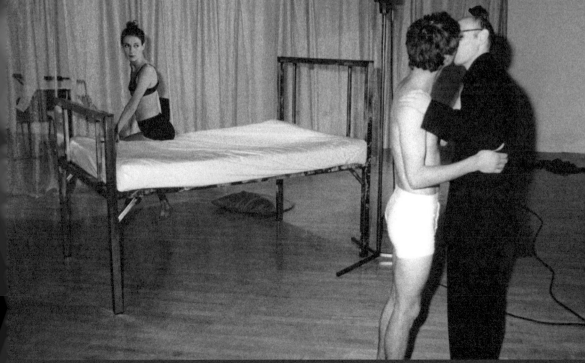

Text extracts

SIMON JONES

With *Do the Wild Thing!* my writing focused for the first time solely on the work's 'situation' – a recreation of an Andy Warhol one-reeler in which an unseen man interrogates two people on a bed about their sex lives. This 'situation' allowed me to push my interest in the metatheatrical to the point where the dramatic scene became coincidental with the theatrical set-up: the 'character' of the Man in many senses became a version of a possible audience-spectator. I realized that by having the Man unseen, reading out his text, his words had the force of a radio play, getting into the heads and imaginations of his auditors in a more intimate way than if he had been visible. Furthermore, the reactions of the Boy and Girl on the bed were deliberately 'cool', their blank faces allowing the auditors to superimpose their own responses to what the Man said. To maximize this queasy boundary between the Man's desires and the spectator's voyeurism, I decided to create a single, interior consciousness for the Man, that was overwhelming in its scale and resolutely unpleasant in its tone. I wanted to push the text past what might be thought as simply representational towards a visceral impact on the auditor, challenging them to position their own engagement with the 'scene' in active relation to his.

MAN: I think tonight … let me see … I'll have you do very little for me. Tonight will be an easy shift. I don't feel inspired. I'm emptied out of fantasies. Such a sickly little word. I'd like to suggest something … ripe. A new position, a new grip. Something unsustainable. But no, nothing … comes to me. Though how many times have I started saying that, and then in the end I've had you up all night? It's having you there, in front of me, before me, does it. Let's sit and wait and see what comes. The raw material's always been an inspiration before. Or the thought of it. Or the mechanics of it. Or the reaction. I like your little looks of disgust. The ones you try to hide from me behind those cool faces. Or maybe you don't hide it. You sneer. I know I'm not paying for your enthusiasm. That's out of my price range. Flesh comes cheaper. Shhh, calm your … whatever. A little retreated space.

For spiritual renewal. It can't do any harm. Out of, away from the everyday, and all that. Just look.

a little laugh

Dear muses. Dearest, as in most costly, we'll begin as we always do, gently. We'll ease everybody in and open up the whole scheme leisurely. We'll tear nothing. Just look at you. You're already in the position I prefer. I don't like that. It's presumptuous. Do I do you a disservice? Perhaps you fell into it naturally. Well, shift.

[both, do; boy, put out fag, throw off packet and lighter JOE, hands on groin. GRACE, lie back.]

That'll do. You look grotesque. I'm going to read you a story. They meet regularly in a motel room. The man just looks and talks. The brother and sister … no. The man suggests to the thirteen-year-old … no.
Am I now ready for the glimpse? That drives desire … whatever. Have I talked myself up to the brink of it? Does the hemline hitch itself accidentally up the thigh? Does the T-shirt slip the belt and ride up the belly carelessly? Who is first tonight? I'm simply asking. I don't know if one can ever really and truly be ready. I think, in all candour, it is an act of surrender. One gives oneself up to the glimpse and the risk of it. Cos flesh can only be forgotten. That's why we never notice the decay. We come to it every time like the first time. Innocent in our need. Surprised in our long anticipation. Degradation all around and our eyes mesmerized by the. We are ready. We must be ready. Ready?
Show me a little bit, honey. Open out like you used to. Cos what else is there to do these nights? Come on, just show me something. Any little thing will do. I'll make out I haven't seen it before. I'll act all shocked. I'll come on all flattered. Gosh, I never knew money could buy me that. You honour me. Do the little girly thing. Pull his … no. Let's not go into detail. Detail makes a story, and stories get human, and I'm not responsible for any of that. I never brought that into the world. I

never construed anything … palpable from the detail of the events in this room. I never demanded that dimension to the situation. Won't be framed. Always been prepared to let it just run. Only want what I can see. Any other seduction is dangerous. My knowledge is intimate in one very strict sense – a close familiarity with your skin. And I have shown you the respect of never getting inquisitive. You, of course, reciprocate. And I think I can say what little of you I know I have come to love. And this familiarity of use has bred a strange kind of devotion. I think, sometimes, I forget I am sitting over here and you are over there. So, honey, open up for me … your little darling bud. Hang it in the air for me. If you can't make me human, make me happy. If it ain't got no soul, it sure got lots a … dre … na … line. I got no handle on right and wrong. I'm a once-round-the-block man, me. But right now, I have a heart in working order. And my heart inclines to you, like a lover's would. And it skips its beat, forces too much blood into my head, like any lover's would. So … show … me. Honey, show me what I … so want to see.

[…]

Be very still. As still as you can. See if you can behave. Don't think what are they thinking as they look at me. Think how can I obey the order so it seems the order was never made. How can I be there before there was there. Be even stiller. Even more still than a body can be. Than the gap of the blinking eye. Seem to be seamless. Like time was no time. Or if you move, think … economy. Think impression … you will make … inevitably … necessarily. It's a mark that doesn't leave a stain. Think … I am looking at me making this move through his eyes. What will strike him? Will he recognize the line? Or maybe just move thoughtless. Shift your weight, couldn't care less how the flesh falls. Why should you? You didn't ask to be looked at. Quite right. A very private little business. Argument withers to nothing in the face of. Just so. Who listens when they can look? Only the blind, you say. Out of necessity. Cos nature's cruel. Who's to say I am not looked upon and blind? That what I think I see amounts

to sight. And where I hide is sanctuary enough from peeping. Who sees me? They're not telling. Don't look at me. Don't move. If you do anything now, you'll just make things. I need some corner of some … that is … not overlooked.
Sometimes to name the deed is enough. Isn't it? Just to give the instruction. Or not even to name it as instruction. Simply to say it out aloud. Or in my special whisper. To know you have done such a thing at such and such a time and place in the undocumented past. To imagine you could do such a thing, if so instructed, in some indeterminate future. That's enough. On quite a few occasions. But then. When confronted with the deed, who knows what'll come to one? When it's done, before me. That very complicated place. When all the talking, the instructing and the describing's done. And it is done.

[both, still]

Do it then. Go on, do it. Only kidding.

[both, shift]

[…]

I while away the in-between time thinking of you two off scene as lovers. In real life, so to. Pretending this indifference, but when unseen, passionate, violently so. As only two can be alone together unoverlooked. A world unto themselves, they used to. Bites and weals and matted hair and fingertips that reek. The only stains you've ever left across your skins. I imply this romance, because before me you appear so indifferent. Like you've clinically excised every trace of love – for want of a – from look, gesture, voice. So absolute is your excision, I surmise you must know what it is you've cut out. This thing called love – for want. And so, I deduce you two to be or to have been lovers, mutual and exclusive. And so, I guess the deeds you do for me are nothing like the way you love alone unseen. And the more intimate my demands, the greater the addition of naturalistic detail, the more you spread yourselves out before me, the less of the really felt I actually see, the further from the truth of you I place myself. But the operative question here isn't to do with how well you perform or how rabid my addiction to verisimilitude. It's how long can you keep this up. Might you not, one night, under the weight of instruction, implode, and let me glimpse the really experienced thing? Might not the accumulation of nuance so approach the facts of your love – ditto, that you cannot help but get confused, and, inadvertently, against your better judgements, do the real thing for me? Forget where you are for a moment. Before whom you. For a moment. Maybe even forget yourselves and let me in. So, my character should be one of vigilance. If this window of opportunity opens shut in an instant, then I have to be ready, don't I, to take advantage? I'm all eyes.

a little laugh

I'm one big raw nerve end, waiting for the synapse to spark. Jump start me into another way of being me. Some outcome my instructions never intended. But then, they say you only see what you're looking for. How will I recognize this thing when it appears? Maybe I missed it. I blink, I'm only human. Maybe it passed me by and I wiped the tape. I'm thrifty that way. It has already happened. Hasn't it? Be honest with me. Ha. You pathetic tosser. If it happened, then I missed it. I guess I'll have to learn to live with that possibility.

[…]

a little laugh

Behold the impossible real. They say there is no such thing. Ha. I wanted to walk amongst the. And be very sublime. And now look at me. No details, no types. I do not want to be read like some rotten and fucking open book. Implausible reality. Occluded, like a … like a … badly fucked-up eye, swollen shut, ouch. I wonder. When you can't work up the. The only limit on this show is my imagination, and I fucked that centuries ago.

You try to get that little spark into those tedious instructions. It's the detail kills it for me. Fantasies should have that broad sweep. They should be realized in an instant. Things don't just drop into place. It takes time. It has to be staged, if you want them to be convincing. To be whole. And sometimes … sometimes … what was conceived in the space – so to speak – of the mind – or the whatever – cannot be … just cannot be … enfleshed. Some detail overlooked. The weight distributed wrong. The joint won't bend that far. And then … compromise buries it. Unpredictable real. You gotta laugh. I have never had a vision. Halfway through my life and I have lost my way and I have never had a. And I had to guess by meticulous procedure, by hiring the best, I could get a little of the man-made. Watch the virgins burst. I'm not pretending it's my first time, so I don't see why you. The reality is all too apparent. The little time delay before you obey. Just enough … just enough to get you noticed. After all, I keep coming back for … more of … the same. And I thought I was gonna come on … never mind. I get to the time and I can't perform. Or rather, not the performance I'd intended. Meandering when I should be to the pointy point-point, like a. I saw I don't know what. What I cannot account for. They did for me. I averted my eyes. And not one vision. Not one thing worth coming out of a night to. But let's not get into that. Whoever said there had to be a. What effect did you have in mind? I said to her and made her cry. Only so many opportunities. It isn't forever playtime night after. It only feels like that, some nights. In childhood. Ditto. How many summers did you have? I had many hundreds. I remember the lot. I remember the sun. And she was no longer there. Put arm out. Nothing. No … body.

[…]

flick lights, side to front

How you have me. How it has me. Yes, love is taxing and tedious to determine, but this desire thing? That should be as easy as boy, girl, fuck. So, he sets it up for a little clarification. That's what he was taught to use pretend for. But faced with the real copy thing, he was phased and fucked about enough to be unable to declare this is what I. And if he had, what could anyone have done with it? Shared in the experience of it? Since when did this desire become an act of solidarity? Faced to face with it, he finds it isn't the thing he thought was driving him here. That sought you two out, and bought you and your time, and costumed you, and made you do for him, ditto. This is of another kind altogether. He doesn't know this except by what it trashes, the wrappings left behind, the carcasses unburied. It is a thing hates him, would happily dance on his eyes and push its long fingers down his throat and up his arse, until they met somewhere in the deep middle, in the stomach area, he guesses. It's a thing so embarrassing it has to be exhibited, so he can talk it to death. Everything that's nice about the world, including oneself, of course, provides, so to speak, a kind of focus for it. You never in your wildest dreams thought you desired this, in this way. Or that the expression of your whatever would end in this, this way. But honestly, put him to the test, he could not name the properties of his desire that are good. He could not say it streams forth into the world and does such and such. It wants a better, hand-on-heart thing to happen. Let's leave him huddling in the darkened room, fantasizing his community of the desirable and desiring, together alone, ferocious and awkward. Let him hide our shame, which is indeed something we do share with him, in the relevance of it all. I came here with one thing on my mind. I had thought about it sufficiently to go into stunning detail. I now worry I'm not getting the effect I was after. That the thing I've made is monstrous. And like all good monsters takes its revenge by pointing out, at the most inopportune times, and to the largest possible public, how far it exceeds the ambition, imagination and inadequacies of its master.

18

The Magnificent Minutiae

SARA GIDDENS

In this Flight, I explore how the smallest of everyday gestures has been used compositionally and my fascination with the extraordinary-ordinary. Starting with Do the Wild Thing!*, I chart how this focusing became a crucial principle in my practice in later works: how focusing on performers' habitual actions, framing them as choreographic material, structured whole shows and required a slowing-down of the pace with which material was unfolded on stage. This led to understanding both the stage and the devising workshop as places in which to dwell, both for ourselves as makers, and then for spectators. I reflect too on how concretizing the smallest of actions in this way relates to how Simon's writing ranges far and wide and moves with a quicker, more febrile energy: in essence, the two different vectors of choreography and writing, flesh and text, become the fundamental axis between which Bodies in Flight's practice 'unconceals' itself.*

Do the Wild Thing! was our least-seen show. We performed it in only two venues: the Bonington Gallery (Nottingham) and Arnolfini (Bristol). But of all our shows it is the one that has marked the most fundamental shift in our work and our collaboration, in our process and product. As a response to the theme of the work – a peep show, *Do the Wild Thing!* began with a methodological shift, a shared script and an agreed structure. Predominantly I worked in one space with performers Dan Elloway and Jane Devoy, who, in performance, barely spoke but could be seen at all times. Simon worked, in an adjacent but discrete rehearsal room, with Jon Carnall who, in performance, spoke almost unceasingly from a stool behind a curtain, and was not seen until the final climatical ending, apart from a brief glimpse of him in the gloom untying Dan in the overture. The trio of classical musicians were separated from the performers by a second curtain (see Figure 17.3). Through these theatricalized means, we created a series of (already impossible) divisions between what is seen and what is heard. Between sound and vision. Between image and word. Between flesh and text. A deliberate attempt to separate the senses to some extent, and in doing so concretize our belief in the live event-hood of performance as an art form where fleshes and senses truly mix.

Back in the 1990s, this separation, particularly during the devising process, felt radical. In hindsight, this seems strange as I have become such a staunch admirer of Merce Cunningham and John Cage's collaborative work. But back then, co-devising in the same space and time had lain at the very heart of our practice in every show up until this point. To work like this, in separate rooms, on separate flights, felt courageous and daunting, yet within days strangely freeing and invigorating; not least in its almost entire removal of a whole layer of 'negotiation' between writer and choreographer, which was often, and continues to be, complex. In retrospect, both the process and outcome heralded a new understanding of the expertise we each brought to our work. Indeed, this deliberate separation of the performative texts of movement and words only served to heighten the tension between words and image, the impossibility of words ever being quite adequate enough to wholly describe or touch upon the utter complexity of an image. Each articulation seems only to intensify the hopelessness of such a task. This inadequacy became a theme we returned to again and again, and certainly lay at the very heart of our collaboration with photographer Edward Dimsdale in *Model Love*.

However, perhaps most significantly for me as a choreographer, the separation of bodies from words in *Do the Wild Thing!* began to reveal, maybe following Heidegger it actively 'unconcealed' (Heidegger 1978b: 161), its own landscape. A space–time in which I could linger, and Jane and Dan were wonderful, committed, brilliantly understated and natural performers to linger with. Both remained utterly open to and playful with their physical expression, restricted as it was to the limits of designer Bridget Mazzey's beautiful steel bed, until the flurry of movement filled the whole space at the end of the show. This restriction became the opening, a place to luxuriate in. I became fascinated with the minutiae, in attending to the smallest of everyday habitual gestures: the curling of the hair behind an ear, the rotating of an ankle, the slightest turning of the head, the lightest of sighs, to the apparently subconscious scratching of the face, all then very carefully and purposefully separated, often stretched out over time as distinct elements; each tiny gesture becoming part of a seemingly never-ending, but deliberately restricted palette of discrete, choreographic possibilities and potential. I employed this strategy of apparent reduction as a direct response to the extremity, the boldness and, yes, the harsh explicitness of Simon's deeply searching and arresting philosophically driven text. To me, it felt impossible and frankly quite pointless to try to match or mirror the grandness and at times brutality of the text through the movement. I had a hunch, and that was all it was then, that my only fertile avenue was to play against the macro, to find richness and density through exploring the micro. With Jane and Dan's willing consent, I homed in on the magnificent minutiae, upon the tiniest of details, somehow already aware that in such details lay all the promise of Theodor Adorno's 'splinter' in the 'eye' and its potential to provide the 'best' and most illuminating 'magnifying glass' (1978: 50).

I became fascinated by how the smallest of actions were somehow unable to avoid, and what's more consistently referred to, the deepest complexity of our mortal shared experiences. I was drawn to the minutiae, to that which writers such as the American performance scholar Andre Lepecki (1999) and the Dutch dance historian and anthropologist Jeroen Fabius (2009) have since called the 'microscopy', where—when each microscopic movement is amplified. Fabius develops this idea further through a reflection upon how the American choreographer Meg Stuart employs a 'reduction of choreographic information' so as 'to create a microscopic effect' (Fabius 2009: 337). 'This microscopy', reflects Fabius, 'is achieved by using nearly still bodies, minimal movements, and exposing both personal and bodily experience' (2009: 336). This commitment to a deliberate reduction of elements within performance became central to my developing choreographic oeuvre and eventually led to the deliberate employment of stillnesses and still-ing, present in many of our later works including *The Dream→Walks* and *Still Moving: Moving Still*.

However, somewhat ironically, I am moving too fast. Back in 1996, I was fixated on the smallest of everyday gestures and how these could be used compositionally to inform and structure the whole work. I was drawn to the extraordinary–ordinary and fascinated by how the ordinary could become so extraordinary when the palette was restricted in this way. The American painter, Allan Kaprow, well known in certain circles for coining the term 'happening' in the late 1950s, was committed to making and promoting live events that focused on the blurring of the line between art and life. Kaprow (2003: 9) advocated that if artists could only let the ordinary show itself, to reveal, to unconceal its very ordinariness, then we (as artists and viewers) can experience and 'devise the extraordinary' outwith attempting to deliberately make the ordinary extraordinary. Indeed, it is through this attention to the everyday, to the ordinary, that we can experience the extraordinary within the ordinary, in Kaprow's words we are then able to 'discover out of ordinary things the meaning of ordinariness' (2003: 9).

It is not strictly true that *Do the Wild Thing!* was my first ever professional choreographic foray into the extraordinary–ordinary. My experience tells me that such methodologies are born and developed in anything but a linear way. It is much more accurate to say that a greater methodological clarity emerged from the making of *Do the Wild Thing!* as a direct result of being with and in the practice. The repeated laying of the table in *iwannabewolfman* is a clear example of choreography focused on taking an everyday ritual and developing it into an increasingly deconstructed choreographic sequence, which moved further and further towards the stylized through repetition, through an insistence upon returning to or attempting to re-create the apparently lost moment. Although I feel uneasy in coupling the beginning of my choreographic focus with the everyday with *Do the Wild Thing!*, I am completely comfortable in writing that the actual naming of this attention to the minutiae through the extraordinary–ordinary began with that show.

This attention to the minutiae heralded another major methodological shift for us as a company, the employment of dwelling. *Do the Wild Thing!* became the first show that I truly dwelt with both materials and collaborators. I am using the verb *to dwell* here to suggest a staying with, a not moving on or away from material, in both a temporal and spatial sense; its usage is heavily influenced by my yin-yoga practice. Dwelling became a central part of our practice, part of an attitude to self and others and those other things and spaces around us. In his essay 'Building dwelling thinking' (1978a), Heidegger argues that we need to think of building as intimately connected to dwelling, and that both building and dwelling are fundamental and in constant relationship to thinking. Heidegger pursues the relationship between thinking and building through dwelling, bemoaning how too often they are separated. He draws particular attention to the importance of the one listening to the other. He elucidates upon this interrelationship, suggesting '[b]uilding and thinking are, each in its own way, inescapable for dwelling. The two, however, are also insufficient for dwelling so long as each busies itself with its own affairs in separation, instead of listening to each other' (Heidegger 1978a: 362).

Heidegger suggests that in order to build a space, any kind of space, 'properly' and with due care and attention, we should come to this by way of dwelling. He states how the meaning of the word *dwelling* has come to be misused by exploring the association between dwelling as a space for a home and suggesting that one is not synonymous with the other. Just because a house may provide a roof over our heads does not mean that we dwell in it. Conversely, a place where we feel 'at home' (Heidegger 1978a: 347) does not mean we stay there.

He elucidates this by way of a carefully crafted etymological journey through Old English, High German, Old Saxon and Gothic, arguing that dwelling is already in relation to another, a near-dweller through the German word *Nachgebauer* (in English 'neighbour') (Heidegger 1978a: 349), and that 'proper' dwelling carries with it a necessity to value and care for those beings and things within our 'domain' (Heidegger 1978a: 347).

Moreover, dwelling illuminated a further useful connection to the creation of space–time for performance. According to Heidegger, dwelling should be intimately connected with that which he names the 'fourfold' (Heidegger 1978a: 352). This 'fourfold' is made up of the earth, sky, mortals and divinities: indeed, space meets time through the sky and earth and in relation to its sun and moon and the passing of the seasons. Through the 'fourfold' space and time are both separate and inseparable. Each part of this 'fourfold' has its own 'oneness' (Heidegger 1978a: 351) yet is utterly inter-connected. Significantly for Heidegger and our developing practice, the 'real plight' for us as humans is that we have lost our ability to dwell, to exist in relation to the fourfold, 'that mortals ever search anew for the essence of dwelling, that they must ever learn to dwell' (Heidegger 1978a: 363). It seemed to us that dwelling was a very useful way to enter the 'domains' of both generating material and supporting collaboration, coupled as it was with an accompanying and necessary care and attention. For now, it is enough to state that dwelling became a central strategy in our approach to creating space–time for the making of performance; and as such the process and practice of dwelling pervades all of our subsequent work.

As I dwelt with the developing material in *Do the Wild Thing!*, I realized that the act of looking and averting the eyes, so often minute actions in themselves, frequently took centre stage, and this too became a significant shift for me methodologically. The moment, a third of the way through when Dan 'the Boy' and Jane 'the Girl' look at one another, when their gaze is reciprocated for the first time, marked the beginning of the employment of a performative action that directed their whole subsequent pattern of behaviour. It was this act of looking, either towards or away from the other, that provided the choreographic imperative, that allowed, maybe more accurately – released, the other to move. This one act(ion) fuelled the whole of the choreographic sequencing until the end section of the show. It drove the entire rhythm of the piece, dictated the pace and even led to the opening up of the playing space, as the two visible performers moved on and around and under the bed and finally through and beyond the now opened gauze curtain. We had created an elaborate theatrical game of cat and mouse, where–when the anticipation of the look and its accompanying pauses, of vastly differing lengths, was filled with subtle or occasionally dramatic shifts of weight, such as rocking or perhaps sighing. This reciprocated exchange, however brief or extended, could not help but draw attention to both the act of looking and, by way of an extension, solicit an invitation to both performers and audiences to become aware of how they/we look at each other within such a frame. Moreover, it led us to consider, as we did in an even more crucial way through *Life Class*, how such 'performances' make up a part of our everyday lives. In effect, it was this employment of the richly simple and simultaneously complex look in *Do the Wild Thing!* that heralded a significant, much returned-to, compositional tool for us as makers and performers.

Fabius writes of Stuart's 'stretching time', of slowing down the action so that the audience 'is given more time to see' (2009: 337), and where–when each movement becomes amplified through this attention to the microscopic, the minutiae. *Do the Wild Thing!* gave me more time, not just to see, but to consider my practice on every sensorial and philosophical level. It gave me a place to dwell and a very particular focus. The subsequent shows *Constants* and *DeliverUs* used technology, specifically very small hand-held cameras manipulated by the performers, to help focus the audience's attention upon the minutiae, to foreground details. By the time we worked on the *Dream→Walks,* a series of promenade performances out on the streets of cities and towns across Singapore and the United Kingdom, I was utterly committed to exploring the potential domain that dwelling together and slowing down, in order to focus on the smallest of actions, could offer. I employed this slowing as a choreographic strategy. In the *Dream→Walks*, it enabled us, both performers and audiences, to *step aside* from the predominant direction of travel, that of moving forward to reach a destination, originally in the morning commute. This slowing down enabled us to dwell together in specific places and invited space–time for reflection. I became so intrigued by the dynamic space–time that such a slowing down could open up for us as both makers and audiences, that whole pieces stemmed from this one concern.

Still Moving: Moving Still, a promenade performance for gallery spaces in Bristol, Nottingham and Birmingham, was made originally as a direct response to returning to *Do the Wild Thing!* This time I worked alone as a choreographer developing a durational site-specific work. For the original Arnolfini version, I worked with two performers, Tom Bailey and Martha King, producing a standalone performance alongside, but separate from, the work of three of the other artists involved in the making of the original work. This time a separation of both artists and media. Stepping outside of the proscenium arch, *Still Moving: Moving Still* was developed for spaces connected to both inside and outside of the galleries, to foyers, stairwells, connecting spaces and onto the streets. Significantly, it was an attention to this slowing, or more precisely to the absolute limits of this slowing, employed to draw attention to the minutiae, and the extraordinary–ordinary around and within the spaces, which led me to name still-ing as a compositional tool. I coined the word *still-ing* to reflect, or at least to try to touch upon, the active, rather than passive or frozen, nature of working with stillness. Still-ing was used as a way to try to acknowledge the minute movements always already contained within each and every attempt at stillness, and an exploration of the palette of stillnesses became the driver for the whole show.

I did not know back in 1996 that finding and committing to the magnificent minutiae would lead me to where I find myself today. I had no idea that I would develop whole shows around the quest to allow the smallest of movements to be unconcealed, or to name and develop still-ing as a choreographic device to allow this to happen. Perhaps this is what can be achieved when one is supported and has the confidence (often through that support) to dwell in the detail, to strive to invite the ordinary to reveal itself as that which it is – extraordinary. Curiously, it was through separation that such a shift occurred. When we prised the movement and the words apart through the making of *Do the Wild Thing!*, many possibilities opened up. The inter-relations between and in-between the two became so much richer. We were not trying to illustrate one through another but, in placing the two side by side, the two could collude and collide by way of a third, the presence of the spectator. Choreographically, dwelling with the minutiae led to a foregrounding and naming of a process that concretized the deconstruction of the performers' own everyday movement, worked through and then given back to them. A process so human, so vernacular, so personalized as to seem, at first, inseparable from them, indeed, second nature. And yet through this methodology, this de-second-naturing, this returning of actions that originated as theirs back to the performers, the transformative nature of the process of performance was once again highlighted.

References

Adorno, Theodor (1978), *Mimima Moralia: Reflections from a Damaged Life* (trans. E. F. Jephcott), London and New York: Verso.

Fabius, Jeroen (2009), 'Seeing the body move: Choreographic investigations of kinaesthetics at the end of the twentieth century', in J. Butterworth and L. Wildschut (eds), *Contemporary Choreography: A Critical Reader*, London and New York: Routledge, pp. 331–45.

Heidegger, Martin (1978a), 'Building dwelling thinking', in D. Farrell Krell (ed.), *Basic Writings*, London: Routledge.

Heidegger, Martin (1978b), 'The origin of the work of art', in D. Farrell Krell (ed.), *Basic Writings*, London: Routledge.

Kaprow, Allan ([1958] 2003), 'The legacy of Jackson Pollock', in J. Kelley (ed.), *Essays on the Blurring of Art and Life*, Berkeley, CA: University of California Press, pp. 1–9.

Lepecki, Andre (1999), 'Stillness and the microscopy of perception', in *5th International Performance Studies Conference*, Aberystwyth, Wales, 9–12 April.

Further Reading

Cage, John (1961), *Silence: Lectures and Writings*, Middletown, CT: Wesleyan University Press.

Bodies in Flight

19 Constants (1998)

FIGURE 19.1: *Constants*: performer Sheila Gilbert. Photo: Edward Dimsdale.

FIGURE 19.2: *Constants*: postcard. Courtesy of the University of Bristol Theatre Collection.

FIGURE 19.3 (next): *Constants*: performers Patricia Breatnach and Sheila Gilbert. Photo: Edward Dimsdale.

FIGURE 19.4 (next): *Constants*: performer Patricia Breatnach. Photo: Edward Dimsdale.

FIGURE 19.5 (next): *Constants*: sound artist Darren Bourne, performer Patricia Breatnach. Photo: Edward Dimsdale.

FIGURE 19.6 (next): *Constants*: performers Patricia Breatnach and Sheila Gilbert. Photo: Edward Dimsdale.

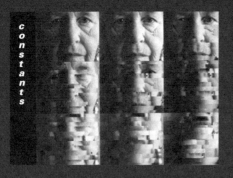

Publicity copy

A future perfect
She is rehearsing her love just one more time. Over three score and ten, now she needs to get it just right. Time is running out for her, as it is for the rest of us. But in this constant instant, this endless replay of those lines he might have said, the moves she kind of made, the images you will see, her time is also filling up and brimming over. Her past pours into the future, which is where we are all going. In this old woman's reverie, memory compresses upon memory, the images so vivid we do not know whether they or she are for real. What actually happened and what could still happen saturate one another. And at this point of letting go, does it really matter whether our memories retell the past or help us write the future?
Collaborating with composer Darren Bourne and multi-media artist Caroline Rye, Bodies in Flight's ninth work challenges the assumptions we make about the ageing process. Two women performers, one twenty-three, the other seventy-four, interrogate the differing capabilities and experiences of each other's lives. Using choreography and text, sound and video interactively, they conspire and conflict to stage our culture's anxieties over, attitudes to and depiction of the old. Their bodies become the intimate site upon which to celebrate the ageing process as both beautiful and terrible, as the one, truly shared experience of human existence.

Here we focused on the ageing body, the body in a palpable state of decay, as 74-year-old Sheila Gilbert made her way from the walls of the space to its 'dead' centre, moving through the seated audience, often using them as physical supports for her painful journey inwards. Collaborating with media artist Caroline Rye, for the first time, we integrated video technology into our making process with Sara choreographing a dance with and for camera. Accordingly, we presented the work both as a media installation (work in progress) and as a performance, and began to understand that a single work can have many different manifestations.

DARREN BOURNE sound composer, PATRICIA BREATNACH performer, SARA GIDDENS co-director/choreographer, SHEILA GILBERT performer, SIMON JONES co-director/writer, CAROLINE RYE media artist.

Performed: Celebration Nottingham – Bonington Gallery (Nottingham) work in progress, Bonington Gallery (Nottingham) show, Arnolfini (Bristol).

20
Set-Up and Situation – Dramaturgy as Transformation

SIMON JONES

In this Flight, I explore the relationship between dramaturgy and scenography in our devising practice, and how that drives the development of material in rehearsals. By breaking the logic that demands dramaturgy determine scenography and its technology, we found an endlessly productive means of exploring and transforming material in the devising workshop. Through works such as Constants *and* DeliverUs, *we developed a methodology that opened up the transformability of materials to a variety of forces – performers, technologies, sites. Whatever provided the richest possibilities for the investigation of material informed the decisions about dramaturgy and scenography, determined how the different materials were to be brought together in the work. I trace how this approach developed into the sited performance* Dream→Work/Dream→Walk, *and became central to how we transformed material across different media in portfolio projects.*

> In one way or the other, the animal is more a fleer than a fighter, but its flights are also conquests, creations.
> (Deleuze and Guattari 1987: 55)

So begins the 'origin myth' of Bodies in Flight: we had been selected for the National Review of Live Art; we had a show – *Deadplay*, but no name; I was reading Deleuze and Guattari's *A Thousand Plateaus* at the time, with its opening riff on bodies 'deterritorializing' down lines of flight. The rest is (this) history, which, as it unfolds, reveals to me so much more than I realized at the time because then I was busy with the making: that the inaugural gesture of Bodies in Flight is *to flee*. In 1989, it was to escape both the conventions of traditional narrative realist theatre and the trendy tropes of physical performance. This impulse to flee whatever threatened to be conventionalized or normalized became a principle that structured how we progressed from one work to another: often by running away from the key elements and style of the previous show, towards something as unalike as possible. Through the series of works, this is most clearly seen in the osmotic edge between dramaturgy and scenography: proscenium-arch configurations would oscillate with environmental set-ups, in-the-round with site-specific, the theatrical with the public realm. In this way, with every successive work, we were progressively loosening the strong bonds between the 'drama' and its 'staging', bonds reinforced by the hegemonic logic of realistic representation. And from this perspective of hindsight, all thoroughly Deleuzian!

I now understand that what energizes this initial impulse, to run from the last work into something completely different in the next, roots us directly into the essence of performance: *to transform*. And rather than shaping the material to realize some already determined, ideal image perfectly and finally, or even some sense of what was fitting or right at the moment, what we felt we needed to actualize was that material's endless transformability. What we discovered was that flipping staging configurations was much more than a whim to enliven the stage design: it was a means of disrupting the fundamental relationship in all performance between the dramatic and the theatrical. In most narrative theatre, the drama of the story and its characters conditions the theatricality of its staging: that these two can be brought to such fusion without actually dissolving the one into the other is the great genius of Naturalistic drama. Consciously we were trying to move our performance away from representation towards *a being in the presence of whatever material as it transforms.* However, along the way we were also prising apart the dramaturgical from the scenographic, allowing each to become intensities of transformation in their own right.

In Bodies in Flight's first series, what we came to call *the situations,* the works' dramatic contexts, were fuzzy and indistinct: *iwannabewolfman* was loosely inspired by a TV documentary about reclusive twin sisters whose hermetically sealed domestic scene was burst open by the arrival of a lodger, and *Beautiful Losers* threaded together its satires on modern living through the figures of evangelical street-preachers. This series culminated with *Do The Wild Thing!,* whose set-up was provided by Andy Warhol's one-reel movie *Beauty#2*, its framing focusing on the 'beautiful' 'stars' and excluding the bitter-sounding voyeur/interrogator; the improvised, desultory dialogue meandering around topics of desire, love and sexuality. Bridget Mazzey's set-design transposed this framing from the movie, its seen–unseen, including–excluding, onto the stage by dividing the space up into three areas: the seen (the mute 'objects' of desire), the hidden (the speaking 'subject' of desire) and the sonorous (the musicians' mood of longing) (see Figure 17.3). This scenography flushed out into the open the erotic force of the performers' bodies so rigorously that we decided to carry this inclusion/exclusion into devising and see where it would take us.

First into two separate rooms: Sara working with Dan Elloway and Jane Devoy who moved and were gazed at, and me with Jon Carnall who spoke and was listened to. In effect, we found ourselves treating the (theatrical) *set-up* as distinct from the (dramatic) *situation* (see Chapter 18, 'The Magnificent Minutae'). However, this went beyond Brecht's 'separation of the elements' because, within each room, the work's different materials developed *in their own ways*. So, when we came together to see and hear what the other(s) had done, we each looked at one another's work *as if for the first time*. This effectively interrupted and challenged how we each separately tended to construct a 'logic', I might even say – an inevitability, for our own material – the moving or the speaking. However, because we limited this sharing (not 'exchanging') of materials to two hours at the end of each week's work, we had neither the time nor inclination to construct an 'über-logic' that knitted the two elements together. In effect, we had to think of each as 'aspects' or 'planes' of (pure) difference, suspending any judgement we may have wanted to make about each other's work. This was only possible because we kept faith in the rigour of the work's (founding) set-up – Bridget's theatricalization of Warhol's cinematic frame: however the choreography and the text developed, both would eventually resonate the one with the other in performance.

Having seen what possibilities emerged by separating the development of the performance's different materials, its channels of communication and performers' skills, we extended this in the next project by collaborating with both video artist, Caroline Rye, whose film *Constants* inspired us, and its 'star'/'subject', actor Sheila Gilbert. Again the impulse to flee had partly driven this choice, because we wanted to escape the (obvious) erotics of the performers' bodies in *Do The Wild Thing!*, by placing a differently sensual, elderly body at the work's centre – literally. Sheila Gilbert was 74 years old and unable to walk far unaided because of arthritis; however, this frailty was countered by her will as a performer to push beyond those constraining physical capacities. So, for the work-in-progress showing at Bonnington Gallery, the blank walls became her support: she walked and wrote upon them. Her walking around the walls opened up a question of duration: how long could she go on? The task of writing demanded its own duration: each time Sheila circled the walls, she wrote over her previous writing. Graphic layers transformed the text over time into a palimpsest: the time of writing rendered visible, reminding us nothing is without time.

Then in the Arnolfini, upon whose walls we were not allowed to write, we decided Shelia had to move from them to the theatre's centre. So, the shoulders of the seated audience became her support; and this necessity led directly to the arrangement of the chairs, the space between them enough for her to pass, but close enough for her to reach to the next shoulder for support, the chairs all facing counterclockwise, so as she moved towards the centre, each shoulder presented itself first. This obliged her to approach each audience member from behind, which conditioned the sense of her passing them, and occasionally her touching them, as if she were already a ghost, sensing her there without necessarily seeing her there, until, that is, she had passed by. So, by this process, all the materials in the show, the (scenographic) arrangement of the space, the video set-up and the (dramaturgical) mood of the text were transformed *by way of Sheila*, whose very personhood became both *Constant*'s set-up and its situation.

For Caroline as a video artist, the focus in *Constants* had been the technology's ability to capture different perspectives on the action *as it happened*, and then to rewind the videotape as if Sheila's performance could be replayed. This pulled apart our sense of time in two ways: first, the ease of reviewing the tape jarred with our felt sense of Sheila's effort in performing: it simply was not possible for her to perform again, to have that time again; and second, the recorded images (a live-relay mix from cameras placed around the space) compared awkwardly and uncomfortably with our memories of the performance each from our own perspective, reminding us that our embodied reflection on time passing is far richer than any captured image. As part of her video rig, and in an attempt to find ever more disorientating perspectives from which to view the performance, Caroline built a small handheld camera (a piece of kit that did not exist at the time!) to relay live images to her vision-mixer. Performer Patricia Breatnach's manipulation of this device as she danced opened up a completely new capacity in videoing performance, so stunning we knew we had to build our next work around it.

DeliverUs, like *Do the Wild Thing!* before it, was inspired by a film: the long, improvised post-coital scene in Godard's *A Bout de Souffle*. Into this intimate scene between two lovers, we introduced two small handheld cameras, the images from which were relayed via a vision-mixer to TV monitors. The performers enjoyed using these cameras, framing themselves or each other, producing images that were richly interesting in the combination of their liveness with the unusual perspective and intimacy. Indeed, the oscillating focus between performer and their self-mediated image became a key dynamic in the dramaturgy. So much so that this undecidability of being both 'inside' and 'outside' of their relationship had to be physicalized in the set-up. In rehearsal, we tried various arrangements of performers to screens to audience seating. Each proved unsatisfactory because the relationship of performer to screen, or screen to performer, dominated, resulting in either audiences or performers being unable to readily access the images, or the images drawing too much attention away from the performers.

The active undecidability we wanted the auditor-spectators to experience through the performance was not achieved until we arranged four monitors in a square, facing inwards. This became the playing space, and the audience arranged on raised rostra around the square, looking into the space and across it at the monitors opposite. By turning the monitors inwards in *DeliverUs*, we produced a technological closed-circuit, within which the audience shared the same physical relationship to the screens as the performers. Furthermore, this set-up intensified the work's situation – its investigation of the ultimate unknowability of any romance, by creating a bespoke performance arena with no entrances for the performers, who were present as objects of visual desire from when the first spectator entered the arena until the last person left. Crowded around them and above them, we peered into the space of their relationship as if it were a world entire unto itself, uncertain whether to access this intimacy 'directly' 'with our own eyes' or 'indirectly' via the camera-live-relay-monitor closed-circuit. Accompanying these vision-mixed images was the awkward bedfellow of the lovers' self-descriptions because the handheld devices also had microphones and amplified the performers' voices.

Both *DeliverUs*'s dramaturgy and scenography had been derived from the unfinished business of *Constants* – our first use of Caroline's handheld camera. We learnt that transforming material was as much about what remains unused or unrealized, as it is about being open to new material (see Chapter 22, 'A Dialogue at the Globe Theatre' and Chapter 32, 'The Transmediated Image'). In focusing on this innovative device in our devising, we were also freeing ourselves from the conventional hierarchies of material in making theatre: for instance, that decide in advance that the spoken word shall determine the gesture or the move, or what technology should be deployed. In *DeliverUs*, this remainder transformed the work in the rehearsal room:

we had to be open to what it was revealing, and then do what was revealed in order to understand it. Once the material is loosened or disassociated from these conventions of meaning-making or theatre production, its capacity to transform and lead a work in ever more creative and productive directions becomes practically infinite. We have found that we are never done with material: it returns across a series of works; or more recently, in what we are calling our third phase of devising appears as multiple, different outcomes in a 'portfolio' project (see Chapter 45, 'Developing a Portfolio'). The material's endless productivity is actually to be found in-between these outcomes: there always remains something in each medium, that the work cannot resolve or bring out fully into the spaciousness of that particular event/performance/outcome. So, it requires that medium to reconfigure and re-constellate itself, in order to express that remainder more openly.

Never more so, than with the multiple editions of *Dream→Work*, which transformed into *Dream→Walk*, an ambulatory performance whose focus shifted from the anonymous spaces of 'global cities' and their technocratic commuters to the specificities of place and their inhabitants' oral histories. In this portfolio project, we found that by dwelling in a public space we were able to transform even the (material of the) everyday into an artwork, for that moment, for those participants as well as for some passers-by. We also learnt that dwelling *per se* is another way of transforming (see Chapter 18, 'The Magnificent Minutiae'). So much so that, for us, every *flight-from* had to end in a *dwelling-in*. However, unlike the everyday where dwelling is being with the same, with family, our dwelling as artists is a being-at-home-with the uncomfortable and the unknown, the unhomely. We make our work in the *now-here no-where in-between* this uncanny dwelling in material and its remains, and our ever-readiness to flee.

Reference

Deleuze, Gilles and Guattari, Felix (1987), *A Thousand Plateaus: Capitalism and Schizophrenia* (trans. B. Massumi), Minneapolis, MN: University of Minnesota Press.

21
DeliverUs (1999–2000)

FIGURE 21.1: *DeliverUs*: performers Mark Adams and Polly Frame. Photo: Edward Dimsdale.

FIGURE 21.2: *DeliverUs*: postcard. Courtesy of the University of Bristol Theatre Collection.

PUBLICITY COPY

a romance

the maths: 1 weekend: 1 flat: 1 locked door: 1 phone off the hook: 1 full freezer: 1 bed: 2 lovers: how many loves?
1: look into your lover's eyes for a very long time indeed: what do you see? 2: study his face like your life depended on it: is his smile your working definition of trust? 3: close your eyes tight and imagine a world without her. (Pause a bit.) Now, that wasn't so hard, was it? 4: why isn't there world enough and time enough and love songs enough for this? By falling in love with love, Bodies in Flight's second collaboration with media artist Caroline Rye continues our fascination with what happens when flesh meets image-text, when the apparition encounters the incarnation. Choreography, text, video interact to explore that interface with the divine that we all experience when we fall in love, the anxieties and ecstasies, the unbearable and yet undeniable undecidability of that first chance encounter that leads to the blissful/terrible [delete as appropriate] forever-after.

Inspired by the long scene of Sunday morning post-coital reverie in Godard's *A Bout de Souffle*, this piece charted the whole arc of a love affair from first-night ecstasies to end-of-romance recriminations. To intensify the focus on minute action and choreography, we built a small theatre-in-the-round in every venue we performed in so that the audience felt they were right in there with the lovers. Audiences who turned up 'in couples' were asked to sit across the space from one another. Thus, they were able, if they had so wished, to re-enact in their own mutual gaze that of the performers, looking over the space of the performed gaze of 'fictional lovers' to perform their own 'reality'. Re-using Caroline's hand-held mini-cameras added a forensic gaze to this intimacy, as the absence of any sound score reinforced the sense of the lovers' self-contained world ... until at the end (of both the show and the affair) the TVs are retuned to whatever was being broadcast at that time on that night.

MARK ADAMS performer, POLLY FRAME performer, SARA GIDDENS choreography/direction, SIMON JONES text/direction, CAROLINE RYE video.

With: JON CARNALL artwork, EDWARD DIMSDALE photography.

Performed: Arnolfini (Bristol), Now Festival 99/Bonington Gallery (Nottingham), Wickham Theatre (Bristol), The Roadmender (Northampton), The Green Room (Manchester).

FIGURE 21.3: *DeliverUs*: performers Mark Adams and Polly Frame. Photo: Edward Dimsdale.

FIGURE 21.4: *DeliverUs*: performers Mark Adams and Polly Frame. Photo: Edward Dimsdale.

FIGURE 21.5: *DeliverUs*: performer Polly Frame. Photo: Edward Dimsdale.

FIGURE 21.6: *DeliverUs*: performers Mark Adams and Polly Frame. Photo: Edward Dimsdale.

Text extracts

SIMON JONES

Having developed a forensic mode of writing that investigated the 'situation' in Do the Wild Thing!, DeliverUs *required something poetic. Since the lovers' 'world' was scenographically and choreographically confined, and the handheld video cameras afforded a literal intimacy of the performers' bodies and actions, I wanted the text to express the interior states or 'worlds' of being in love – the emotional and imaginative. This poetry countered the scenography's physical proximity of audience-spectators to performers and the apparent reveals of the live-relay video. Amplified through microphones built into the handheld cameras, the text also felt mediated, working against both this physical intimacy and the sense of eavesdropping into the lovers' thoughts. Furthermore, in clearly defined shifts of mood and register, the text compressed the whole arc of their relationship into an hour, dislocating narrative time from theatrical time, producing a dream-state that mirrored the hallucinations of love.*

```
POLLY: head goes blank
       tape goes blank
       screen goes blank
       go blank
       and these aren't the words I'd use
MARK:  attention, world
       let's mix
       the one image upon the other
       the one superseding the other
       the one body upon the other
       the clinch, the clasp and clutch
       the cleft cleaving
       of bodies however intimate still separate
       howsoever indistinguishable still alone
       let's mix
       let this mix
       here now
       stand in for all the great mixing
       done everywhere else that is not here
       at every other time that is not now,
       for instance, the great mix of Europe with Asia,
       all the euro-oriental kids fucking,
       or the Pacific with the Indian,
```

          or the African and their Americans.
          O endless and unstoppable fuck
          of nations and peoples and ideas and hopes and salva-
          tions
          here now
          at furthest throw and deepest reach
POLLY: let's mix
MARK: o my wild heart open and mix
          and cease to live solitary
          but cast and spread yourself upon the swell
          let's mix
          here now at furthest throw
          some part of everybody else
          and still only now
          a world unto ourselves
          this interference of flesh
          the noisy mess of flesh
          the piss and shit
          the spunk and spit
          the cunt and tears
          the blood in blood
          o reckless exchange of flesh
          us, palpable idea of love
          us, palpable beauty
          palpable fecundity
          palpable futures
          mix
          mix and fuck
          and fuck and mix
          and make no end
          especially last night
          and no end to this morning lay
          let's make no end
          to the mess in this bed
          to the mix in our heads
          and, to forgetful flesh
          let's never remember who we are
          let's never go to work again
          let's never pay the bill again
          let's never holiday with mum and dad
          let's never ever leave this bed
          cos that light's not the sun
          and that sound's not our world

           and everything we need is here
           and everything we want at hand
           and everything elsewhere only imaginable
           only here the palpable idea
           and the babbling flesh of love
POLLY: the world gets inbetween us
           it interferes with us
           we interfere with it
           let's mix
MARK: how come the world was before you?
           How come the sun sets without you closing your eyes for sleep?
           Or how come the trains run when you're not going out today?
           How come research institutes the whole world wide bother about the future, when you have not yet made up your mind?
           How come?
           How come I dream your dreams and breathe to your rhythm and dance with your steps and laugh at your jokes and …?
           How come?
           How come I haven't seen or heard or felt or smelt or tasted until now?
           How come I never had a body, a head or cock, some lips or fingertips,
           till I compared myself to you and found myself
           Found myself wanting
           Found myself wanting you?
           How come you came and made me up anew
           Made me up a new world, like the old, but true?
           How come?

           […]

           Suppose there is a world without these walls
           and you play some part in it.
           Suppose there are others who have an interest
           a care or a stake, in you.
           Suppose you reciprocate
           suppose you come when you are called
           and it's not my voice
           cos I am here

        in what remains
        and you are somewhere altogether elsewhere
        somewhere other where I am not
        cannot be
        somewhere deliciously your own, your very own
        say you answer
        (why shouldn't you?)
        say you say yes
        it's possible.
POLLY: Suppose it's you who says
        you are not the interesting person
        all of a sudden
        to change your mind
        and say
        I am no longer interested in you
        a simple enough statement
        I'm tired of it, I need to go to bed
        or some such
        I'm busy, I'm washing my hair tonight.
        And then I am as nought
        all of a sudden
        suddenly blank
        suddenly an only here-and-now blank in the world.
        And what can I do about it
        but moan and wail and other tedious and embarrass-
        ing effects?
        You could not account for the interest accumulating
        so why should I expect a coherent narrative when it's
        spent?
        Love comes, love goes.
        No sensible behaviour at either end
        but to take pleasure in the lovely in-between
        ahhh, that closing space
        all used up by reality
        all swallowed up by ideas
        the joy-curse of word upon word, scribbling and
        smudging, graffiti in the gap.
        Nature abhors a vacuum
        so let life eat up this love
        as time fills space
        and ideas flesh out reality
        and bodies write their own ends
        and persons end up other than they might have been.

This in-between
all over in an instant
since you cannot measure time in a blank space
the counter doesn't run over the blank tape
and when you finally get it
as you must surely finally get it
the idea of your love
the name for it
the engine that lets it fly
it's already over and done with
bar the shouting and the scars, the memories and the regret.
And they call it a leap of faith. That's what politicians do, hand in hand with terrorists.
Or the leap into the void. That's for artists feeling blue.
But for us, there's no future in leaping. Cos lovers, if that indeed is what we are, only leap to end it all, when they finally get it, as they must surely finally get it, that they cannot make that other world in their own impossible image.

22

A Dialogue at the Globe Theatre (London)

POLLY FRAME IN CONVERSATION WITH SIMON JONES

POLLY FRAME studied Film, Theatre and TV at Bristol University. After graduating, she went on to work professionally as an actor and voice-over artist, both in the United Kingdom and internationally. Her theatre credits include Hamlet, After Edward & Edward II, Sir Gawain and the Green Knight, The Odyssey *(Shakespeare's Globe);* Sometimes Thinking *and* I Think We're Alone *(Frantic Assembly),* On The Exhale *– a solo show and Fringe First winner (China Plate/Traverse Theatre),* After Miss Julie *(Young Vic),* Earthquakes in London *(National Theatre) and* Macbeth *(Chichester, West End & Broadway NY). Her television credits include* The Great, The Crown, Grantchester, Ray and Gaynor, The Tunnel, Man Down, Silent Witness *and* Servants. *She has worked with Bodies in Flight since 1999.*

Here Polly discusses how her work with Bodies in Flight has impacted her portrayal of classical roles.

SIMON:
I'm interested in your experience as an actor working with different texts in different ways, such as a brand-new text, or a text from the classical canon as you're doing now playing Gertrude in *Hamlet*.

POLLY:
I'd say there are two things I have been drawing on from my experience with Bodies in Flight. Working on this production of *Hamlet* (Shakespeare's Globe, 2022) and a previous production of *Macbeth* (Chichester Festival Theatre 2007/West End/BAM & Broadway NY 2008), they have both been quite bold in re-ordering the text in places. So even though it's a classic text, there's been a much freer approach to working on it: for example, inserting lines from different scenes, using repetition or moving characters into scenes they don't originally

appear in, to make a kind of 'psychic space' for the other characters. So, particularly with female characters like Ophelia and Gertrude, in order to show the misogyny more clearly, but also to fight back against it. I really recognize that from working with you. Trying out sections of text in a different order with Bodies in Flight felt a great way to access the personality of the character and often helped unlock something in my understanding of what that character's journey was through the piece. It's an alternative process to working on a text as a fixed entity and taking a more linear route through it. You use the text in a way that feels right for you as a performer so that meaning and response to it merge and the way of working on the script feels a lot more malleable.

SIMON:
I was wondering what that freedom is. To find a through-line to a character that maybe the text doesn't automatically or readily reveal?

POLLY:
Yeah, I think that's exactly it. A freedom to explore different pathways and possibilities. The way Bodies in Flight uses repetition is important here: when reading a text, repeating certain lines or repeating somebody else's lines helps to get a sense of what you're leaning into, what you're trying to say. I was very comfortable working in that way and think it's a great tool for rehearsing a classic text.

SIMON:
And when you're working on new writing?

POLLY:
That depends on the personality of the writer and if they're involved in rehearsals, how happy they are to listen and respond if things are feeling stuck: for instance, working with playwright David Greig on *Solaris* (Edinburgh Lyceum and the Malthouse Theatre Melbourne, 2019). As an adaptation of the original science-fiction novel, there was a great deal of conceptual and emotional complexity the characters had to wrangle with, and David was very generous in his approach to working this through with us actors. For me, a good collaboration, like that, is always about trying to find a way to access the truth.

SIMON:
Often with Bodies in Flight, it's about sustaining a mood through language. There's not a plot as such. There's a certain arc of thought, but it plays more like a mood. And I was just thinking of *The Secrecy of Saints,* the solo piece you did with Bodies in Flight.

POLLY:
There's a kind of feeling of suspension if you're doing a one-person show. I imagine it like being in space, you start, you lift off, and then you're not quite sure how fast you're going. *On the Exhale* (Traverse, Edinburgh 2018), as a solo piece, was very dynamically paced, and the drive was to play against the mood of the character's interior life. She had lost a child, but drove the action of the play by refusing to be 'emotional'. So, although it was terrifying to perform, the journey was clear and urgent and gave the piece a definite momentum. The difference with a Bodies in Flight text is, you're on a journey, but it's harder to articulate what that journey is. It feels perhaps more dangerous to perform because there isn't a clear plot to anchor you; and, although meticulously scripted, you have the sensation of being out of control. The mood shifts can feel almost reckless because there isn't an obvious route through them.

With all the classical texts I've done, mood works differently. I've found Bodies in Flight's approach to text has been helpful, because when you first look at *Hamlet* on the page, it looks like poetry. It can be much harder work, for me anyway, than modern dialogue. There's such a fine line between falling in love with the sound of the language and keeping it in this vibrant state where it isn't poetry but a very active expression of thought. That was a very clear note for all the Bodies in Flight texts: to be muscular with the language and resist dwelling in the poetry. I remember days of rehearsals with you saying, don't get stuck in a tone with it! That really helped me to access the truth and keep the performance energized.

SIMON:
That's really interesting because I think that the tone comes from how I write it. Because I'm not an actor, I tend to surf a tone in the voice in my head. So, for me, the actor's job in Bodies in Flight is to say this text back to me, and then turn to face the audience. You're in that unique position of having to make the text work for an audience. Because as you just said, it doesn't automatically work. The text I write is not dramatic in that sense. One could say the same about Shakespeare's because the language is so alien. Everyone just stops listening and only hears this Shakespearean pentameter. *Skinworks* was the show where you could think of each block of text as a soliloquy.

POLLY:
Skinworks made us each very self-reliant as separate performers. We needed each other's exactitude to bounce off, but ultimately we had to adopt a very singular approach to our own journey through the piece.

That felt a direct reflection of the show's content exploring online gender and sexuality. So, there was a weird technical and fictional duality that I really enjoyed.

SIMON:
After *Skinworks*, we made *Who By Fire*, subtitled *An Opera*. Your description of this singularity, this autonomy, but nevertheless being part of a larger group presenting the work, reminds me of the operatic. The soliloquy is the aria. You are the focus; and all the attention is on you, even though you're part of a collective.

POLLY:
Sara's approach to choreography accentuates this. The attention she places on a performer's own physicality works like a telephoto lens. The division of focus that happens when you have these very small physical moves with the heightened, operatic text is really exhilarating. You have a hugely heightened awareness of everything that you're doing on stage, which is not a self-consciousness. It's the opposite of that, it's like a mindfulness, an awareness of being very, very present!

SIMON:
I remember that moment in *Skinworks* when you did the text 'This body feels so strange tonight'. You were doing this weird, insect-like crawl on the floor, speaking this text about having an out-of-body experience. And yet, you seemed to be so *in* your body. For me, that speaks to this hyperawareness of your technique as an actor, because you're having to deal with Sara's micro-choreography as well as my excessive text, all these different technical regimes. This is not to say these are unrelated, of course, but not in a naturalistic expression when what's going on in the character's subconscious comes out in their body language. It's not that kind of connection.

POLLY:
And yet, it always felt right. I found a kind of comfort in the physical side of the performances, even when the movements seemed ugly or brutal. The text would often drive the thoughts into darker places, so the limitations of my own body felt safe! It's quite difficult to explain. There was a lovely tension and separation between the body and text which, at the same time, felt absolutely indivisible. And, for me, that's what it means to be a performer: you are in a heightened, often exulted state; and yet you are limited by your own body. You are in the zone, but also technically making sure you're not fucking up and, at the same time, thinking this is so strange! I really enjoyed that with Bodies

in Flight – the intensity of that strangeness. Because the shows didn't have a conventional narrative structure or character definition, the boundaries for us as performers felt less solid and that was exciting.

SIMON:
I'm wondering how that works with a classical character like Gertrude. I'm thinking of the common tendency nowadays to naturalize Shakespearean poetry and make it 'relatable'.

POLLY:
The approach for me has been the same. My body and voice have a specific biography, that I can't hide, which then informed how the text resonated with me. So, it was less about making the poetry 'relatable', but more about committing to the effect it had on me as an actor. In *The Secrecy of Saints*, the physical journey demanded of me as a performer had a direct effect on how I responded to the text. Beginning the show muffled and bound in layers of clothing to ending it physically free and unconstrained had a very visceral effect on my relationship with the text. That way it not only remained truthful to perform but also allowed that truth to exist in more obscure or complicated forms of communication.

SIMON:
There was also bravery in what you were doing to find that kind of truth. Interestingly, a common reaction to our work in the 1990s was that it was cold. I used to think, how can that be? I mean, as far as I was concerned it was all felt. And it may take performers, such as yourself, to hunt out that emotion and make it work for an audience. I'm thinking particularly of the run of works you made with Bodies in Flight from *DeliverUs*, through *Skinworks* to *Who By Fire*. At that point in your career, you were very concerned with finding the truth of something, and that was good for me as a writer because it helped me to find out how to make the emotion connect. So much so, that, by the time of *Who By Fire*, there was a complete shift in the way that people responded to the work. They found it moving and emotional, even though I didn't feel like I changed anything that I was doing as a writer. It was the performers who provoked that shift.

POLLY:
For me, counter-intuitively, it was how we used technology in those shows, particularly video, that significantly influenced how the emotions connected. In *DeliverUs*, we used the cameras in a very explorative, almost tactile way. We created the images, and the way we

interacted with the technology formed a performance space, that felt very intimate and honest, and allowed a kind of playfulness from us as performers that felt very natural. The abstracted quality of the images and the textural nature of them, I think, allowed the audience to share that intimacy with us without feeling self-conscious.

I sometimes think of the journey we went on with the technology in those shows like the evolution of AI. There's the creation/wonder stage, a battle for control, and then a separation that feels both mature and steeped in sadness! In *Who By Fire*, the imagery felt very much like a separate entity on stage on a range of differently sized screens, as opposed to a tool used by the performers. The technology this time felt self-contained and provoked a humility in me, which was a really interesting place to be in performance, it felt very naked.

SIMON:
That brings me back to the technicality of an opera singer. The awareness of the technical challenge and then the dramatic truth combine to make the integrity of the performance. That's what I've always hoped Bodies in Flight would aspire to: you would always find it true, but never for a moment forget the performer's technical command.

POLLY:
The poetry never felt indulgent to perform. Like you say, there was an exactitude that the choreography and technical stuff required in every performance, and that demand for precision was both difficult and exhilarating. And perhaps, as a consequence of that, I found the 'operatic' nature of the text very liberating.

Further Reading

Wallace, Clare (2013), *The Theatre of David Greig*, London: Bloomsbury.

23

Dialogues & Duets

JOSEPHINE MACHON

JOSEPHINE MACHON is a writer, practice-researcher and educator and Research Resident at Guildhall School of Music and Drama, London. Author of The Punchdrunk Encyclopaedia *(2019),* Immersive Theatres: Intimacy and Immediacy in Contemporary Performance *(2013) and* (Syn)aesthetics: Redefining Visceral Performance *(2009, 2011), she has also published widely on experiential performance. Joint Editor for* The Palgrave Macmillan Series in Performance & Technology, *a commissioned contribution from Bodies in Flight is included in her co-edited collection,* Sensualities/Textualities and Technologies: Writings of the Body in 21st Century Performance *(2010). Josephine first began researching Bodies in Flight's work in 1998.*

Here Josephine returns to DeliverUs, *to consider how embodied experience, recall and remembering position the audience as archivists for the work.*

at (preposition): expressing location or arrival in a particular place or position. 2. expressing the time when an event takes place.

dwell (intransitive verb): 1: to remain for a time; 2a: to live, reside; b: to exist, lie; 3 (- *on or upon*) a: to keep the attention directed; b: to speak or write insistently.

BEGINNINGS ...

As this book is a testament to, Bodies in Flight's work can be tracked through its rich repository of images, interviews, play-texts, published analysis, soundtracks and video, stored at the University of Bristol's Theatre Collection. Reviewing my own journey with Bodies in Flight takes me back to the turn of the millennium when I first accessed VHS recordings of the company's, then, full back catalogue. Fast-forwarding through all my encounters with the live projects to *Flesh & Text* in 2019, the exhibition that marked Sara and Simon's thirty-year-plus creative partnership allows me to reflect on the importance of documentation as artistic practice in Bodies in Flight's history. The now obsolete CD-ROM *Flesh & Text*, the original iteration of this exhibition and progenitor of the company's current website, serves as a reminder of the ethereal ways in which live performance endures, suspended in time and memory, like those past electronic interpretations that remain captured yet unseen in a digital ether.

Together, Sara and Simon have created a body of work that is '(syn)aesthetic' (Greek, *syn*, 'together' and *aisthesis*, 'sensation', 'perception'). This term defines an experiential style of practice *and* an approach to analysis where sensual approaches in form lead to a quality of experience that is *felt* in immediate appreciation and so influences subsequent affective interpretations (see Machon 2011). Bodies in Flight's singular style of intermedial practice plays across the senses in audience perception. It destabilizes the live moment, opening up boundaries and definitions of the 'live(d)', accentuating connections and gaps between 'the moment' and 'the momentary'. It draws the spectator into the active relationships that traverse the corporeal and textual, the analogue and digital. Given this, beyond physical exhibitions and virtual repositories, a Bodies in Flight archive might also be retraced through the bodies of those who experienced the work, who were *at* the event. Here *at* encompasses both location and temporality, both of which are embedded in the very definition of 'dwelling', as espoused by Bodies in Flight. My focus here is to acknowledge the significance that Sara and Simon place on the spectator's internalized inhabiting of – or *dwelling with/in* – their work, both at the time and in retrospect. Drawing on my live(d) experience of *DeliverUs*, I intend to show how sensual archives can take flight once again through the process of attentive recall. I intentionally, fluidly, switch between past and present tense to communicate the now–then–now nature of embodied analysis. To further evoke this, any right-aligned text from here on denotes my first-person recollection with upper-case text indicating speech taken directly from this original production.

TO *DELIVERUS* FROM *(SYN)AESTHETICS* ...

... Space & Spectator

Inspired by Jean-Luc Godard's film *Breathless* (1960), *DeliverUs* resonates with the philosophy, the lover's journey and the linguistic play charted through Roland Barthes' *A Lover's Discourse* (1978). It begins and ends with HE and SHE in bed, yet rather than remaining in the electric glow of first lust, their interactions quickly progress from consummation to accusation. The pre-recorded film sequence that closes the piece depicts the goodbyes and regrets at the end of this affair. Seated in a square theatre-in-the-round, above the performing space, suggesting surgical theatres of old, this spatial dramaturgy set the spectatorial relationship and invited a viewing that was active and involved. With cameras and monitors visibly surrounding the playing area (a white square that would eventually become the screen onto which that final film was projected), from the outset, our attention was caught within and between the lens and each frame. Spatial design set the context and themes as much as it held the intermedial dialogues and duets that played out:

> HE and SHE lie
> coiled in white, cotton sheet
> seated above, all around
> we look down on them
> subjects
> physically, forensically, exposed
> LET'S MIX
> THE ONE IMAGE UPON THE OTHER
> THE ONE SUPERSEDING THE OTHER
> THE ONE BODY UPON THE OTHER
> monitors screening white
> and
> every now
> and then
> a flash of flesh
> from where the camera is hidden
> beneath their sheet
> beside their skin
> intimate clandestine revealing

... Bodies & Words

In *DeliverUs*, the performing body becomes a living canvas upon which expressions and experiences are inscribed. Sara's attention to the language of the body, magnified through digital and video monitors, focuses on a use of repetition that intentionally exploits Jacques Derrida's concept of *différance* (1978). It exposes the problems of meaning-making inherent in human communication while emphasizing the artistic potential that this opens up through a performance style that simultaneously defers and invites interpretation. Sara's micro-choreography draws the spectator into the intricacies of pedestrian movement, amplifying the physicality of each gesture, of motion. This micro-choreography pulls focus. It carefully 'sights' the body by leading the spectator's gaze. Concurrently, expanses of the body, mirrored and magnified on screen via handheld cameras, serve to deduct individual identity and unequivocally display flesh as medium, canvas, so 'site' of that gaze.

> SHE centres herself centre-stage
> writes her own body
> decelerating the pace
> her own chosen rhythm speaks
> sensually circling
> lunging-slow
> side-to-side
> reve(a)ls in
> her unmediated body

The moment of this dance was pronounced and explicitly removed from any lens or screen. I felt the sensual locomotion of her side-to-side lunge, cradling the moment in an unfettered and relaxed second position. I was attuned to the sensation of this movement and felt traces of equivalent motion in my own body. Both watching and *sensing* the (e)motion of that moment perfectly articulated the feeling of that state of love, tenderness, happiness, contentment and pleasure. Removed from the mediated, the performing body encapsulates and transfers sensual experience, *'cites'* it in the perceiving body of the spectator, accentuating the reciprocity of the live(d) encounter. This sense of marking, in time and *within* bodies, is made more intense by the intimate relationship set up between the audience and the performers:

> In close proximity
> to their bodies in close proximity
> next to them
> above them
> over them
> on top of them
> we overlook and look over SHE and HE
> lying in each other's arms
> we provide the frame of their bed
> the walls of their room

> the perimeter of their playing space.
> We are simultaneously
> confidantes
> voyeurs
> the wall that shields them from the outside world
> the outside world

Simon's writing interweaves diverse linguistic registers, shaping them within and around the moving bodies in a visceral-verbal poetic style. These written scores weave together themes and crystalize sensory experience, rather than structuring linear narratives or naturalistic characters. Speech here 'pleasures' and 'discomforts' via a voluptuous 'disfiguration' of language (Barthes 1975: 14–37). In content and form, it is commensurate with the erotic, sensual body and congruently explored, enjoyed and taken to extremes.

> US, PALPABLE IDEA OF LOVE
> US, PALPABLE BEAUTY
> PALPABLE FECUNDITY
> PALPABLE FUTURES

When delivered or 'written aloud' an audience can hear 'the grain of the throat, the patina of consonants, the voluptuousness of vowels, a whole carnal stereophony: the articulation of the body, of the tongue, not that of meaning, of language' (Barthes 1975: 66–67). It double-plays the definition of dialogue as 'intercourse' and indulges in sonority; in word as sensual-sound-capsule while also pleasuring itself in its power to convey and complicate meaning, requiring *sense*-making within interpretation. Bodies duet and dialogue with the speech, just as SHE and HE duet and dialogue with each other in the space.

> OUTSIDE THE ONE AND ITS OTHER
> YOU THE OTHER OTHER
> YOU THE WOUNDED
> BECAUSE YOUR VIRTUAL HALF NEVER MATERIALISED
> OR RATHER, THEY CAME AND THEN THEY WENT

... Flesh & Tech

The interplay of live and pre-recorded video, crafted by Caroline Rye, de-familiarizes the live choreographed bodies in the same way that the heightened language of Simon's text disfigures the words. Flesh duets with camera and screen. This live and live-screened choreography demonstrates a playing with the (im)mediate, exposing methods of representation and live(d)ness in performance. The spectator is required to make decisions about which bodies to view. This generates a further in-betweening, mixing, retracing and redoing between the performing bodies, the perceiving bodies in the audience, and the monitor(ed) bodies of both; flesh fused as sight/site/cite of the performance.

The handheld camera, manipulated by HE and SHE, isolates sites of the body and cartographies across the flesh:

> SHE takes the mini-cam
> lens magnifying
> her writing on his body
> with her fingers, palms, marker-pen
> mapping the physical relationship
> citing herself upon him
> ('I woz ere' on his foot
> 'and here' on his throat
> and here, and here
> and here ...)

The mediated body both elaborates and fragments the live body, renders it unusual, as it reduces sections, pauses, holds and expands the corporeal in the performance moment, in space, playing the live performer off the mediated image, playing traces of performance moments off the continuing performing present. It suspends spectators in the here–now–then, making them attend to their dwelling-in-and-on chosen moments of the performance, citing the experience within bodily memory. It creates a performing space and a spectator position that are always both live and mediated, then and now, fragmented and montaged, magnified and reduced – a duetting in form that sees flesh become text become flesh become screen become text become flesh.

> SHE ignores live-HE
> to interact with
> video-monitor-HE
> HE ignores live-SHE
> to interact with
> video-monitor-SHE

This intermedial interaction distorts the way in which the relationship 'on show' is received, giving attention to notions of role-playing, broken communication, barriers, mediation and the idolizing of the image – *the idea(l)* – of a lover. What this play with the live and mediated body enforces is the fact that these people, like the speech they utter, can never be contained or explained completely. The live, choreographed body – moving, breathing, in varying degrees of nudity, is forensically 'real' and very present in front of our spect*at*orial gaze. Yet it is also always a representation of a body in a performance, also always a live-screened image, also always a pre-recorded film subject. *DeliverUs* here is intrinsically unsettling. Unsettling to view it up close (in explicit close-up) and personal. Made aware of our live presence, the simultaneous together-yet-apart, subject–object voyeurism foregrounds our active spect*at*orship as we notice ourselves self-consciously choosing where to place our attention:

> held in the projected video image
> reflected back at ourselves
> our own micro-choreographies
> writ large on the screen

ENDINGS ...

> AND LAST, A GHOST, THE AFTER-IMAGE

DeliverUs is an intimate tracing of a relationship that is clinically analytical *and* sensually tender. The white sheets and the way in which the audience is positioned looking down into the theatre highlight this 'screening' of an internal examination. At one point, with the unsettling intimacy of an endoscopy, via the handheld camera operated by SHE, we see down HE's throat, the tunnel to the oesophagus. This physiological moment inhabits the emotional and physical and evokes the sexual. The movement of his tongue in his throat, the secretion of saliva, is juxtaposed by the tender tracing of each body by the other body. The probing of the camera is played against the choreographed, consensually exploratory hands of the live performers, revealing and revelling in the surfaces, contours and textures of each other's flesh. This intimate investigation of the anatomical form serves as a paradigm for the piece and corresponds to our examination of the anatomy of this relationship, closely monitoring each moment as it plays itself out.

DeliverUs epitomizes how spectators are intrinsic to the *sense*-making that is invited in Bodies in Flight's work. Retracing my experience of it here goes some way to marking the simultaneous passing and continuing presence of all those moments of performance that have been shared.

To dwell in and upon those moments again,
here,
now,
they become live(d) again.
SHE and HE
breathing talking laughing moving
holding
moments
picture snapshot onscreen smiling
they lie, roll, crouch, stand, move
white floor canvas
becomes screen
the after-image
diaphanous film
HE and SHE
image overlaid bodies overlaid
S/HE
Lyingrollingmovingleaving
traces ghosts
present absent
leaving traces
present
absent
HEAD GOES BLANK
TAPE GOES BLANK
SCREEN GOES BLANK
GO BLANK

References

Barthes, Roland (1975), *The Pleasure of the Text* (trans. R. Miller), London: Jonathan Cape Ltd.

Barthes, Roland (1978), *A Lover's Discourse: Fragments* (trans. R. Howard), New York: Hill & Wang.

Derrida, Jacques (1978), *Writing and Difference* (trans. A. Bass), London: Routledge.

Further Reading

Crossley, Mark (ed.) (2019), *Intermedial Theatre: Principles and Practice*, London: Bloomsbury Publishing.

Machon, Josephine (2011), *(Syn)aesthetics – Redefining Visceral Performance*, London & New York: Palgrave Macmillan.

…Bodies in Flight

24 Double Happiness (2000)

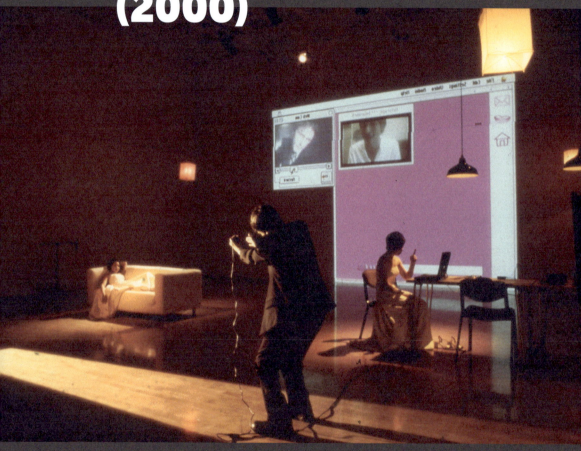

Figure 24.1: *Double Happiness*: performers Marianne Wee, Benjamin Clough, Dan Elloway and Kaylene Tan. Photo: Edward Dimsdale.

Figure 24.2: *Double Happiness*: postcard. Courtesy of the University of Bristol Theatre Collection.

Figure 24.3 (next): *Double Happiness*: performer Marianne Wee. Photo: Edward Dimsdale.

Figure 24.4 (next): *Double Happiness*: performers Marianne Wee and Benjamin Clough. Photo: Edward Dimsdale.

Figure 24.5 (next): *Double Happiness*: sonic artist Chong Li Chuan, video operator Ben Davies, lighting operator Jessica Morris, performer Kaylene Tan. Photo: Edward Dimsdale.

Figure 24.6 (next): *Double Happiness*: performers Marianne Wee and Dan Elloway. Photo: Edward Dimsdale.

Publicity copy

a transport
an international web & performance collaboration with spell#7 (Singapore) fluffboy visited hunny.bunny's website. shygirl7 met wasabi69 in a chatroom. Now it's double happiness twice over. But real life's messy. Do you know where he's been? Does she?
Across continents where differences of language and culture, shoe-size and disease-resistance create turbulence in the flow of information and capital, Double Happiness *jacks into the body that braves time-zones and economy class to get fleshy with another.*
This web-event & live performance mixes text, movement, digital sounds & video to distill WAPness into a distinctly wet-ware double-take on 21st century sex.

This marked our first international collaboration and explored the then-novel world of internet dating with an inter-continental double wedding celebrating the possibilities of the world-wide web and cheap jet travel to bring communities and cultures together. We continued to develop our integration of new technologies into our working method by using webcams and a specially authored website that extended and blurred the boundaries of the performance: for the first time, the platform for the work moved fluidly from theatre space to online environment.

CHONG LI CHUAN sonic artist, BENJAMIN CLOUGH performer, DAN ELLOWAY performer, SARA GIDDENS choreographer/co-director, KHOO EE HOON production manager, SIMON JONES writer/co-director, DOROTHY PNG lighting designer, PAUL RAE director, KAYLENE TAN performer, MARIANNE WEE performer, HANINDAH ZAINOMIUM new media/graphic designer.

With: BEN DAVIES video operator, EDWARD DIMSDALE photography, JESSICA MORRIS lighting operator.

Performed: The Black Box, Fort Canning Centre (Singapore), Digital Summer/Contact Theatre (Manchester), NOW/Breathing Space, Bonington Gallery (Nottingham), The Drama Studio (Loughborough), Breathing Space/ Arnolfini (Bristol).

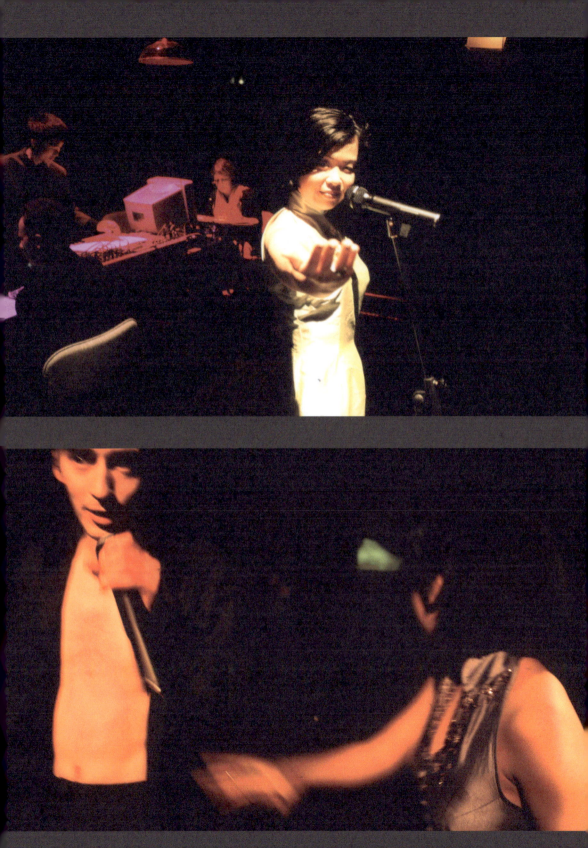

25
Beautiful Losers Re-worked

KAYLENE TAN

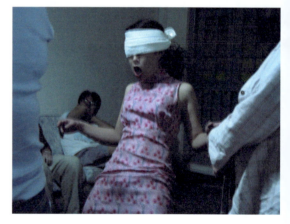

FIGURE 25.1 (top, left): *Beautiful Losers*: performers Gerald Chew, Kaylene Tan, and musician George Chua. Photo courtesy of spell#7.

FIGURE 25.2 (top, right): *Beautiful Losers*: performers Gerald Chew and Kaylene Tan. Photo courtesy of spell#7.

FIGURE 25.3 (bottom, left): *Beautiful Losers*: performers Gerald Chew and Kaylene Tan. Photo courtesy of spell#7.

FIGURE 25.4 (bottom, right): *Beautiful Losers*: performer Kaylene Tan. Photo courtesy of spell#7.

KAYLENE TAN has created performances, audio and site-specific works as a writer, director and performer with the Singapore theatre company, spell#7. She is particularly interested in sonic experiences such as audio walks, tours and headphone theatre. Her works include Desire Paths *(2004–14), a binaural audio walk of Little India,* Sky Duet *(2008), an audio experience set on the Singapore Flyer (Singapore Biennale),* Dream→Work/Dream→Home *(2009), an audio walking performance in Chinatown (Singapore Arts Festival). In 2019, her headphone theatre production of* In the Silence of Your Heart, *commissioned by Esplanade Theatres on the Bay, won Best Sound Design at the Life! Theatre Awards. Recent projects include* Devil's Cherry *(2022) for the Singapore International Festival of the Arts, creative residencies at the National Library Singapore and at the State Library Victoria (2023), conceptualizing and scripting the National Day Parade 2024 in Singapore.*

Here Kaylene writes about collaborating with Bodies in Flight and spell#7's 2003 re-working of Beautiful Losers, *transposing it to a Singaporean setting.*

Are you ugly, desperate, impotent? Welcome to spell#7's epic tragi-comedy of domestic proportions: Beautiful Losers. *Other frequently asked questions include, 'What do you do when heaven breaks lose in your family home?' Don't touch it. Stand well clear and make a date with the* Beautiful Losers, *8–18 January at 65 Kerbau Road in Little India. Tickets at $18 and $15. We know that sometimes, the last thing you need in your life is a miracle (Radio advertisement for* Beautiful Losers, *2002).* I showed my 15-year-old the CD-ROM of *Beautiful Losers*, a companion to the performance spell#7 staged in 2003. 'What is a CD-ROM?', she asked. Yes, it is a relic. Excited by what were then new technologies, we decided to make an interactive CD-ROM, to extend the experience of the *Beautiful Losers* performance – who needs programmes!? In the CD-ROM, a man and a woman (Gerald Chew and myself) appear in seven different houses in search of relics. Users were encouraged to scroll across panoramic photographs of homes to locate relics, such as a knife, biscuit tin, a lucky cat, an inflatable bear, a kindergarten graduation photo and a bottle of gin. A line of text and a sound effect would be triggered when a relic was found. They were in search of … what was it? Salvation? Redemption? Love? Something like that. *HIS: Although there has been a general decline in official relic veneration, the popularity and notoriety of some have never been more pronounced. Caption, What is a relic?/ HERS: The material remains of a holy person or objects sanctified by contact with* *their body. / HIS: Caption, What does a relic do for me? / HERS: Edifies me. Stimulates fortitude. Generally mediates grace in a fucked-up world. Children can get a handle on heaven with a good relic.* Not sure if the CD-ROM did anything for my child though. Fresh-faced and in the United Kingdom for an adventure, learning to run away from Singapore, I studied drama at Bristol University. Feeling out of place – Loser. There I saw the BIF show *Rough*. What was that? Mind blown. I don't remember the show now, but the black-and-white publicity image – a few people around a bed? Kinda sexy. Could I … would I make theatre like this? How do you even begin? I stumbled through university in a haze, losing faith in theatre, feeling like I'd never make a show, thinking maybe I could be a photographer or something else instead. Maybe I'm just nostalgic. Because I met and fell in love with Paul Rae who later moved to Singapore, and we formed spell#7 performance in 1997. The early days were spent working through our influences, working out how to work with each other, and finding things we wanted to say. We made theatre that was noisy, fast and loud; we spoke into microphones, danced earnestly and ironically, and experimented with multimedia. We created site-specific performance – in a church, a disco, a convent, on the streets – because we couldn't afford to rent theatres. Our performances were devised, texts written and performed by ourselves and with a few regular collaborators. After two years of frantic theatre-making, we were sick of ourselves, so we took a break – Paul decided to do his Masters in the United Kingdom and I tagged along. We lived in Bristol for a while and hung out with Simon and that's when we decided to collaborate and make *Double Happiness*, a cross-cultural internet romance. Double happiness (Shuāng Xǐ) is a decorative symbol (not a real character) that is often used in Chinese weddings: it consists of two happinesses, 喜 (Xǐ). 喜喜 – Happiness ×2. Twice the fun? Half the team were from Singapore and the other half were from the United Kingdom. As with new partnerships we were getting to know each other, each other's approaches and ways of working, and this was my first time working with Sara and my first encounter with speaking Simon's text. We had a creative development in the United Kingdom, played with these new technologies (a webcam on a very long USB cable – a relic!), machine voices (hey Siri – we were there first), lots of running around, exhausting physical rehearsals. And then the text … Is there a way to say these lines? There's a lot of it, where do I stop, where do I breathe, what's the rhythm, emote or not to emote? These are the questions. Then, oh well, just say them, and they spill out, the lines – nicer with a microphone. I like microphones. I liked working with a choreographer. I'd never paid such close attention to movement and Sara was all about the details. Movement+Text – separate but necessary in a BIF show: it needs the breathing space or one moves the other, colliding then drifting apart, standing alone. We premiered in Singapore and toured in the United Kingdom. We even had a website (www.doublehappines2.net) – gone now, another relic! Old technology seems to outlast the digital. We created chatroom conversations, back stories and video calls for the characters fluffboy (Benjamin Clough), hunnybunny (Marianne Wee), wasabi69 (Dan Elloway), shygirl7 (me). It was part of the show experienced in private in another space. I have many good memories of the production, but was it 喜喜? Collaborations are tricky; we were still figuring out who spell#7 was, still learning; and because BIF had a much stronger identity and the text seemed so dominant, those factors led the overall direction of the production. *I advise you burn, don't cool, never again cool* … It wasn't the end. There was something about a Simon Jones text that was attractive to Paul and me. What would we do if we had full control of one? How can we make it our own? In 2001, spell#7 was granted arts housing on Kerbau Road by the National Arts Council Singapore. It was a two-storey shophouse in Little India, a vibrant ethnic enclave in the centre of Singapore. The spell#7 office was downstairs, and we used the upstairs as a rehearsal and performance space. It was not an easy space for performance as it was long and narrow with a limited capacity of 30. We wanted to make a show for the Kerbau Road space. We wanted to make a show that was not devised. We wanted to focus on making a polished performance and creating an intimate and intense experience. Enter *Beautiful Losers*. I liked the title and knew the Leonard Cohen novel. I didn't see the original version of *Beautiful Losers*, so I approached the text with a blank slate. Paul saw the production and remembered the promenade staging and the proclamatory style. What was it about? I asked. He couldn't tell me, something about losing things? As a two-hander, the text seemed manageable. When I read the script, there were several themes that appealed. Firstly, faith – Singapore is a religious country with many faiths co-existing. In the 2000s, there was a growing trend of evangelical churches in Singapore. It is also a superstitious country, with many people in search of quick fixes, or getting fixated on magic objects. Secondly, failure – as a very success-driven country, in Singapore if you fail, you lose. So, the idea of beautiful losers in Singapore was very appealing! I saw *Beautiful Losers* as a story about a couple in search of hope and goodness, a couple trying to save themselves, and themselves from each other – and failing. We cast Gerald Chew as the other loser. He was a well-established TV and theatre actor. More of a mainstream, popular theatre actor. But he was willing to try something different, and we thought he would add something to the show.

Two beautiful losers scour the city for the relics of faith. As they bear witness to the heaven held in these everyday things, they deliver up lessons on impotence, the afterlife and other modern headaches. Not only do they share their prophecies and revelations with us, but also their take-outs and titbits. During one of these lessons something bad happens and all hell is let loose. We can't say any more about that now... (Beautiful Losers, *publicity blurb*). Having tackled a Simon Jones text before, my strategy this time was similar. I let it move me, move through me. Words enter. Exit. It's a wave, and another wave. Sometimes, it wasn't about the meaning of the words, but where it took you as you were saying them, and then the movement followed. *No matter how shitty shitty panties I get, I will not surrender my tongue. Not to you. Have every organ else, but my licker, my lapper-kisser, my lover, my halloo-er, my word-maker, world-ravisher. Have the whole holy carcass else. Not the clacker, not the teaser, not the lovely lovely soother in the panic-fucked night.* Gerald had a different approach, he tried to get into character and bring emotion to the lines. We were more interested in him saying the lines as himself, as Gerald the performer rather than Loser 1. At times we wondered if we had made the right decision to cast Gerald. But he found a balance between acting and performing, brought a sweet puppy-dog vulnerability to the role and was nominated for a Life! Theatre Award for his performance! We staged *Beautiful Losers* as a site-specific performance. A voyeuristic journey into someone's house. Audiences were ushered to the entrance of the Little India Mass Rapid Transit (MRT) train station, which had not yet opened to the public. The MRT staff opened the shutters and revealed the two performers (myself and Gerald Chew) and a musician George Chua. *Welcome losers!* Audiences were taken down an alley, through the back entrance and up the stairs. They entered what looked like a home. A sofa, sideboard, half-eaten dinner on the table, a bed. (This physical experience was something that they would experience again when they went home and accessed the CD-ROM. This time, they were the Losers.) The performance style was intimate. We pulled audiences aside and whispered secrets to them. At times, it was declamatory, ironic and playful. *Most miraculous.* The audience is brought in, and an hour and a quarter later sent away, now wondering whether there is more to our world than we'd previously thought. 'There might not be a "plot" as such, but the universe created in this production is utterly complete and believable' (*The Flying Inkpot Review* n.pag.). This morning I ask Paul what he thought of *Beautiful Losers*: I like it. It worked! There was something about the domestic environment that made the performance very charged; there was a lot at stake – that search for meaning and belief, especially in a place like Singapore, he says as he makes his way out of the flat. Working with Bodies in Flight has shaped how I approach text and what it does to the body and the bodies experiencing it. *Beautiful Losers* was the beginning of an ongoing exploration of intimate, text-focused performances. spell#7 began the *Duets* series in 2004, focusing on pared-down, minimal works with a small number of performers. I also began to work with audio walks and headphone experiences. Paul and I moved to Melbourne in 2015 and that marked the end of spell#7. In 2022, we returned to the intimate private world of a couple struggling to make sense of their lives and their relationships in *Devil's Cherry*, a performance for the Singapore International Festival of Arts. In the headphone theatre show, a Singaporean couple, Debbie and Mo are drawn to the beauty of the Australian landscape, the vastness and the abundance of nature. For them, it is about freedom and escape from Singapore and their mundane existence. But when they are removed from what is familiar to them and when they are given the space to 'spread out', their personal demons surface. It is the physical conditions of the land in all its beauty, harshness and cruelty that bring out their demons. And what lies beneath. The beautiful losers continue to haunt.

Reference

Samuel, Jeremy (2002), 'Fabulous Review: *Beautiful Losers* by spell#7', *The Flying Inkpot Theatre Reviews*, 10 December, https://eresources.nlb.gov.sg/webarchives/2022-07-12%2020:35:07.000/wp/details/http:%2F%2Fwww.inkpotreviews.com%2FoldInkpot%2F02reviews%-2F02revbeaulose.html. Accessed 22 November 2024.

26
Flesh & Text: A Document (2001)

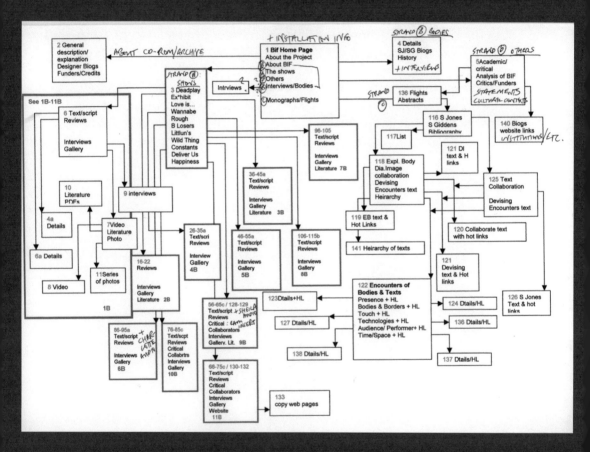

FIGURE 26.1: *Flesh & Text*: CD-ROM architecture schematic plan with handwritten annotations. Courtesy of the University of Bristol Theatre Collection.

FIGURE 26.2: *Flesh & Text*: CD-ROM cover. Courtesy of the University of Bristol Theatre Collection.

When we started making work in 1989, we were sceptical about documentation, fearful that the documents of performance would be used to replace the performance itself and that it was easier to watch the video than go to see the show. This meant that the archival remains of those early works were patchy and incomplete. In 1996, with *Do the Wild Thing!* we realized that companies that had good documentation were better able to thrive, so we decided to ensure that all our future work would be well documented. We produced multi-camera video records alongside catalogues and booklets of scripts and images.

In 2001, in collaboration with Iain Simons from Suppose Design and Tony Judge, we made *Flesh & Text*, the first CD-ROM collection of archival materials from one performance company. Covering our first eleven shows, it included scripts, publicity copy and images, photographs, video, interviews with members of the company, written reflections from a range of commentators, and two extended hyper-texts from the co-directors that linked together the various documents to tell the many stories of the many bodies of Bodies in Flight.

Today, developments in software mean that this document is inaccessible – the fate of much digital art and archives.

DARREN BOURNE sound design, EDWARD DIMSDALE photography, SARA GIDDENS co-editor, JULIAN HANBY packaging design, SIMON JONES co-editor, TONY JUDGE producer, design and construction by SUPPOSE.

Exhibited: Arnolfini Gallery (Bristol), Bonington Gallery (Nottingham), National Review of Live Art (Glasgow).

27
Skinworks (2002–03)

FIGURE 27.1: *Skinworks*: performer Polly Frame. Photo: Edward Dimsdale.

FIGURE 27.2: *Skinworks*: postcard. Courtesy of the University of Bristol Theatre Collection.

FIGURE 27.3 (next): *Skinworks*: performers Polly Frame, Doug Bott, Tim Atack, Kaylene Tan and Neil Johnson. Photo: Edward Dimsdale.

FIGURE 27.4 (next): *Skinworks*: performer Polly Frame. Photo: Edward Dimsdale.

FIGURE 27.5 (next): *Skinworks*: performers Neil Johnson, Polly Frame and Graeme Rose. Photo: Edward Dimsdale.

FIGURE 27.6 (next): *Skinworks*: performer Kaylene Tan. Photo: Edward Dimsdale.

PUBLICITY COPY
A valentine
Three handles appear in a chatroom, they're anonymous, they're anybody, everybody, they're angels, demons, they're hermaphrodites, they're making a new kind of love mailing valentines into the void.
Three performers cruise the web, crashing chatrooms, flipping identities, spinning yarns, beguiling, ensnaring unsuspecting novices, seducing each other, pushing imagination beyond the tech spec.
No flesh given, no harm done.

Made as a collaboration with the band Angel Tech, filmmaker Lucy Baldwyn and new-media artist Nicholas Watton, the show continued our exploration of cyberlove by turning the online into the actual: we physicalized a sex chatroom in the performance space. In this way, we investigated the shifts in contemporary identity construction: how new desires and moods of love emerge from the irresponsibilities of sex without bodies. Partly made in Chicago and the United Kingdom, the work developed into a series of linked outputs – a radio broadcast, installation, lectures, web and performance events across the United Kingdom and internationally in Brisbane, Chicago, Victoria (Canada) and Singapore – thus pushing the boundaries of what constituted performance, and demonstrating how different media could dialogue with one another to produce an expanded, portfolio work.

TIM ATACK sound, LUCY BALDWYN video, DOUG BOTT sound, POLLY FRAME performer, SARA GIDDENS choreography, NEIL JOHNSON sound, SIMON JONES text/direction, GRAEME ROSE performer, KAYLENE TAN performer, NICHOLAS WATTON new media.

On video: Mark Booth, Benjamin Clough, Stephen Fiehn, Stacy Goldate, Olen Hsu, Malin Lindelow, Tyler Myers, Ethan Roeder, Hamza Walker, Christopher and Ria.

With: EDWARD DIMSDALE photography, JULIAN HANBY graphic design.

And additional text by: Mark Booth, Stacy Goldate, Olen Hsu, Ethan Roeder, Hamza Walker.

Performed: Arnolfini (Bristol), BAC (London), Colchester Arts, Crewe & Alsager Arts, ICA (London), Hoxton Hall (London), Now Festival/ Bonington Gallery (Nottingham), Wickham Theatre (Bristol), School of the Art Institute of Chicago (USA), Year of Living Digitally Festival (Singapore), Speculate & Innovate (QUT, Brisbane), Collision Interarts (Victoria, Canada).

Text extracts

SIMON JONES

The situation of actualizing a chatroom in the performance space freed up my writing to explore the 'metaphysics' of internet communication: I deliberately riffed off the 17th-century English metaphysical poets in how I structured the texts and 'investigated' the topic of internet dating. I was profoundly aware of how the performers actually speaking out loud these texts amongst an audience was so challenging. So much so, we took measures to 'aestheticize' their delivery: the performers were dressed as if at a cocktail party; they never physically touched each other or the audience; they moved slowly in between audience members seated on separate chairs; they used microphones to address the room, but never an individual. At the beginning, we also used others' improvisations on internet dating, often humorous, to lead the audience gently into the piece.

GRAEME: no one is really here
          are they?
          how can they be?
          really here
          really anywhere
          just the mood of the event
          the buzz or hum or vibe of the room
          you were really there!
          pah!
          you expect me to believe that
          to act on that
          to found a philosophy on that

THE BAND: you're my cookie lover
          I know you inside out
          I printed off your cookies
          I let the cookies lead me to what your heart desires
          to where your soul abides

KAYLENE: I'm really selfish … but I'm honest about it and some people think that I'm mean, but it's really that I'm honest. I can't stand people who are needy. I have a lot going on in my life and I don't really have a lot of time for people who

|||||||||don't also have a lot going on in their life. So, I guess I'd like my date to have a life and not try to live through me or expect me to live through them.

POLLY: Cyberlove is a beautiful thing, cos it's like fictional love. It can be anything you want it to be. Cyberlove is exploring fantasy. It is like a dream, a shared dream. There doesn't have to be any inhibition, any limitation to it, no fear about what's gonna happen, about where it's gonna go, cos as long as it's all virtual you can create your own world … with no worries.

GRAEME: between the face and cock
or cock and cunt
or cunt and arse

KAYLENE: a whole world
between the ear and eye
or word and mind
or tongue and flame
o holy you
let the monsters in

GRAEME: I am versatile … versatile bottom … looking for a pretty aggressive top who also likes to be bottom sometimes. Er … big … big into … playing with toys. You gotta be open to that. Anal massage is definitely a plus. What else? Dark hair is good. Blond hair is good. Latin blood's very good. I guess I said that already. Erm. If you're into role playing, I can definitely do that. And would definitely be attracted by … I'm looking for somebody who is definitely very sexually liberated. Basically that's it. You have to be comfortable with your body. Take care of yourself. Eat well. Definitely drugs and that kind of thing is not for me.

KAYLENE: I … spend … well … what do I like to do? I play music … I like to listen to music. I like to go for walks, long walks actually, with no particular aims, destinations. I'm a collector. I collect lots of … just … most people would, I guess, think it was junk … people's old … old belongings or … so, I do a lot of that. Takes up quite a bit of time. Yeah, okay.

POLLY: this body feels so strange tonight
ill-fitting
like I'm performing it rather than living it
a quasi-thing hardly crediting this quasi-real look
somebody, look at this
halfway through a riff that's suddenly playing itself
makes you kind of queasy cos you know you're in for the ride
but high so high
cos it can't be you that's doing these things
you can't be held responsible
sex without secretions, ha
a world of blame and not a single guilty soul

[…]

THE BAND: I'm Barbie
doll me up
dress me down
spank me hard
fuck Barbie
Barbie's fucked

POLLY: all intimacies now so blasted
so spread about the world
like you slip in this smear of intimacies
maybe you surf them
the interiors of people's hearts
the spill of their desires
the liquidized hope of each shared secret betrayed
this world now turned inside out
all closenesses exteriorized
all hearts on sleeves
all genitals on webcams
show me, boys and girls
pull back the folds of skin and show me … what?
how the world came to be so … so empty … of love
(now that was simply put)
I see your fingers' tips pulling at yourself
they say this is me
this is the very heart and soul of me made visible

transmissible
unmissable
download me
print me off
and if you take to what you see
save me
somewhere deep in your hard-drive
protected by passwords and firewalls
and if you think you like what you see
bookmark me
cos I'll be there
waiting for your return hit
with my fingers about my sex
pulling back the fold of skin
ready to show how very much I love you

KAYLENE: I can't be cool and oh so contained like.
I splurge. I seep. I leak all over you
every hole dripping with the gore of my soul
this holy mess
my body is not a containment area
it is not secure
my body is a catastrophe that hasn't waited to happen
a bomb that's gone off
whoops
my body is not a temple
no health here
only the just-about staving-off of death
only the constant and unregulated exchange
this wide open border of love
and the torn open arse of the betrayed
whoops
I am both
abuser and abused
object subject
an outer in and the inner out
my skin is the only thing around that's unreal
it's a chimera that dissolves at the lightest touch
the lover's sigh upon the neck and whoops! access to the soul
hacked right in, fingers in the trough of my personality, fiddling away

I share these genes with most of the rest of creation
I drop these jeans for all the others
I'm not proud
you fuck me over
you will fuck me over
I will be fucked over
by you
and I will love it
I do love it
and I will beg for more
and I will weep
and make a mess upon your doorstep
or in your bathroom if you let me get that close
I'm incorrigible
there is no exclusion zone around me
there is no love without me
and where I am is love

GRAEME: and to what forms of abuse did she put herself cos she thought no harm could come when there was no exchange of flesh – exchange, ha
so deliberately submit herself, open herself out and let his words – for that's what they were, as she thought it must be the male of the species, so desperate and exacting were its desires render her most hidden places most public, sometime just the two of them he promised, othertime the whole chatroom packed with anonymous handles each, she imagined, had to imagine, tugging at themselves as each detail of the abuse unfolded, too caught up in the systolic rhythm of the chat, as it tried to cross the current of the traffic on the web that night – was it a night for all of them?
held together in that one strict sense, our own customized darkness, to enter a reply most times, sometimes wanting a private chat when he had done with her, when he was spent, and she would commit herself to yet another opening, yet another detail to the flesh she once had, no longer really there, no longer her own, no longer real, but lost in impossible detail, flesh she could never, indeed, have had, implausible flesh, that seemed the only variety that

could now convince, the only stuff somewhere about this globe somehow substantial, somehow realizable, so calculatingly and haplessly, so casually and momentously give her whole self, her whole holy carcass over, her one true soul over to this man, for let him at the very least be that, for his purposes, for him to do the deed, for his use, and after all, since no DNA exchanged – ha, no flesh given, no harm done.

KAYLENE: how could it be
that I remember you there
when you have never been there?
recall the flavour of your skin
the taste of your mouth
that particular liquidity to your kiss
or the temerity of your ass
or the absurdity of your cock
I feel those things
I feel I know those things
the trail of hair down your belly
the bony rib-cage
I should have felt
your stubble burn
your spunk splash
your tears' salt
I would not have imagined
all the languor of that morning
all fuck the night before
the entire scope of that thing
you called your love for me
I could not have had that put into my mind
by some idle chat
at the dead of night or turn of day
you could not be so present to me now
fiction though you now are
had you not been immemorial you
in some now long forgotten place
at some now long lost time
fiction though you are
you were real
my soul founds itself upon that

[…]

POLLY: if I were to admit
               you had gotten under my skin
               that would be as much as to write
               that skin were real
               which is more, much too more than the total
               possibility of me
               and yet you have been thereabouts
               for some time now
               a presence without sense
               a motive without goal
               a sin without its sinner
               and a love without its soul.
               Such poetry ha
               you draw off me
               like I never had
               never could have had
               just some few hapless tappings at the keys
               like there was particular you
               just a spell-check away from perfection.
               I was enjoying the ride
               or was it the fall?
               if I ever had a mind
               and there was something worth standing for
               or was it just standing in for?
               for what it could have been we thought we felt
               cos others too might have felt something like
               at some other time and place
               between some other times and places
               (words to that effect)
               for sure we are not alone
               they are gathered hereabouts
               in the darknesses
               in the hush
               countless others maybe for whom a not dissimi-
               lar issue has come to mind
KAYLENE: this is not a hand
               this is not a face
               where am I?
(POLLY: she wants answers)
               this is not my body
               how the lungs squeak
               and this jaw clicks
               like I never had

                never could have had
                this is not me
                I am elsewhere here
                a speaking without a voice
                a moving without a body
                o lend me your face
                that I might smile upon the world
                give me your lips
                so I can sigh upon my lover's neck
                let me have the use of your tongue
                to help me phrase a time and place
                adequate to this love I bear
                but cannot bear alone
                this is not a prayer
                and this room is without

GRAEME: don't hurt me anymore
                I can't take anymore pain
                can't you see I distress easily?
                when I come I hurt
                don't even think about it
                that's abuse too
                no touchy touchy
                much less feely feely
                I bruise when you think about me
                I read your emails and my eyes bleed

THE BAND: this valentine just for you
                the unwanted for the inattentive
                this electronic for the narcotic
                my insomniac's love
                cos all sleepers must eventually wake
                all silences eventually speak
                and all the dead will live again
                and go to work and play and love.

28

Being In-Between: Collaboration as Non-Collaboration

SIMON JONES

In this Flight, I propose a new model for collaboration in performance-making as a complementary working – in effect, a non-collaboration. This underpins the second series of Bodies in Flight's work where we sought out a range of new collaborations across art-forms and media. It also marks a shift in our rehearsal practice towards discovering how the material each artist brought could be allowed to express itself in the fullest possible ways whilst also working with all the other materials in the space – a dwelling alongside. This effectively made these materials starting points, rather than solutions, for the issues explored in the work, marking yet another shift from our earlier shows. Finally, this approach to developing material has implications for how we viewed each show as discrete, changing our understanding of how material re-appears across a series of works over time.

Common sense suggests that the performing arts are a highly collaborative endeavour. On the one hand, methodological manuals advise theatre-makers how to develop the collaborative spirit of an ensemble, with the aim of easing inter-personal communication and improving the 'transparency' of meaning-making and decision-making within the given aesthetic process, all pointing towards the performance as a single, defined, mutually understood objective. On the other hand, motivational and team-building coaches, employed by corporate and public-service organizations, use those very same actor-training exercises to improve the 'bonds' between staff, thence maximizing their productivity (and profitability), again with the underlying (and often explicitly stated) assumption of a common goal. So apparently compelling is this understanding of both the centrality of collaboration to performance and its fundamental purpose being to define the process and its outcomes as shared, that, for many years of making theatre, I did not question these tenets, despite ample evidence from both rehearsals and performances that this paradigm was profoundly flawed. In this Flight, I want to propose a radically different model for working together in performance-making, predicated not on the commonly understood but on the impossibility of ever sharing common ground or even common goals: a model of collaboration *as complementary working*, in effect – a coming-together of 'unalikes'.

Here, I am using 'complementary' in a specific sense borrowed from Quantum Mechanics.

> At the quantum level, the most general physical properties of any system must be expressed in terms of complementary pairs of variables [e.g. momentum and position; energy and time; continuity and discontinuity], each of which can be better defined only at the expense of a corresponding loss in the degree of definition of the other.
> (Bohm 1960: 160, my gloss)

In other words, the more we examine the abundance of material in the rehearsal room, the more we are obliged to focus on specific aspects, necessarily excluding others. It is physically impossible to understand the material in its entirety. Physicists will use different instruments to measure different aspects of their experimental 'object': for instance, the (famous) wave-particle dichotomy which demonstrates that something as ubiquitous and 'self-evident' as light behaves in one of two mutually exclusive, contradictory ways, as either particle or wave, depending on the equipment used to measure it. These mutually exclusive aspects cannot be measured, I might say – cannot be made to appear, at once: one has to choose which one to 'realize' through measurement. They only exist as a 'complementary pair' in theory, *until* the instant they are measured, appearing then as *one or the other*. For me, this complementarity inherent in all materials is so vital to making theatre. I would even propose that it is performance's generative principle: this profound *being in-between* is the very thing that both artists and audiences seek in performance: *the intermingling of un-alikes*.

Material's fundamental complementarity energizes and drives all performance because theatre is the art form *sine qua non* of mixing. Its basic set-up materializes this ontology of being in-between in a particularly intense way since it foregrounds not only its eventness but also its happening in that time and in a certain place; and also the manner of its mixing of persons, their fleshes and histories, their desires and prospects. This intensification is not simply one particular relation between a material, its expressing by means of a single object, and the solitary viewer, such as the relationship of viewer to painting, but a compounding of the sensations of *the relation between relations*. One fundamental in-between, that of different kinds of material, each with their own means and media, such as the visual, the sonic or somatic, their own middles that meddle each in their own curious ways, is compounded furiously in the 'heat' of the event with another in-between, that of the gathering of persons, each aware of the others *as persons* each in their own right (see Chapter 48, 'The Dare of Other Voices'). In the theatre event, we put ourselves forth in this doubled sense: *into the midst of various middles amongst others*. We come together to experience, each in our own way, these various in-betweens being revealed, disclosed and even deconstructed, before us.

In the performance 'itself', both artists and participants achieve a heightened attention, a kind of mood, as described by Heidegger as an 'attunement' to the work. This 'sensitivity' has been identified by scientists across many different natural systems, when one organism or system encounters another, sometimes called 'sensitivity to initial conditions' or 'the butterfly effect'. In performance, this is often experienced as a plenitude, an overwhelming of the senses, leading to either an abandonment or a resistance to what the work expresses. In a devising process, in which hierarchies of material are jettisoned (see Chapter 20, 'Set-up and Situation'), we needed to find an organizing principle that helped us explore the potential of the different kinds of material in the rehearsal room, without slipping back into the normative conventions and practices of [say] 'logocentric' or 'representational' theatre. The duet or pairing provided this 'sweet spot' where we could both manage the plenitude and keep open the possibilities of combining the different materials, such as flesh and text, text and music, music and video.

Taking Bodies in Flight's core pairing – of choreographer and writer, I came to understand that Sara 'saw' bodies differently from me. She understood them as somatic gestures *through* space and time, whilst I saw them as images *in* space and *out of* time. The performers literally right in front of us in the rehearsal room were actually bifurcated beings: since we each understood them in our own discrete ways, they were able to defy natural laws and exist in two complementary aspects simultaneously. Sara was able to move them in ways I could not imagine, and I encouraged a voicing she could not evoke (see Chapter 13, 'Speaking in Texts' and Chapter 18, 'The Magnificent Minutiae'). From this profound observation about the material *in-between-nesses* produced from our (non-)collaborating, we realized that collaborators worked each in their own media, and each had their own discursivity, their own middle that meddled – the choreographic, textual, sonic, musical, pictorial, fleshy. This led us to seek out further collaborations across media and skill sets, which explicitly sustained the open relations between different kinds of material and their composition in the performance, integrating technology into our methodology, folding back into the event not only material captured live but also material from rehearsals, thus layering different times from the show's making into the performance itself. We worked with musicians, sonic and video artists, photographers and, more recently, gymnasts, performers whose bodies were expert, amateur, young, old, who could sing, dance, play or tumble.

In encountering media in which we were not experts, each of us had to cross a void in-between channels of communication, producing a kind of speaking without a common language, making these collaborations endlessly productive, non-resolvable, complementary and compossible. In theory, they should not work, but in practice, the work works precisely *at the point* where we cannot: impossible collaboration happens in the non-collaboration which had always been right in front of us in the rehearsal room. However, it is not enough simply to recognize one's collaborator's expertise, to acknowledge the profound otherness of their material. We had to find ways of holding open the undecidedness in-between different materials, and we had to learn to *be with* their otherness in the rehearsal room as the material disclosed itself. This *dwelling in* the different materials' othernesses we called *a dialoguing*, inspired by the physicist David Bohm's writing on First Nations gatherings in North America.

> The basic idea of this dialogue is to be able to talk while suspending your opinions, holding them in front of you, while neither suppressing them nor insisting upon them. Not trying to convince, but simply to understand. [...] That will create a new frame of mind in which there is a common consciousness. It is a kind of implicate order, where each one enfolds the whole consciousness. With the common consciousness, we then have something new – a new kind of intelligence.
> (Bohm 1998: 118)

This radical suspension of judgement enabled each collaborator to approach one another's material as a touching without ever reaching, daring each to leave the comfort of their own expertise and move into a being in-between, an *inter-esse*. In rehearsal, these crossings-across are always underway and never undergone, always in action and never done, sensing the matter materializing, rather than the ostensible appearance of matter materialized, the quasi-thing that can only be pointed to. These approachings are thus *pre-position-ings*, before the performer takes a stand or the auditor under-stands, before the place is occupied, the point is made, when-where 'we' 'know' 'where' 'we' 'are'. And yet paradoxically, this 'knowing' can only be achieved *by way of decisiveness*: deciding when and how to bring the duets of material to realization in performance becomes a profound mix of ignorance and experience, courage and daring (see Chapter 13, 'Speaking in Texts'). During the performance, the non-collaborators play between this point of *not yet having come* into focus, of *not yet having understood*, suspending it sometimes for as long as they dare; and the *instant of making the decision,* when–where what was potential in the material is actualized.

To date, our most explicit non-collaboration has been the performance-installation – *Do the Wild Thing! Redux*, which pulled apart the different materials and their respective media to expose the 'gaps' between not only media but also times of performing and collaborating. Four of the original collaborators extended *Do the Wild Thing!*'s ideas of non-collaboration (see Chapter 20, 'Set-up and Situation') by working independently until the day of installing the work. Returning to the archival remains of this peepshow about desire and voyeurism, each produced a separate new work in their own medium – dance, photography, text and video. Our collective brief was that each non-collaborator would take their own inspiration from their first involvement in *Do the Wild Thing!* and, where possible, pay particular attention to those elements of the archive each produced. The show, which now appeared through the perspectives of each work making up the installation, existed between the media as an expression of in-betweenness 'itself'. The illusionary centre, the real of the work-object, was evacuated to the edges of multiple viewpoints, expressions of each non-collaborator's journey between the non-communicable parts, the aspects of the re-dux/re-turn.

As an *approaching*, each non-collaborator's work touched without ever reaching the 'original' performance: to begin again towards the emptied scene. *Redux* did not provide a more complete version of *Do the Wild Thing!*, as film directors might like to think their redux does – a version more original than the original. It actually opened up more gaps, exposing the show's auratic mask of originality, its documents' claim to be *the* work, by pointing to multiple, possible future works. In this way, our stepping aside and disentangling resonated with the 'original' process of both making and documenting, disclosing the incompletenesses in between and within media – the middles of middles. The artists' indirect relation to the archive, thence to all technologies, says something more about performance: that it is made out of this non-collaboration *as indirectness* (see '*Do The Wild Thing! Redux*' in Clarke et al., *Artists in the Archive*, pp. 212–17).

This dwelling in non-collaboration's in-betweenesses happens not only 'within' the osmotic envelope of any one project or performance but also across a series of works, concerns over different materials emerging from the mix into clearer focus in one show, then fading into the background of another (see Chapter 45, 'Developing a Portfolio'). Much scholarship has been done on the production processes of repertory companies, from Shakespeare's Kings' Men to twentieth-century regional Rep in the United Kingdom, where the same artists honed their shared aesthetic in a series of works, a familiarity among the 'collective' producing 'shorthand' approaches that enabled plays to be rehearsed and staged within a week. Very little has been written about the commensurate benefits to established experimental ensembles, such as Forced Entertainment, who are, to all intents and purposes, a repertory company. Bodies in Flight's *Unbox Me!*, made in just two weeks because of commissioning constraints (February 2023), exemplified this open-ended non-collaboration.

In accepting the commission, we knew we could not employ our usual extended development period consisting of workshops and periods of reflection over many months (see Sara's *Still Moving: Moving Still*). Part of the dare was to explore how much of our methodology we carried within us, how much could we discover in returning to an accumulated, aggregated, articulated body of work to produce new work, not a repeat or revival: to what extent was Bodies in Flight *a unique practising* held open over time? The condensed making revealed to me the deeply embodied rigour and strengths of our methodology, forcing us to cut straight to the challenge of placing old material in a new context, to embrace and revel in the risk of the performance moving through a series of representational modes: from Naturalism (from the opening of *Who By Fire*), through forensic analysis of circumstances (from the middle of *Model Love*), through a hallucinatory journey into the self (from *The Secrecy of Saints*), to the direct address of a new 'political' consciousness (earlier glimpses of which appeared in *Rough* and *Double Happiness*). The courage and richness of *Unbox Me!* proved to me the benefits of holding our non-collaboration open over an extended series of projects with an ensemble of regular artists, infused along the way by new (non-)collaborators. It demonstrated a fundamental mood to artists working together, not predicated upon common ground, but upon revealing impossibly from out of unspeakable and non-communicable complementarities what the work can do amongst the wills of its makers: an endless capacity to transform and become anew, *to live again*.

References

Bohm, David (1960), *Quantum Theory*, London: Prentice Hall.

Bohm, David (1998), *On Creativity*, London: Routledge.

Clarke, Paul, Jones, Simon, Kaye, Nick and Linsley, Johanna (eds) (2018), *Artists in the Archive*, Abingdon: Routledge.

Further Reading

Barker, Clive (1977), *Theatre Games: A New Approach to Drama Training*, London: Eyre Methuen.

Berry, Cicely (1973), *Voice and the Actor*, London: Harrop.

Callery, Dymphna (2001), *Through the Body: A Practical Guide to Physical Theatre*, London: Nick Hern Books.

Graham, Scott and Hoggett, Steven (2014), *The Frantic Assembly Book of Devising Theatre*, Abingdon: Routledge.

Hodge, Alison (2010), *Actor Training*, London: Routledge.

Lehmann, Hans-Thies (2006), *Postdramatic Theatre* (trans. K. Jürs-Munby), London: Routledge.

Rodenburg, Patsy (2002), *Speaking Shakespeare*, London: Methuen.

Rowell, George and Jackson, Anthony (1984), *The Repertory Movement: A History of Regional Theatre in Britain*, Cambridge: Cambridge University Press.

Zarrilli, Phillip (1995), *Acting (Re)Considered: Theories and Practices*, London: Routledge.

Bodies in Flight

29
Who By Fire (2004–05)

FIGURE 29.1: *Who By Fire*: performers Benjamin Clough, Tim Atack, Doug Bott, Polly Frame and Graeme Rose. Photo: Edward Dimsdale.

FIGURE 29.2: *Who By Fire*: postcard. Courtesy of the University of Bristol Theatre Collection.

FIGURE 29.3 (next): *Who By Fire*: performers Polly Frame, Neil Johnson, Doug Bott, Benjamin Clough, Graeme Rose and Tim Atack. Photo: Edward Dimsdale.

FIGURE 29.4 (next): *Who By Fire*: performers Tim Atack and Benjamin Clough. Photo: Edward Dimsdale.

FIGURE 29.5 (next): *Who By Fire*: performer Graeme Rose. Photo: Edward Dimsdale.

FIGURE 29.6 (next): *Who By Fire*: performers Doug Bott, Neil Johnson, Polly Frame, Graeme Rose and Tim Atack. Photo: Edward Dimsdale.

WHO BY FIRE (2004–05)

PUBLICITY COPY
An opera
The party's done.
Five hangers-on share bizarre stories of accidental deaths, killing time before going home, on the eve of something big. Facing the void: like children facing the future, lovers facing each other, the old facing death.
Combining the music of the band Angel Tech with the intimate performance style of Bodies in Flight, this is another powerful piece of performance, where everyday materials – simple language, mundane actions and gestures – fuse into poetry. The performance centres on that strange in-between time after the party's over and before the day that just won't dawn.

Beginning with a long, improvised dialogue between performers and musicians, this show blurred the distinctions between who did what on stage to produce a rock opera on our fascination with how people die and how that most personal of all life events is shared. This grew out of our growing concern with the theme of generations, with ageing and how one generation passes on its knowledge to another. This show moved from the private language of pre-verbal twins to the frail voice of an old performer singing a shanty to her lost love. It became not only about death but how we acquire and then finally lose our capacities and skills, life as all possibility, then all memory. This inter-generational theme was further developed by Sara in her three-screen video collaboration with Tony Judge – *Triptych*.

TIM ATACK sound, DOUG BOTT sound, BENJAMIN CLOUGH video/performer, POLLY FRAME performer, SARA GIDDENS choreography, NEIL JOHNSON sound, SIMON JONES lyrics/ direction, TONY JUDGE video, GRAEME ROSE performer.

On video: Mark Adams, Sheila Gilbert, Ella Judge, Sam Lambshead, Alisdair McKee, Tom Wainwright.

Performed: Opera 2004/BAC (London), Mayfest/Bristol Old Vic, ICA (London), Wickham Theatre (Bristol), Sensitive Skin Festival/ Powerhouse (Nottingham), Bretton Hall (University of Leeds).

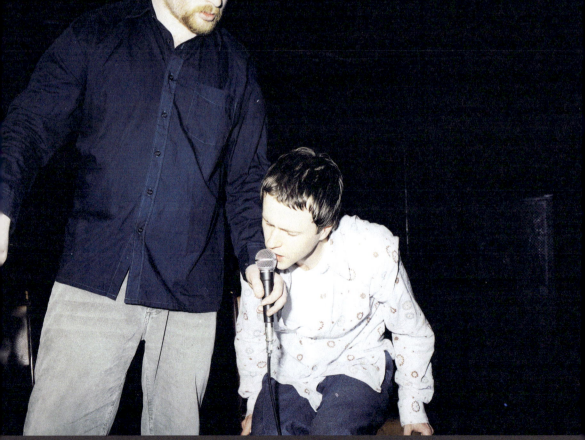

BATTERSEA ARTS CENTRE MARKETING TEXT

The Pub Conversation: *Tell us about the show as if you were describing it to a mate in the pub. This is not marketing copy! We would just like you to describe the show and why you are doing it as if in normal conversation.*

Who By Fire is a work of music theatre. It combines the music of the band Angel Tech with the intimate performance style of Bodies in Flight. We've always been about uncovering the hidden, unspoken feelings and passions in everyday events. That's why we've made a lot of works about love, some about growing old, others about grief and loss. We've talked about living in cities, about feeling always in transit, never feeling like you're at home. These are feelings that we feel everyone feels, and those are our concerns. This show explores that strange time in every celebration, like Xmas Eve, New Year's Eve, when the party's done and you suddenly feel really emotional because you realize you're on the edge of something new, something just starting – rebirth, a new year, whatever: you're supposed to be celebrating it, and suddenly you realize you don't really know what it is, what it should be. This strange sense of being at a loss about the future often involves you remembering key times from your past. You're exhausted after partying; you've drunk too much; but you don't want to go home yet; then all this past floods back and all this scary possibility of the future floods in.

As with all our shows, we take the unfinished business from the previous work as the starting point for the new work. In *Skinworks*, we ended with an exhausted text about the empty feeling you get after having surfed the web – all the possibilities of human life/sex/passion/desire have been revealed to you on that tiny screen, and then you think – where else is there to go? That feeling of facing the void, facing the future that seems too empty to bear, is what forms the foundation for *Who By Fire*. Although that feeling may seem bleak in its emptiness, there's also hope there: the dawn will come; things will start up again; you are on the eve of something, in there at its beginnings. Your job is to find your place in newness.

In terms of the style of the show, we focus on taking what we think of as everyday material – simple language, everyday actions and gestures – and distilling them into poetry and choreography. It's a process of framing the essence of everydayness in such a way that it makes you look at your own life and the passions that drive that in a new, refreshed way. We don't have a point of view nor an argument: we try to open out a feeling and passion and hold it up for exploration. That's why we often go for non-formal audience-performer relationships, trying to break down the conventional divide between the auditorium and the stage so that we can get right into people's bodies – their heads and hearts. We can be very intellectual about our work, and we're certainly not ashamed of the fact that our shows are hard work for both audiences and performers alike, but we believe that makes them good and worthwhile, and we believe that's why most of our audiences come back for more.

30
Who By Fire: Very Slow Decay

SLEEPDOGS: TANUJA AMARASURIYA AND TIM X ATACK
IN CONVERSATION

TANUJA AMARASURIYA is a director and dramaturg. TIM X ATACK is a writer and composer. They work across screen, stage, audio, games and XR and are co-founders of Sleepdogs, whose projects include the sci-fi theatre show Dark Land Light House *and the film* All My Dreams on VHS. *Tanuja has worked with Dominic Cooke, Danusia Samal, Die Güte Fabrik and Improbable, among many others. Tim's writing includes* Forest 404 *for BBC Sounds and the Bruntwood Prize-winning play* HEARTWORM. *From 2002, Tim collaborated on several projects with Bodies in Flight as one third of the band Angel Tech, alongside Doug Bott and Neil Johnson.*

In this conversation, Tim and Tanuja share recollections of Who By Fire *from the perspective of performer and audience.*

TIM:
Here are some of my strongest memories of performing *Who By Fire*.
   1. There was a fifteen-minute conversation at the top of the show, delivered at 'room volume', where we all sat around and talked about death. It had an early-hours, post-party kind of air to it and a few of us had instruments we would occasionally strum. Then there was an unexpected gearshift where over about ten to fifteen seconds we suddenly became a band. The guitars would be turned up, someone grabbed a mic, and I'd leap towards a drum kit and start blatting at it furiously. I always used to love this moment: it felt irreverent and on edge. The choreography of how and when we began playing was forever in danger of tripping over itself. But I'd spend the first fifteen minutes trying to forget it was approaching, worried I'd give off an energy that would give it away.

2. During a song called 'Ahhh She', Ben Clough would give out a lustful breathy ode into a microphone while I manipulated the boom stand, throwing it into more and more unlikely and uncomfortable positions (see Figure 29.4). I always liked to imagine I was invisible for the duration, that all the audience could see was the stand moving around by itself, like a construction crane. I knew I couldn't be invisible, obviously, but somehow it helped.

3. With the previous project we'd collaborated on with BIF, *Skinworks*, I felt I knew what I was 'representing' or conveying when I moved or sang. In *Who By Fire*, I didn't so much, and generally, I preferred that. It felt a lot more like being in a band and less like being in a devised performance company. You can be in a really good, really impactful band and never have defined your goals, never really spoken about what you want to 'say'. It felt like that at the end of most performances of *Who By Fire*.

What are your strongest memories of watching it?

TANUJA:

I feel like I'm always trying to get the sense of that performer-manipulating-mic-manipulating-performer moment in everything I direct. I don't mean copying it literally but drawing on the feel of it. There's a real sensuality in that moment, which I think comes from the tension and surrender in it: the intensity of focus required to sing and follow, Ben's body being led by his mouth and your body being led by your hands, the strangeness of the movement that comes from following the motion of the mic stand, the strange machine of it. I mean there's a whole load of stuff accumulating in that moment, of course, but it's really the dance of it and the moving parts of that dance, which are still so vivid for me. I don't remember what the song was, or how far into the show it happens. But the feel of that moment remains strikingly alive for me. It's one of my favourite theatre moments ever. I don't know if this is something developed in my remembering of it, or if it was something I felt at the time of watching it, but in my mind, it has the dream-like quality of the memory of a party. I don't know about you, but my memory of parties is often a collection of disparate intense experiential snapshots. That's what *Who By Fire* feels like in my memory – the memory of a party.

I'd always found Bodies in Flight's shows interesting, but somewhat cerebral and emotionally distant. *Who By Fire* felt very different to me. And I remember a lot of people making the same observation at the time. I found it emotionally vulnerable and immersive. I remember there being these big, surprising shifts in energy and focus throughout the piece, which I loved. I think there was perhaps something a little 'uncontained' about it, and I love that kind of thing.

TIM:
Yes, I think there was that sense of a memory or memories, changing, fading perhaps, but sometimes sharpening. There was a map to the soundtrack too, a design, where it slowly moved in stages from the completely 'live' to the electronic, to the purely recorded. So 'Ahhh She' was in the last third; the music was in a territory I'd describe as somewhere between Massive Attack and Plaid. Doug was behind a laptop, using Ableton Live to switch between different intensities of beats. I can't remember whether that soundtrack map was planned, or a nice accident responding to the practical needs of the show.

In fact, the main memory I have of the construction of the show is that most of the decisions were made after rehearsals, over a drink. If I'm honest I was frustrated by this at first, but soon realized the benefits that kind of approach brings. The rehearsal room was largely a place of experiment, of running things in different ways, with only the occasional examination, some sparse but decisive 'more of that' or 'not that' from Sara. Then out of the room, we'd pick it all apart, under less pressure. That's liberating in a way, and we've often ended up doing something similar in Sleepdogs rehearsal rooms. We'll regularly talk about how it feels, but less so about what it means, not until we have a bigger picture. It makes me think of the 'Rules for Students and Teachers' by Sister Corita Kent, the list John Cage popularized: Rule 8 – 'Don't try to create and analyze at the same time'. They're different processes.

TANUJA:
A friend, a fellow artist, recently said to me – 'there always seem to be ghosts in your work'. It surprised me because I didn't realize how visible that was. It's not really a conscious thing, but I think it ties into what you say about our Sleepdogs conversations often being more about how it feels, and less about what it means. I don't really know what 'haunting' means, but I know how it feels. I think lots of contemporary theatre gets fixated on presence as immediacy, but I'm more interested in how presence lingers: accumulation, fade, memory, ghost. That journey of the *Who By Fire* soundtrack that you describe – from the 'live' to the purely recorded – feels like ghosts. Sure, it's not only about the textures of the music but also about the materiality of the music. This interest in the materiality of sound is definitely inside so much of Sleepdogs work.

You describe the musical territory of *Who By Fire* as somewhere between Massive Attack and Plaid. Was that intentional? How did you arrive at that?

TIM:

Yeah, I meant by the time it got to 'Ahhh She', we'd hit that electronica territory. But the musical genres were all over the place. We had some Mountain Goats emo-ish punk, some Bad Seeds brittle rock, Polly even sang us a kind of Weimar ballad, 'Temptation', that I was worried had a bit too much of Coldplay about it. But happy to say, Polly's clear and unshowy vocal steered us well away from that. Actually, the chord sequence from 'Temptation' eventually made its way into 'The Measure', a track for our Sleepdogs dream-pop odyssey *A Million Tiny Glitches*. Similarly bittersweet, similarly not Coldplay.

The strangest number was 'Lament', which Doug meticulously constructed from samples of Sara's kids vocalizing at bath time. I think they were less than two years old then. He built up a whole melody from tiny fragments of their burbling and set Simon's lyrics to it. I have no idea how you'd categorize that sound. Bubble bath opera.

The shift from one aesthetic to another wasn't a planned thing as I recall, beyond us just kind of accepting we'd be doing it. But it's interesting how musical genres get used in performance. Pop is often used as a shortcut to some emotion, an attempt to unify your audience into a state of mind, but that usually backfires, in my humble opinion. Good pop means so many different things to so many people, you'll summon up a billion atomized emotions. In *Who By Fire*, I reckon what really sold us on each genre shift was finding something that helped embody that part of the text or the show. So, for instance, in the slow group dance at the end where all of us were pacing back and forth in unison (see Figure 29.6), that was connecting with something naïve, sentimental, maybe even maudlin in the song. Earlier, when Graeme Rose was raging around hurling this snarling existential invective all over the place, we went towards one of those Nick Cave wig-outs, like the Bad Seed's version of 'Stagger Lee'. Neil was certainly giving it some proper Blixa Bargeld guitar shredding. Soundtrack-wise, I don't think I've ever done anything quite that varied since. In our Sleepdogs' scores, we tend to unify the aesthetic a lot more, but I'd say that's because we often world-build through sound. There were a lot more questions about presence and absence throughout *Who By Fire*: the slippery, the flickering, the moving in and out of focus. So the music went along with that.

TANUJA:

Yeah, my memory of *Who By Fire* is that it definitely had that sense of elision, like you notice things have changed, but you didn't notice the point at which they changed. I guess that's kind of 'undramatic' (or anti-dramatic?) in conventional terms. Normally that would probably be 'dramaturg-ed' out of the play: 'Be clear about what changes in the scene! Be clear where this character makes this decision!' But I guess that comes from looking for a narrative in a conventional 'hero's-journey' way, which would obviously be a category error for *Who By Fire*. In my memory, the show was more like a photo album. Or actually, it's more like the photos that you leave out of the album, the ones where people aren't looking at the camera, or everything's blurred or off-centre, people caught off guard. It's funny to find myself describing the show that way because I remember the images as being very precisely choreographed. But I think it comes back to that thing you mentioned previously: about drawing focus to how it feels, rather than what it means.

References

Sister Corita Kent's list, https://www.openculture.com/2014/04/10-rules-for-students-and-teachers-popularized-by-john-cage.html. Accessed 8 May 2024.

Further Listening and Reading

'Ahhh She' (instrumental), https://soundcloud.com/neiljohnson/ah-she. Accessed 8 May 2024.

'Temptation', https://soundcloud.com/neiljohnson/temptation. Accessed 8 May 2024.

More on Sleepdogs' processes in this talk by Tanuja, http://sleepdogs.org/2020/10/breaking-theatre-is-more-fun-than-making-theatre/. Accessed 8 May 2024.

Bodies in Flight

31 Triptych (2005)

Figure 31.1: *Triptych*: video montage. Still courtesy of Tony Judge.

Figure 31.2: *Triptych*: video montage. Still courtesy of Tony Judge.

Figure 31.3: *Triptych*: video montage. Still courtesy of Tony Judge.

Triptych is a single-screen video work, re-entering material used in *Who By Fire*. It concerns itself with articulation: specifically, how we might find our physical and emotional voice, and how this may change as we age. Working with three women performers of very different ages, the work explores how the smallest of actions and sounds can refer to, perhaps touch upon, the complexity of our shared, mortal experience. This work invites audiences to slow down, to still, to notice, to remember, to perhaps recall, and in doing so to re-engage with themselves and the people and places around them.

TIM ATACK sound/performer, DOUG BOTT sound/performer, BENJAMIN CLOUGH performer, POLLY FRAME performer, SARA GIDDENS choreography, NEIL JOHNSON sound/performer, SIMON JONES lyrics, SHEILA GILBERT performer, CALLUM JUDGE performer, ELLA JUDGE performer, TONY JUDGE video, GRAEME ROSE performer.

Exhibited: Goldsmiths University (London), Quake (Dèda, Derby), Arnolfini (Bristol), Banff Arts Centre (Canada), Artist Researcher in Performance Symposium (University of Bedfordshire), Artistic Doctorates in Europe Symposium (Middlesex University, London), Flesh & Text: 30 Years of Bodies in Flight (Wickham Theatre, Bristol), Lakeside Arts (Nottingham), Anglia Ruskin Gallery (Cambridge), PR1 Gallery (Preston).

32
The Transmediated Image
TONY JUDGE

TONY JUDGE has worked in film and television for 40 years, specializing in arts, music, performance and artist's film. He trained in fine art (sculpture and the moving image) and has exhibited and screened internationally. He has video works in the permanent collections of galleries including MOMA (New York) and ICA (London). His current research includes the recycling and transmediation of performance and materials for multi-screen and installation. Tony was a Senior Lecturer in Filmmaking at Leeds Arts University and founder and creative director of Creative Forum, a commercials and documentary production company whose clients have included Pepsi, Guinness and Ronseal. He has worked with Bodies in Flight since 1989, documenting, archiving and collaborating, most recently on Life Class *and creating* 30X3, *a three-screen archival video work for their 30-year retrospective exhibition* Flesh & Text.

Here Tony explores the creative re-use of video in his work with Bodies in Flight.

As a filmmaker, through my long collaboration with Bodies in Flight, I have been concerned with exploring ways of transforming material, moving material from one medium to another, or from one time and place to another, through re-using, re-purposing and transmediation. This is particularly interesting within a performance-based context because it is a medium very much of the here and now, an event in a specific place and time, but it also hopes to happen in another place and time, a strange paradox. I began with Bodies in Flight as a documentor, recording *Deadplay* in 1989 at the Third Eye Centre in Glasgow, when I had been commissioned to document shows at the National Review of Live Art. At that point, I was focused on trying to capture what was going on within the movement, the text and the staging, and to represent that on screen, to be true to the performance, and the audience experience of the performance, but also as a mediated process. By the time I produced Bodies in Flight's archival CD-ROM *Flesh & Text*, the documentation had started to contribute more creatively to the process, as it moved into a new format, a new purpose and a new way to engage with the shows, not just through the CD-ROM itself but also through the subsequent presentation of materials from the CD-ROM in accompanying installations. This recycling and re-purposing through an archival process, through different ways of manipulation and through different ways of experiencing that content, as a viewer and an audience, invigorated a new kind of working.

One of the things that fascinated me in the process of making the CD-ROM was that I re-purposed the material into bite-sized pieces, manageable chunks of data, driven by the technology's interactivity at the time, allowing the viewer to take their own *flight* through the documents. This opened up so many potential routes through the material that it felt infinitely productive. Moreover, you could explore it as a conventional archive, but at the same time, it was immediate and accessible. The irony with using 'new' technologies to compress and display such data is they become obsolete, and what is easily accessible then becomes totally inaccessible. The CD-ROM's functionality was probably ten years. However much I tried to future-proof, I had to accept this captures a moment in the here and now, much like theatre does.

This re-purposing began to inform how I recorded the work in the first place, particularly where I placed the camera, from whose perspective, i.e. audience/viewer/participant. Do I place the camera on stage? If so, what does this do to the dynamic and geography of the performance space in relation to the viewer? This conundrum, the choreography of the camera in relation to the action, the environment and the text, was a central concern for me on *Who By Fire* as a video artist, in addition to documentor. Bodies in Flight was interested in working with three generations of women: Sheila in her 80s, Polly in her mid 30s, and Ella, a toddler; capturing this on film to be used in the live show. Gathering imagery of the women around Sheila's cottage garden and by the sea, I explored how the camera searched for an image and how it found its focus. This became key to the development of the whole show. I looked for the stillness between the performers' actions: in these moments, I placed footage from the three generations of women. This began visually with a deliberate hunting for the image through the lens, abandoning conventional filmic composition, such as the rule of thirds or focal lengths, in favour of happy accidents, out of which striking images appeared: for instance, when Ella used

Sheila's Zimmer-frame as a walking aid (see Figure 29.2). These images combined into a narrative framework of tracking and observing the performers through their presence and movement in the landscape.

When I saw the first performance at the Bristol Old Vic, the video material on TVs felt flat and formal: the screens needed their own characterization and interactivity. So, I explored the piece's generational theme by experimenting with the relationship between performer, monitor and scale with different screens, from the small handheld to the CCTV monitor, to the projected (see Figure 29.6). I used the performers' relationship with the technology to create opportunities to record and playback imagery or trigger pre-recorded imagery: for example, Graeme Rose would cradle a small monitor in his hands, whilst a large image of found footage was projected on the rear screen (see Figure 29.5). This image then moved around the space, bouncing between the monitor and the screen. At that time, physically holding a moving image in the hand was comparatively new: here it was achieved by re-purposing inexpensive screens intended for in-car entertainment. Because Bodies in Flight was never shy of technology, I re-purposed DVD players, the closed-relay cameras and the projection, and made the performers' engagement with this technology central to *Who By Fire.*

Both Sara and I felt the video material had unrealized potential as part of this stage work. Sara wanted to explore how to present her choreography beyond live performance; I was interested in choreographing as a filmmaker. So, to make the video installation *Triptych*, we re-edited documentation of the live performance, alongside 'found choreography' of Ella's natural movements on the beach, in the garden, by a fire and in the snow, to create a new narrative and choreographic focus. In this way, the project *Who By Fire* became about how material gets changed and repurposed and how the video developed from straightforward projection on stage to being manipulated by performers, to a stand-alone installation.

In contrast, *Gymnast* began with the intention of multiple outcomes in different media across various settings, what Bodies in Flight calls a 'portfolio' project. The gathering of material is built on this evolving methodology: I felt greater freedom to develop visuals that would be mediated into the various performances in different ways. A crucial new aspect was allowing the material to emerge, as this time we were not working with professional performers in a studio, but gymnasts in their training spaces. This meant spending appropriate time and space with the participants, a range of élites and amateurs from clubs in the East Midlands: for instance, Joshua Avallone whose speciality was the pommel horse. One time, he performed a routine for the camera, which he didn't think went well. He dismounted from the pommel and stared at me, completely locked on to the camera, revealing something extraordinary about the way gymnasts could engage with a camera, perhaps because they're confident in front of people, comfortable with being scrutinized to the nth detail (see Figure 40.4). For me, this extended gaze into the camera exploded the constraints around documentary making and the interview process, becoming not only a powerful image in the piece but a compositional strategy throughout its many versions, which in turn was re-purposed for Joe's gaze in *I'd Like to Call You Joe Tonight* (see Figure 43.2).

For Sara, this elongated gaze into the camera was analogous to her choreographic approach to the gymnasts' routines: they were doing the thing that they do, but for a longer duration, in a different combination: a subtle drawing-out of certain elements which previously may have lay hidden in plain sight. I felt I was capturing action that is often at the margins and ignored, thus creating new and authentic possibilities for the material. I edited the footage of the gymnasts' training sessions so that it focused on and visually extended the apex or the fulcrum of their routines, to mirror the choreographic strategy Sara had been developing with the gymnasts. In performance, these artificial durations were then interrupted with behind-the-scenes footage of their preparations and anecdotal interviews: for example, a beautiful moment when the gymnasts were relaxing, lolling against the pommel horse. Simply juxtaposing that video material, whilst the live gymnasts were doing their routines on the beams, demonstrated how this methodology can take the habitual and re-arrange it to draw attention to its gracefulness. It also allows the work to remain responsive to different staging opportunities, as *Gymnast* was presented and performed in galleries, theatres and working gymnasia: an artwork that could at any moment become a performance, or the performance could shift into installation. Often the installations in galleries would contain a live element of gymnastics or singing, producing more of a sense of a happening, working between installation and performance. This transformative attitude to the material even resulted in one performance in a gymnasium without video (Mayfest, Bristol, 2013). Beforehand, I had thought it was going to be flat, but the combined elements of live choir, audio from pre-recorded interviews and live gymnastics in their intended setting were compelling. I didn't feel excluded because it felt like another transmediation.

I was able to develop this transmediating further as part of *Do the Wild Thing! Redux*: a project which invited me to re-visit my role as documentor of the original 1996 stage work. *I'd Like to Call You Joe Tonight* pushed re-purposing material by re-staging the performance entirely for the camera, thus exploring more fully the interplay between the three characters. Rather than the work's peep-show situation, or the documentary's 'outside', observational point of view, each performer had their own camera, from which we saw what they saw of one another. Moving between flat-screen TVs placed around the gallery was as if stepping into the play of gazes between the characters, whilst listening to their intimate thoughts and musings on located speakers, allowing the viewer to take on each character's point of view (see Figure 43.1). Whereas the original work's set-up riffed on the conventional 'fourth wall' with performers relating only to themselves and each other, this new configuration allowed the viewer to occupy any one of their gazes and watch the scene from their perspective: the very thing that theatre can't do. I was able to push the original's exploration of the power play of gazes further by including the viewer's active complicity in the voyeur's ethical dilemma. For example, when the viewer saw what the Woman saw, occupied her point of view, they couldn't see her – the object of desire; however, they did see the Man looking directly at them. So, the viewer's own agency in directing their gaze was troubled in a specifically mediatized way.

This is where I first thought about re-purposing material as *re-entering* a work, which is to understand that there is always something inherent in the material, which has yet to be expressed: it needs you to find that different way of unconcealing. Such potential re-mixes are fascinating, especially within an enduring collaboration, such as that with Bodies in Flight, always taking risks with technologies, inviting collaborators to push the limits of their own and each other's medium. Now I realize that to re-purpose and re-use, to be able to re-enter work, there needs to be a substantial body of work in the first instance. Bodies in Flight's commitment to long-term collaborations, as part of their methodology, has allowed me over the years to enjoy re-entering many works, each with their own diverse possibilities for re-invention.

Further Reading

Giesekam, Greg (2007), *Staging the Screen: The Use of Film and Video in Theatre*, Basingstoke, Hampshire England: Palgrave Macmillan.

Bodies in Flight

33 The Secrecy of Saints (2006)

Figure 33.1: *The Secrecy of Saints*: performer Polly Frame. Photo: Edward Dimsdale.

Figure 33.2: *The Secrecy of Saints*: postcard. Courtesy of the University of Bristol Theatre Collection.

Figure 33.3 (next): *The Secrecy of Saints*: performers Polly Frame and Neil Johnson. Photo: Edward Dimsdale.

Figure 33.4 (next): *The Secrecy of Saints*: performers Neil Johnson and Polly Frame. Photo: Edward Dimsdale.

Figure 33.5 (next): *The Secrecy of Saints*: performer Polly Frame. Photo: Edward Dimsdale.

Figure 33.6 (next): *The Secrecy of Saints*: performers Polly Frame and Neil Johnson. Photo: Edward Dimsdale.

THE SECRECY OF SAINTS (2006)

PUBLICITY COPY
*A work-in-progress for Inbetween Time Festival of Live Art & Intrigue 2006
For BODIES IN FLIGHT, a new work emerges partly from the previous show's unworked material. In this work-in-progress of THE SECRECY OF SAINTS, choreographer Sara Giddens and performer Polly Frame re-use the video footage of the inter-generational relationships between three women from our recent opera* Who By Fire. *Writer Simon Jones and musician Neil Johnson (from the band Angel Tech) add new text and music to this re-working to make an in-between work, especially for this major Live Art festival. Here, we begin THE SECRECY OF SAINTS' exploration of the instant when two strangers' accidental eye contact morphs into the mutual gaze of lovers.*

This one-woman performance used wireless video technology and a poetic, allusive text to explore the inner workings of the mind of a recluse, isolated from and fearful of the world. This became a metaphor for the fragility of anyone's identity, the precarious relationship between our senses, our environment and the stories we tell ourselves to give us a feeling of solidity and integrity. Performed four times in one day in a gallery space of Arnolfini, it became a hallucinatory experience for the performer, moving from a closed, anxious figure, physically constrained, to a rapturous, open person claiming her space before her public.

POLLY FRAME performer, SARA GIDDENS choreography/co-direction, NEIL JOHNSON music, SIMON JONES text/co-direction.

With: EDWARD DIMSDALE photography.

Performed: Arnolfini (Bristol).

Text extracts

SIMON JONES

These work-in-progress performances were intended to be the beginnings of a larger portfolio project that explored how we interacted in the everyday, including pop-up installations in empty shop units, online video and performances, inspired by the various people I encountered on my daily walk into work. We did not get the funding to proceed. So, what remains is this small piece imagining the 'inner life' of one of these people. Riffing off Beckett, I pushed my writing into a more intense psychological space where even language itself was detaching from everydayness and morphing into something solitary, almost non-communicative. To imagine a life profoundly alienated from others, I set myself strict linguistic 'rules', such as, always in the third person (see Beckett's Not I*); verbs were only to be conjugated in the infinitive or gerund, emptying the images of a specific sense of time or place; punctuation was to be avoided as much as possible, to give the performer Polly Frame as much latitude as possible in how she spoke the text. What we did carry forward was the individual's relation to public space in our later portfolio project –* Dream→Work/Dream→Walk.

```
she less than a person
not quite all there
blurring into the background
into the crowd presently
just passing through
going down
without touching the sides
capacity only to avoid
as if this peopled place be a void
and emptiness the rule
replicant selfing
minding now
as if for the first time
the gap
between the selfing now presently
and the once image of the self
the she she to have thought she to have been
she used to think she could have been
and now
in this place
```

nothing but the code playing itself out
unravelling itself
from the tiny knot
she to have thought her soul-thing
(to quote) 'the event of my soul in the world'
her words to have said then
but not so much now
just the code
the mumble of ons and offs
adding up to this her last great routine
and then a zero slipping
and time entering her formula
and what she to perform
not quite the self she to have been
the hollowness this time not quite her own
(no one else's, mind you)
the click of ones and noughts
the rattle of her bon-mots
the flourish of her turns
the crushing inevitability of all those her calamities
not quite now her own
but this other playing right alongside
and not quite doing it so well
letting the inside down
and causing all these smiles to harden
sparkling eyes to glaze
disbelief to be suspended
just that little bit further out of reach
she to have loved and come and been
better than the lot of them
better than the lot of you
better than the lot
you lot
my lot
her all
all been and come and done and gone

falling still
and no hope to end
be said whoever to have fallen
and come to an end
but still
the slow unending falling

some hope earthwards
but no hope to end
and the faintest sensation
of atmosphere not quite
itself still
but then that apprehension
itself a delusion
encouraged by the relative movement
of this to-be-endured unendurable falling
against that the barest perceptible
of media through which a body to fall
o heavenly! a body!
one delusion coming upon another
one manufactured hope built upon another
the one mixing so intimately
with the other
that the whole thing
(the body of it, as it be)
giving off the appearance of a truth
she being she
because she to feel herself falling
she feeling herself falling
because of the sensation of the air
(or whatever it be)
moving ever so slightly against the body
(so previously conjugated)
o miraculous logic!
one presumption pissing out of a supposition
it just as easily being
her fixed
and the atmosphere-thing moving
(one time called a breeze)
or she and it both falling
but at different rates
the air slower cos greater bulk
(see how truth springs eternal!)
and the nausea?
be that to be felt as a sensation
separate from the sensation of the relative movement
of a body in its medium?
if there to be no apprehendable movement of air, the
sensation of nausea by itself still to give away the fall?
maybe that

(if that be indeed separable from other sensations)
being the effect of disorientation
the utterly being unable to discern
a way
maybe then no falling
but a wandering
sickening in its aimlessness.
and that to be any more of a comfort
than the fall with its promised end?
(though no verifiable evidence of either)
and comfort to be more or less
the bottom of it all?
the end before the end
the end of an end
the sensation of an ending
mercifully underway
although felt as a suffering
before she even to have known she did not could not know it
small hope to be had there

smelling now the burn of the sun on her arm
in deepest midwinter
the coiling up of every time
stored in this flesh
the capture and grab of every doing
accumulated and rolled over in this flesh
haphazardly carelessly uncomprehendingly
waiting for the doubled doing
of recognition and return
when this flesh yielding
bringing forth a deep past
appearing here now
what being still once there
but not surely in the actual fact of it
(whatever that be
maybe the atoms and the molecules or other imaginary objects)
actually here now smelling the summer sun
but some sensationing
inbetweening whatever actual to be
and whatevering possible to be
(let's call it realing

since she is really feeling it now)
and no capacity like the flesh
the great sump and froth of naturing
to store up and bring off endlessly
and recklessly
not to bother
the heaviest weight of pasts
and the hairiest rush of presents
such a great device to do that
she thinking and smelling her skin
all that has been is shall be
disclosing through this here now
if only she submitting
herself to herself
find a way through to her self
that she feeling so here
her here
and nowhere else's
and what diverting her she should step aside and avoid
and turn back to her here
and how to find the way back
to the middle of everything doing
be amidst the lost
and still there her here

[…]

understanding now
that there was no one
to whom she to unburden
that for each
she to have to refrain a little
keep a portion back
of her misery
of her assessment of her prospects
of the ruins previously known as her hopes
each dear confessor having a certain territory
or character or mood
that they not to brook
a no-go zone
of uncomprehending bigotry or ignorance
or just plain reasonableness

not entertaining
the complete expression of her despair
so she to have to withhold herself
a little
draw back from the brink
and water down the history or the prognosis
omit some particular aspect
apparently minor
supposedly transitory
nevertheless singular
the detail that conjured up the devil of this her despair
its personalized entry-code to the quick
of her soul and the sump of her heart
and each to get something of the whole
like a shattered hologram
a unique perspective on the calamity
enough to engage each taste
but never enough to frighten them away
and she to have believed up until now
that parcelling out her woe in this way
to suffice
until the end
either of woe or of her or of both
but now
she to understand the full horror of the absence of love
for only a lover
would have had the care or courage or grace
to have heard the whole story
only the lover
would have attended to every last word
as if their life had depended on it
only this lover
would have had the volley of follow-up questions
would have indulged the endless effort of imagination
put to work on every cul-de-sac of supposition
only her lover
would have shed real tears
or their credible approximation
in an entire and impossible empathy
would have wanted to help
regardless of consequence
(at any rate, at the point of the offer of help)
would have ravelled up

their ambitions and their hopes
their resolve and the energy and occasion of their singularity
with the fears and regrets
the faded visions and compromised victories
that made her up
that were all hers
and where would that lover be?
and without the dear lover to whom to confess
she being but now a broken person
in pieces, incomplete and barely so begrudgingly, insufficiently heard

[…]

song and there
    his soul would come to rest
    and spend itself
    and spend itself and end.
    and him
    all astonishment
    all surprise
    all love
    in the world of her lovely eyes.
    all in that face
    that he must not, would not
    be able to compare
    should that face of innocence
    bring in a world of want.
    since he will not compare
    all delight
    since he will not look elsewhere
    all hope
    since he will not shut his eyes
    all life.
    and him
    all astonishment
    all surprise
    all love
    in the world of her lovely eyes.
    in the world of her lovely eyes.
    in the world of her lovely eyes.

Bodies in Flight

34
Model Love (2008–11)

Figure 34.1: *Model Love*: performer Tom Wainwright. Photo: Edward Dimsdale.

Figure 34.2: *Model Love*: postcard. Courtesy of the University of Bristol Theatre Collection.

PUBLICITY COPY
A lovers' manual
Somewhere between soundbites, sonnets and songs, Bodies in Flight's fifteenth performance work – a dark and surreal exploration of modern dating – begins with a mysterious book of photographs – a lovers' manual – claiming to record that exact moment when two strangers' eyes meet and it's love at first sight.
Known for their innovative collaborations with sonic and visual artists, Bodies in Flight are for the first time working with a photographer – Edward Dimsdale whose bespoke photo-books are at the passionate heart of this new work.
Part investigators, part impersonators, three performers bring to life his unique series of images with Bodies in Flight's characteristic mix of live music, poetry and high-octane performing. Raiding dating sites and surfing handy hints on how to speed-date, MODEL LOVE *guides you through the maze of rough-and-ready, disposable self-portraiture towards the holy grail of all lonely hearts – romance.*

We began with three location shoots – a hotel room, a library and a lake. These became three books of photographs, from which we developed the work exploring how our ready-to-hand technologies of image-making produce multiple self-portraits with multiple potential performances of self. At the end of the show, we invited audiences up onto the stage to examine the books at close hand: their animated interaction with the images inspired us to continue developing the work into an installation and a one-man show that focused on the many ways in which the images are manipulated, printed and consumed. In addition to the two performance versions and installations, Simon took Sara's choreography to make a video with Tony Judge, entitled *Hymn*.

EDWARD DIMSDALE photography, CATHERINE DYSON performer, SARA GIDDENS choreography/co-direction, SAM HALMARACK lyrics and music, SIMON JONES lyrics and text/co-direction, GRAEME ROSE performer, TOM WAINWRIGHT performer.

With: TIM BISHOP production assistant, JON CARNALL print artwork, PAUL GEARY video documentation, TONY JUDGE video-edit and website, KATE YEDIGAROFF producer.

Performed: Arnolfini (Bristol), Alsager Arts, Technologies of Transmediality (Bristol), Wickham Theatre (Bristol), Ustinov/Bath Theatre Royal.

Installation version: Burst/BAC (London), Quake (Dèda, Derby).

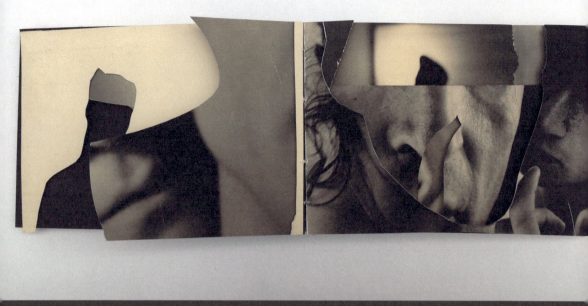

FIGURE 34.3: *Model Love*: Book Two. Image courtesy of Edward Dimsdale.

FIGURE 34.4: *Model Love*: performers Sam Halmarack, Graeme Rose, Catherine Dyson and Tom Wainwright. Photo: Edward Dimsdale.

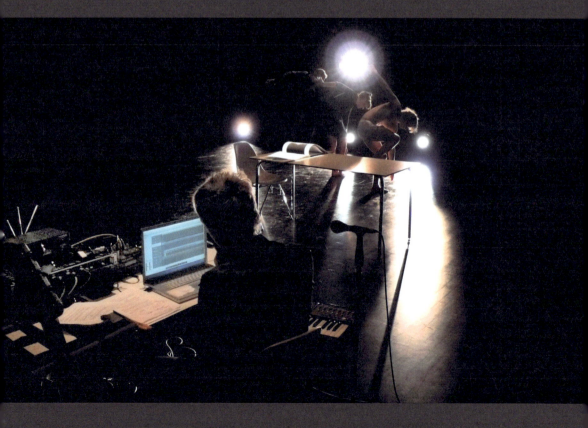

FIGURE 34.5: *Model Love*: performers Sam Halmarack and Graeme Rose. Photo: Edward Dimsdale.

FIGURE 34.6: *Model Love*: performers Tom Wainwright, Catherine Dyson and Graeme Rose. Photo: Edward Dimsdale.

Text extracts

SIMON JONES

This collaboration began with Edward Dimsdale's three books of photographs, each derived from a location shoot involving three performers, alluding to some kind of three-way relationship, very much in the manner of Antonioni's film Blow Up. *Once I had prototypes of the books, I started writing. Since each book was in a very different format, I became fascinated by the materiality of the collections of images, how the books were to be handled in the performance. I imagined three very different relationships to these objects, and thence to the very idea of an image. The first extract relates to the Second Book, a small volume detailing an encounter in a hotel room (see Figure 34.3). It records how performer Graeme Rose substantially fragmented and reordered the text as he developed his forensic, but finally hopeless searching for 'evidence' of love in the images. The second extract is part of a score for the durational installation version presented at Burst (BAC London).*

```
O, where is she? Come out, come out, wherever you. Daddy
wants to. There it is. There. I have it. I can feel it.
No? Yes! No.
```

re-enters with the 2nd book

```
O, that false and fatal promise that truth lies in wait
somewhere deep within this to soothe the restless soul
of the good man.
Nothing. Nothing but the surface. The grains on the
surface. The granulated surface.
What is this surface? A thing I can touch? I can feel
the paper, the ink.
```

opens book

```
I can see the picture. But … where is the image?
Endlessly undone in its constant reappearing.
In and out of focus. In and out of the shadows.
At the edge of the wood. The cruel light and the welcom-
ing dark.
Fixed and flowing, the part and the whole.
```

There can be no world without an image of that world, and no image without a world. So, no picture of paradise possible, only endless imaginings, images of imaginings, that cannot be returned to life since they have never lived, they were born still.
Adrift at sea, inconsolably lost, hopelessly incompetent, shamelessly ignorant, gloriously ugly, and forever weak, endlessly world-without-endlessly weak. And on again to the blur …

[…]

Yes. If I am here and it is now and I am looking around about the thing of me mine own and my hands are moving these other things about and these fingers that are also to me now mine and here to feel all the world that is hereabouts now amenable to what is me … (anyway) what I am taking for the here now and me in all probability … then … then I feel, despite the overwhelming lack of proof that …
And now coming across this the not-me me who appears to have been at someplace once, another other somehow part of me …
I do not recognize, or rather, I recognize but cannot return the how he came about into the world, apparently with these features, all (of course) highly debatable, the not-me me staring belligerently back at me, or plaintively, or accommodatingly, or so very occasionally so very self-assured in his not-me-ness (it fucks me over).
And every time I look back, my certainty as to his falsity, loosens a little, frays at its less-than-sharply-focused edges.
I can't look. It's not that I don't want to look.
I just can't. It makes me sea-sick, so much to-ing and fro-ing, going and coming, in and out of focus.
As he remains the picture of self-assurance, (as it were) the call to life, to get on and forth and do and be.
And me … feeling the gap widening, the comparison testing the elastic limit of credulity …

Look for Questionable Characteristics in Your Communication: As you chat via email and on the phone, you may be able to start to pick out characteristics of the other person. Are they controlling? Do they seem to anger easily? Do they avoid some of your questions? These can be questionable characteristics that tell you it's time to move on.

… especially when third parties have the opportunity to place the thing up against the flesh and speculate on how any human thing could have come so far from that to this and still be living and being and daring to show its face outdoors.
I blame the technology.

[…]

And now I suddenly feel as if the whole of my life, the whole (anyway) up until the here-now, were a terrible imposition … on others' kindnesses, their good will, the extra place at dinner and the meat cut that little bit thinner, worming into their allotted span on this surface … like the whole thing, the wholeness of it, were this impropriety on life … my life … me an impostor … from the very off to the very now-here.
And I shall be found out. In fact, that is the precisely the fear I am living in … of being exposed as the impostor.
Any day now. Maybe even tonight.

By following these tips, you'll help protect yourself from being an easy prey to someone who may have ulterior motives. With an average of one hundred plus marriages a day from online dating, you can see that the experience can be both safe and rewarding. Keep it safe!

[…]

I can smell her. She touches me. I swear I can feel her … the effect of her … the things that were effective about her … that appeared to be around about her … the things that are affecting me here now and that I am making the properties of her there then. Those things

I am remembering against my better judgement that hurt me there then into adoring her, into coming back upon her for more of the same, endlessly to need to have again her, the again at her, and never having enough and knowing any other single thing worth having as much in all of this world … and lost …

picks up book off floor + takes gloves off

… and just the surface left … just the pattern interpreted of the spread of oxidation of the molecules of the chemicals hit by the photons that glanced off the skin lovely certain intangibility of skin and still I cannot go anywhere else about the surface.

Lesson 2: Ease on Down the Road: When you're first getting acquainted with someone it's best to get to know them gradually by communicating via email and IM. Be on the lookout for any inconsistencies in your correspondence with someone, or in their online profile.

So, this proximity an apology for the never-to-materialize, never-to-show-itself. This intoxicating propinquity and consanguinity. The tracings of the tracks of every person's gaze, the caressings of those gazes, their careless attentions and the little lookings back and lookings over – what a miraculous machine. I can taste it, rub it between my fingers' ends … and still not have it, hold it and caress its hole and not have it, lie close to it at night, guard it with my life, stake everything else on it, the futures of my children, and never to have it, never to have the being at one with it. Only alongside it, the being at otherness, forever spooning in each other's lonelinesses a perfect picture of togetherness, the loving couple, my image and me.

INSTALLATION VERSION/BURST FESTIVAL, BATTERSEA ARTS CENTRE

General rules

1. DURATION 4 HOURS
2. TAKE A BREAK WHEN YOU NEED TO BY SIMPLY EXITING
3. PURSUE YOUR OWN CYCLE OPTIONS IN ANY ORDER

4. BE MINDFUL OF OTHERS & THEIR LEVEL OF ACTIVITY
5. DON'T ADD TOO MUCH ACTIVITY TO THE ROOM
6. THE ONLY SYNCHRONIZED COLLECTIVE ACTIONS ARE THE DANCES & SONGS: DISCO – DANCE SIDE-BY-SIDE; TANGO – CIRCLE & DANCE; SAD SONG – LOOKS & FOCUS; LIGHT IS CRUEL – SINGALONG CHORUS

Catherine's action-cycle-options

ENTER→APPROACH BOOK→DO NOT TOUCH IT→EXIT
ENTER→APPROACH BOOK→SIT & LOOK AT IT→SAY SOME TEXT [INTIMATELY TO ANYONE WHO MAY BE NEAR]→EXIT
ENTER→APPROACH BOOK→SIT & OPEN IT & LOOK AT IMAGES→EXIT
ENTER→APPROACH BOOK→SIT & LOOK AT IT
→GO TO HANGING PRINTS→TAKE ONE DOWN
→SIT AT TABLE & SEW IT INTO BOOK→EXIT [+WHILST OFF, ADVANCE DVD]

Graeme's action-cycle-options

LOOK AT BOOK→GO TO SCREEN-WALL→LOOK AT EVIDENCE→EXIT→RETURN & TAKE BOOK IN CIRCUIT AROUND ROOM→RETURN TO VISUALIZER
LOOK AT BOOK→GO TO SCREEN-WALL→LOOK AT EVIDENCE→PRINT A POSTING, TAKE IT TO TRAY OF POSTINGS→RETURN TO VISUALIZER
LOOK AT BOOK→RIP A PAGE FROM BOOK→GO TO SCREEN-WALL→ADD IMAGE TO WALL→MAKE CHALK LINKS BETWEEN EVIDENCE→RETURN TO VISUALIZER
[SAY TEXT AT ANY TIME, QUIETLY, LOUDLY, NEVER DIRECTLY TO ANYONE]

Sam's action-cycle-options

COMPOSE A NEW POSTING
→PRINT A POSTING, TAKE IT TO TRAY OF POSTINGS
→TAKE A PHONE-PHOTO OF OTHER TWO
OR
→COMPOSE A NEW POSTING→SING ONE OF TWO SONGS→TURN A PAGE OF BOOK 3
OR
→COMPOSE A NEW POSTING→PLAY DISCO OR TANGO TRACK→TURN A PAGE OF BOOK 3

35

Rendering Visible

PAUL GEARY

PAUL GEARY *is a lecturer in Drama at the University of East Anglia. His research focuses on the senses, politics and performance philosophy. He is the author of* Experimental Dining: Performance, Experience and Ideology in Contemporary Creative Restaurants *(2022). Paul worked with Bodies in Flight to document a number of shows and was a researcher and production assistant for the Cardiff edition of* Dream→Walk.

Here he writes about Model Love *and technology, particularly its exploration of the photograph.*

I am re-watching the documentation, aware that I lingered behind the camera, like the figure behind the curtain in Do The Wild Thing!, *orchestrating the image according to my own desires of what to see. The footage externalizes my memory, allowing me to access the show again, fixed in place. Yet each time I watch it, it appears new to me, yields something new. As if responding to me, the figure on stage (on screen) speaks out:*

> Down to the second of what you did is documented, and still nothing known.

1. 'RENDER IT VISIBLE'

> Something hiding in plain view, mocking me, evading all my efforts to render it visible.

This line, spoken by the figure on stage in *Model Love*, as he inspected and reflected upon a series of photographs, encapsulates a key concern of both the show and Bodies in Flight's interrogative artworks. To render is to bring into being, to portray artistically or to perform, to translate, to covertly send abroad for interrogation, or to melt down and clarify. The rendering, in each of its characterizations, forms the knowledge-work of *Model Love*. The show took as its focus the visual – the privileged form of knowledge in the West, with its implication of distanced critical observation – and subjected it to the investigation of an artistic rendering. The relations between the photograph and knowledge, memory and love were teased out, no longer continuous and taken for granted, but brought forth in the show as complicated, unstable, in flux, and the subject of interrogation, as the figure on stage mused on his own relation to a series of photographs. The photographs, themselves a rendering of a moment of past love, did not provide an easy index of the past. Instead, they were the source of concern and anguish, an index not of what happened, but of the fallibility of memory and being unable to say, with surety, what happened where, when and with whom. The image of a former lover became fraught with the same relational issues (of misunderstanding, complexity and anxiety) as the live encounter. And the figure on stage struggled, as much as the photograph, to render thoughts, feelings, and what is known, visible and tangible.

2. PHOTOGRAPHY

Model Love's investigation of the photograph dealt with its connections to memory, knowing and love. In principle, the photograph concerns itself with knowing, seeking to render a stable document of the known, abstracted from experience, replacing or augmenting memory as record, documentation and evidence. Something known is rendered visible; or rather, the image fixes in place a promise of the stable and known. Yet, as *Model Love*'s reflections demonstrated, it can only ever be partial, elusive and evasive. Watching the show, we are never able to step into the image, to know it from the inside, to know what was outside of the frame. All we can do, all the figure on stage can do, is reminisce and wonder about what might lurk underneath the surface of the image. The photograph remains a ghostly haunting of something lost, and a tantalizing play of possibles: possible pasts, possible interpretations, possible thoughts and feelings behind the façade.

Model Love opened with extracts of dating profiles. Although the show pre-dated the advent of Tinder (2012), it anticipated the superficial and imagistic logic that underpins Tinder and similar apps. They reduce the user to a photograph and short description or attempt at generic flirtation, further distilling the logic of website-based dating profiles to a condensed sketch. *Model Love*'s presentation of excerpts from dating profiles, one after another, drew our attention to the common tropes of how we curate an image of ourselves for an unknown other in the hope of ... love? connection? a relationship? Whatever the motivation, it is the construction of the image that is important here. The snapshots are funny – a parody – yet believable. And, for me, something unsettling emerges. While watching I chuckled at these profiles, yet IRL (the simplistic rendering of 'in real life' that makes light work of something complex and fraught) am I not presented with the same problem? Others, even lovers, are only available to me as curated images, a body and text, which I am required to interpret. Yet there remains a difference between the live encounter and the photographic (re)presentation. Both may be subject to forensic investigation and interpretation, as happened throughout *Model Love*, but the live allows for exchange, empathy and rapport, while the photograph remains unresponsive. *Model Love*'s absence of an interlocutor who can speak back (unlike the second figure on stage who merely repeated and mirrored in a musical form – another model of the photograph) is palpable, exposing the distinction between the live body and the abstracted photographic representation.

As the figure on stage took selfies, we saw a direct relation between the image and referent or subject, and the severing of that relation motivated the subsequent reflections. The image became the '[n]ot-me me': related, a likeness, but not the same. It became '[n]othing but the surface, the grains on the surface, the granulated surface'. Abstracted and pixelated, rather than the continuous flow of bodies in time, '[e]ndlessly undone in its constant reappearing, in and out of focus', the photographs were severed from their referential events. The figure was frustrated by his inability to capture himself, to take the 'perfect' shot, to adequately render himself as a representational image. The instantaneous technology of the mobile photographic device, the ability to review the photo immediately and to be confronted with the disjunction between external image and internal sensation, between representation and first-hand experience, served to exacerbate the frustration and failure. The photographic technology failed at rendering decisive truth, producing only a kind of likeness.

Like the mouth in Not I, *the eye appears strange, abstracted. As I watch a visualizer turned towards the eye of the performer, and that eye appears on screen (see Figure 34.5), I wonder: do I come into being through the mouth or the eye, through seeing or speaking? I linger in and behind both. Both mediate my encounter with a lover and mark the boundary between us. I try to see through a lover's eyes, to reach out through words. A part of me comes into being in this relation.*

She touches me. I swear I can feel her. The effect of her.

3. BECKETT AND HEIDEGGER

In his reflections on Samuel Beckett, Simon writes that –

> Beckett remorselessly and relentlessly pulled focus from the object of study to the plane of the lens itself: a Modernist struggling with the obfuscation of the medium – whatever medium – and the resultant confusion of communication, striving to produce with each newly inevitable failure a less corrupted description of being in the world.
> (Jones 2007: 94)

In *Model Love*, Bodies in Flight continued this struggle, where the photograph was both the object of study and part of the medium of the work itself. *Model Love* sought to investigate our technological being in the world, citing both the artist-philosopher, Samuel Beckett, and the philosopher-artist, Martin Heidegger. Like the man thrown on stage in Beckett's *Act Without Words I*, for Heidegger our foundational experience is finding ourselves thrown into a world. In *Model Love*, with each turn of a page that reveals a new photograph, the figure is thrown into the world of *this* image, trying to make sense of what he finds there. Like the compulsive, yet insufficient attempts to (re)produce himself as an image, he seeks truth, revelation or substance in images that set up their own world. Yet the images have withdrawn from this world into their own insular, self-contained world. They proliferate possibilities of potential meanings, a 'great flow of actual possibles', betraying their apparent promise to picture plainly.

The visualizer's close-up image of the performer's eye in *Model Love* seemed to reference directly the abstracted mouth in Beckett's *Not I*. Simon reflects that Beckett uses the mouth as the 'most erotic of body openings – the lips, the tongue, the teeth, the dark cavity within' (Jones 2007: 99). The eye in *Model Love* countered this, by replacing the mouth's eroticism with the eye's voyeurism, which can look, but not give back in the way the mouth can. The eye is the mirror of the photograph: the latter can only project out; the former only receive.

Both mouth and eye are synecdoches of our relations with others. *Model Love* investigated the eye and the photograph as a somehow deficient mode of being with others, like Heidegger's deficient mode where others are treated like equipment: through the equipment of the camera, the other is disclosed to us as some*thing* that we pass by and pass over, fixed in place and known (see Heidegger 1962: 157–58, 160). *Model Love* intervened, drawing out this deficiency of the photograph. It followed Heidegger's directive that, when being with others is experienced in this way, '[b]eing-with-one-another must follow special routes of its own in order to come close to Others, or even to "see through them"' (Heidegger 1962: 161). Bodies in Flight's 'special route' is to offer a fraught and anxious imagining of the other, the lover, as Simon's text wanders over the surface of Edward Dimsdale's photographs, attempting to see through them, to see from another's perspective.

In June 2011, *Model Love* was presented in a double bill with Beckett's *Krapp's Last Tape*. In both, memory is mediated by an external technology: for Beckett, through the audio-tape recording; for Bodies in Flight, through the photograph. Both works engage with a double revealing of memory technologies, exploring both what is revealed *by* the technologies, and revealing the workings of the technologies themselves. For Heidegger, technology offers a way of revealing, of bringing forth into unconcealment (2011: 222): modern technologies reveal the paradigmatic demand that nature supply energy to be extracted and stored, yielding useful resources (223). The quotidian ideological framing of technology promises continual improvement, efficiency, help and utility. But these technologies of recording – the tape and the photograph – fail to extract and store in a useful way, rupturing the ideological myth. Their failures to conform to technology's modern demand – their inability to capture, store and subsequently revisit the past – reveal the very demands we make of them: technology's false promise to preserve. In *Krapp's Last Tape*, the eponymous figure reflects on the disjunction between then and now, 'that stupid bastard I took myself for thirty years ago' (Beckett 2006: 222); in *Model Love*, the man reflects on the photograph that '[y]ou are almost like her, and I, almost like him'. In both cases, there is some continuity of identity, from past to present, but something irrevocably changed. The document uncannily reveals the separation of then and now, of who I was and who I am, of what was captured and what was lost. The failure to render the self truly visible in the image, and the fraught interrogation of the rendered image, reveals the contrivance of both the camera and the knowledge-claims that rest on its light work.

References

Beckett, Samuel (2006), *The Complete Dramatic Works*, London: Faber and Faber.

Heidegger, Martin (1962), *Being and Time* (trans. J. Macquarrie and E. Robinson), Malden and Oxford: Blackwell Publishing.

Heidegger, Martin (2011), 'The question concerning technology', in *Basic Writings: from* Being and Time *(1927) to* The Task of Thinking *(1964)* (ed. D. Farrell Krell, trans. D. Farrell Krell and W. Lovitt), London and New York: Routledge.

Jones, Simon (2007), 'Beckett and Warhol, under the eye of god', *Performance Research*, 12:1, pp. 94–102.

36
Finding Suspension
SARA GIDDENS

In this Flight, I dwell upon moments of suspended stillness, and the employment of still-ing as a choreographic strategy. Through a detailed analysis of two actions, one in Model Love, *the other in* Gymnast, *I describe how stillness is always a process of still-ing, which should not be thought of as punctuating or separate from movement, but as an integral form of movement towards an impossible or theoretical point of stillness. As such, still-ing provides me with new ways of focusing attention in my choreographic practice. Furthermore, I locate this still-ing in the context of dance studies' use of phenomenological framings of stillness. I discuss how phenomenology helps me to relate still-ing to broader questions of space and temporality in performance.*

In 2008, I was working with performer Tom Wainwright on *Model Love*. I was focusing on developing choreography from the minutiae (see Chapter 18, 'The Magnificent Minutiae'), from a series of stunning location-based photographs that Edward Dimsdale had taken to inform our first workshops; a penchant for detail I had carried forward through all my professional works since *Do the Wild Thing!* However, working with Tom, who had recently trained at Circomedia (a circus school based in Bristol), opened up another movement vocabulary, and this led me to dwell upon a very specific moment of suspended stillness, the handstand.

A handstand is an extraordinary feat for most adults. Tom and I found, or more accurately settled upon, this particular handstand through long improvisations (see Figure 34.1). Its place as part of my choreography was a great surprise to me. It was so extraordinary amongst my practice of choreographing with and from the everyday, and the routine gestural. Yet it was to this instant of suspension, this point in-between, and to the most barely visible of movements that I was drawn. Although I would not have named it as such then, and it feels important to note here (again) that the practice has so often been the starting point from which my investigations and research flights have begun, I was drawn to the phenomenologist Edmund Husserl's notion ([1931] 1981), where–when I could visibly see a performer's insistence upon, and commitment to, both 'keeping still' and 'keeping-in-operation' (Husserl 1981: 250). Husserl uses the act(ion) of walking ([1931] 1981: 248) to elucidate this. What is at play here is a dynamic between a moving body and an actively stationary body. I was transfixed by all the uniquely different tiny adjustments Tom needed to make, in order to hold that 'sculpted' pose still, to not fall, to not fail. A literal manifestation of a high point. I was captivated by all the activity around and about the apparent suspended stillness, where–when the musculature remains active and attentive. I was fascinated by all the activity concerned with actively not moving, and with each 're-alteration' required to approach or even touch upon a 'sense of rest' (Husserl [1931] 1981: 245).

This handstand became a very significant punctuation point in my choreography for *Model Love*. It was a pause in-between the more visible movement, yet still very much part of the dance. A still-ing in what became an otherwise fluid choreographic sequence of five minutes. The handstand functioned as an interruption in the flow. Such a moment of suspension, with all the muscular effort required, reveals how such instants are made up of deliciously imperfect repetitions as Tom attempted, but could never fully succeed, to hold on to the exact same moment. Each instant draws my attention to all the idiosyncratic tiny differences. A collection of quasi still points, still-ings, active and aware, certainly not fixed, and far from frozen. In the *Four Quartets*, Eliot's relentless and quite brilliant reflection upon 'the still point of the turning world' (1974: 191), he describes such a moment as 'neither arrest nor movement' (1974: 191); not quite either, though the promise and reminder of both. A still point where there would 'be no dance and there is only dance' (1974: 191), where–when the world keeps turning both around and because of this still point, consistently inviting and allowing change.

The scholar Susan Jones, in her elegantly crafted writing, describes this still point as 'neither still nor in motion, yet both' (2013: 223). She argues for the influence of dance upon Eliot's poetry and cites 'biographical evidence' (2013: 227) of his attendance at numerous performances of Serge Diaghilev's *Ballet Russes* between 1909 and 1929. Indeed, Jones challenges the performance scholar Andre Lepecki's propensity to wed the more knowing use of stillness with modernism and to separate stillness from movement. Crucially, although Lepecki talks of still moments in ballet, he suggests they are mere 'pauses' (2006: 340), not part of the dance, whereas for Jones and me these 'instants' are 'both of the dance' and 'are the dance' (2013: 227). Jones continues with her argument by identifying moments of 'balance' (2013: 227), or I might add following my studio practice with Tom, stillness held in suspension. She recalls how such moments were knowingly present in ballets such as *The Sleeping Beauty* (1890). She uses Marius Petipa's choreography for Aurora's first entrance as a specific example. Jones talks of these moments in (the) ballet as 'full of potential', where the 'musculature remains alert' and 'where the possibility of movement fills the stillness' (2013: 227). Although I resist her somewhat dualistic split of 'the mind of the dancer reaching within, towards and beyond an apparently temporal confinement of the body' (2013: 227), I welcome the acknowledgement of this knowing 'presencing' (Heidegger [1956] 1978: 151) and 'unconcealment' ([1956] 1978: 161) of instants that are 'full of potential' (Jones 2013: 227). Eliot, Lepecki and Jones reflect the complexity and delicacy of the inseparable relation between stillness and movement, of 'keeping still and keeping in operation' (Husserl 1981: 245), so very palpable in Tom's suspended handstand.

The philosopher Edward Casey's essay 'Taking Bachelard from the instant to the edge' (2008) is useful here. Casey's essay, weaving between time and space through a comparison of the properties of instants in time and edges in space, begins by leading us to Gaston Bachelard's challenge of Henri Bergson's treatise (Bergson 2001, first published in 1889), that instants are distortions, distractions. Casey calls them 'infinitesimal pause(s)' (2008: 2), signifying very little. On the contrary, he asserts that Bachelard believes that an instant is 'where time's action is to be found and [...] where change of any significant sort is located' (2008: 2). Bachelard affirms this through his writing in *The Intuition of the Instant* (1932). Casey writes that suspension has edges, as 'an event has closure, but the closure is not itself closed' (2008: 12). Each closure is different for each person at any event and, I would suggest, creates an opening, or at least the possibility of an opening, into another event. Casey continues by reflecting that there is no single edge of time, no end to time, but there are edges within time. This notion of continually shifting boundaries, rather than any fixed, static, single border, is significant. When viewed through this frame, it is no wonder that my analysis of instants of suspended stillness, such as Tom's handstand, revealed such idiosyncratic edges. Each still-ing was already always differently nuanced, suspended as we were in each unique encounter of each live moment. Each still-ing could not help but reference its alteration and movement, either within itself or in all the activity around it. Moments or instants of stillness, connected to the domain of suspension, seem to take us, as they did me, by surprise, as they literally and metaphorically interrupt the flow.

Our later project, *Gymnast* began from this developing fascination with stillness and stilling. We worked with élite and amateur gymnasts and an eighteen-member choir. I will focus upon one moment, where – when the drive for stillness, however impossible, foregrounded each minute movement. The poster of *Gymnast* shows Jake Houtby (an élite gymnast from Notts Gymnastics Academy) balanced precariously in a planchet, between two wooden rings, hung from straps from the ceiling five-and-a-half metres above the floor (see Figure 40.2). The planchet, a variation of the plank position I practise so frequently in yoga, is more commonly known as the crucifix position. Crucifix, from the Latin *crucifixus*: the crucified Christ, caught, suspended between heaven and earth. And the gymnast, suspended here, almost beyond the mortal, towards the Olympian. I am still struck by this image, though to be technical, the crucifix position is held (more commonly) vertically; indeed, the more vertical the better, with the rings as still as possible. Indeed, the aim of the rings exercise is to keep the actual rings as still as possible during any routine. The body can move, often in extraordinary ways, but the rings should remain still, hence their name 'The Still Rings'.

The rings demand the highest level of strength of the six pieces of apparatus in men's gymnastics. What this image triggers for this choreographer, involved in this practice, is a Husserlian moving in-between 'keeping still' and 'keeping-in-operation' (1981: 250). What is judged in gymnastic competitions, although probably not expressed as such, is in fact an extreme example of the Husserlian alternation between a body moving and the apparatus being kept as still as possible. Inevitably as gymnasts work on the rings, this alteration is present not only in the relationship between their body and the equipment but also between two states of the body, between swinging and attempting to hold stillness in suspension. Thus, this alteration re-emerges between the large-scale fluid movements and the pose that is used to punctuate them. Such a moment of still-ing, that is, moving towards or away from an impossible stillness, such as the planchet or Maltese cross (where the arms are much further apart), reveals an inherent contradiction. Such a still-ing requires a huge amount of muscular strain, which can be seen through all the tiny adjustments in the body. It takes enormous effort to hold a planchet or cross, and it places a huge demand on the upper body to hold the horizontal or vertical body as close to the edge of stillness as possible. Once more, still-ing draws attention to movement. During performances of these routines, gymnasts are usually working to conceal the movement necessary to maintain, what I now know to be, an impossible still point, an active quiet.

These two instants of suspended stillness in my practice, performed by Tom in a handstand and Jake on the rings, were twinned with muscular and psychological effort, both in their execution and in the training or rehearsal. I am reminded of the effort needed to create space–times to dwell, and the learned understanding that stillness and ease should not be coupled together lightly. Moreover, these vertical instances of suspension from *Model Love* and *Gymnast* seemed steadfast in their insistence to hold on to a moment in time and simultaneously attempted to defy the inevitable pull of gravity. Such instants seem to challenge certain givens: that time is horizontal; that dance is or should be made up of clearly visible movement. They both worked in contrast to the flow and fluidity of the choreographic sequences they were part of, and in doing so, I would argue, they punctuated space as well as time. Indeed, such suspended instants of stillness seem to balance on the edge of both time and space, though Casey argues (2008: 13) that we cannot simply replace instants for edges, as there are no instants in space, whereas edges can be both temporal and spatial. Edges in time just keep on going, as each edge reveals more edges, such as day turning into night, next week into next year. Moreover, separating out instants of suspension, like separating out time from space, could only ever be a temporary measure.

I came to recognize that any moment of suspended stillness was a balance, a complex point in-between what had been and was to come. As in absence and presence, stillness and movement are hard to force apart for long, and if they can be separated, they are separated by mobile boundaries, rather than fixed borders. I was certainly drawn to these instants of suspension in relation to both their temporal and spatial properties. It was here in these vertical instants, suspended, on an always already different edge, that stillness was both so palpably present and always already absent. It was, and is, through such balance points, moments brimming full of memories and expectation, that the complexity of each and every presencing could be revealed, and as such, such moments of suspension unconcealed so much. Indeed, for me to remain open to what might spring up or emerge in the first place, I had found it necessary to suspend my own critical judgment as best as I could. In hindsight, I had approached still-ing in suspension from my own place of suspension.

My practice has led me to this ever-deepening investigation, and not only contributed to my understanding of my perception of movement, but it has also helped me to develop and name what I now call a *palette of stillnesses*: namely stillnesses held or caught in suspension; stillnesses characterized by a softening or a letting go; and stillnesses coupled with difficulty or tension. Significantly for me, this palette, still characterized by its delicate, slippery and ephemeral nature, formed the choreographic and compositional drivers and basis for a further three bespoke, site-based durational promenade pieces: *Still Moving: Moving Still*, made for Arnolfini (Bristol) in 2012, Nottingham Contemporary (2013) and Birmingham Conservatoire of Music (2018). Each gave me space–times to extend my study and employ this palette of stillnesses, specifically into how still-ing can draw attention to the extraordinary in ordinary places, to how people use their everyday space, and even to movement itself.

References

Bachelard, Gaston ([1932] 1979), *L'Intuition de l'instant* (trans. M. Jolas), Paris: Gonthier.

Bergson, Henri ([1889] 2001), *Time and Free Will* (trans by F. L. Pogson), New York: Dover Publications.

Casey, Edward S. (2008), 'Taking Bachelard from the instant to the edge', *Philosophy Today*, 52, pp. 31–37.

Eliot, T. S. ([1944] 1974), *The Four Quartets*, London: Faber.

Heidegger, Martin ([1956] 1978), 'The origin of the work of art', in D. Farrell Krell (ed.), *Basic Writings*, London: Routledge.

Husserl, Edmund ([1931] 1981), 'The world of the living present', in F. Elliston and P. McCormick (eds), *Husserl: Shorter Works*, Notre Dame, IN: Notre Dame University Press, pp. 238–50.

Jones, Susan (2013), *Literature, Modernism, and Dance*, Oxford: Oxford University Press.

Lepecki, Andre (2006), *Exhausting Dance: Performance and the Politics of Movement*, London and New York: Routledge.

37
Performance/ Photography/ Photography/ Performance [And On/And On]
EDWARD DIMSDALE

EDWARD DIMSDALE *is Professor of Art & Contemporary Visual Culture, and Head of the Graduate School, Cambridge School of Visual & Performing Arts. As a freelance photographer, he has exhibited his photography widely, and his work is held in public and private collections. Exhibitions include* Agulhas *at HackelBury Fine Art (London); and* Picturing Eden, *a five-year touring museum show curated by Deborah Klochko for the George Eastman House, Rochester, NY. A photographic publication,* Stilled, *was published by Stanley Barker in 2017. Ed has contributed to numerous publications, including* Hotshoe *magazine, Ian Macdonald's* Eton *(IM Press, 2007), Lam Pok Yin and Chong Ng's* The Untimely Apparatus of Two Amateur Photographers *(Jiazazhi Press, 2019) and Kim Thue's* Lode *(Serpent's Tail, 2022). He has taught at the Cambridge School of Art (Anglia Ruskin University), the London College of Communication (UAL), the University of Coventry, the Bartlett School of Architecture and the Slade School of Art.*

Here Ed discusses his long collaboration with Bodies in Flight, focusing on the development of his role from documentor to co-maker of work.

FIGURE 37.1 (next): *iwannabewolfman*: performers Charlotte Watkins, Katherine Porter, Simon Pegg, Jon Carnall and Barnaby Power. Photo: Edward Dimsdale.

It is in vain that we say what we see; what we see never resides in what we say.
(Foucault 1966: 9)

If you want to see the world, close your eyes, Rosamonde.
(From *Le Gai Savoir* [1968], directed by Jean-Luc Godard)

1ST PHOTOGRAPH: *IWANNABEWOLFMAN – A FARCE* (1991)

As the three figures in the foreground move towards the right-hand edge of the frame of the black-and-white photograph, they begin to disintegrate under a phenomenal gravitational force operating from beyond the event horizon of the image, which is apparently pulling the figures towards incipient annihilation. Meanwhile, towards the left-hand edge of the frame, and moving fast in the opposite direction, other figures (two? three? hard to determine) are similarly at the brink of being sucked out from the frame, apparently subject to the similar centrifugal forces being exerted elsewhere. And yet, an equal and opposite force appears to be keeping the figures in stasis. What balancing force is this? Whilst disaster cannot be entirely averted, it can perhaps be stayed for a while – perhaps indefinitely.

Of course, that's just storytelling. This photograph is really just a smudge of an image deriving from movements in a space (the Wickham Theatre, University of Bristol) at a moment in time (sometime in 1991), and actually brought about by the laws of light and optics, in which the slow shutter speed required due to the low-lighting conditions has served to smear movements which might otherwise have been more sharply delineated. More specifically, it is an analogue print from a 35 mm film negative stock produced by Kodak, rated at ISO 400, called Tri-X, which was, after being exposed in a Canon F1 camera with a 35 mm lens, processed in a developer called Rodinal at a 1+25 dilution, for approximately 9 minutes at 20°C. The resulting negative was washed, dried and stored in an acid-free negative storage bag, along with many other such negatives, and then very occasionally sought out to be printed or scanned, with the resulting image used for various purposes. In the case of this image, it has been used as performance documentation (silver gelatin print on resin-coated paper); digitized onto a CD-ROM (no longer accessible); as a silver gelatin print on fibre-based print; and as an image selected for this book. It also exists as a paper negative, which was used for making a paper positive print for an exhibition, many years ago.

For reasons I don't fully understand, it has always seemed to me to be an important photograph in terms of collaborating with Bodies in Flight. It was taken the first time that I worked with the company, so in that sense, it represents the start of what I could never have anticipated at the time would be such a long-term and foundational experience for me, both personally and professionally. The photograph reminds me, more than many others, that the definition of a photograph is actually very simple – it is light, modified by objects. It also reminds me that a photograph is always a performance. Or rather, it is invariably the result of innumerable processes and operations (in themselves, performances), which culminate in what we might understand as the *experience* of a photograph. In this respect, photography is a subset of the category 'performance'. And yet, the stillness of the photographic image sits in paradoxical relation to the liveness of the theatrical (even that incorporating mediated elements). As such, the photograph's potential for material *as* performance is all too often overlooked, in favour of its capacities to produce materials *of* performance (in terms of documentation) or provide public relations materials *for* performance (in terms of posters, leaflets, social media posts and so on).

2ND PHOTOGRAPH:
SKINWORKS – A VALENTINE (2003)

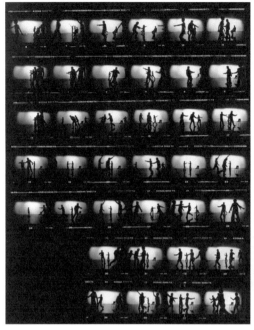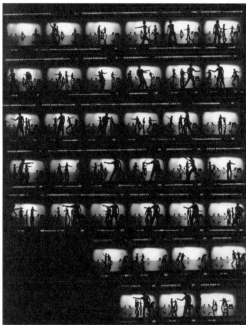

The following non-exhaustive, unordered litany is an attempt to suggest some equivalences between contexts of theatrical performance and photography:

Moving. Standing. Watching. Reacting. Resisting. Conspiring. Taking. Surveying. Yielding. Scrutinizing. Freezing. Making. Viewing. Executing. Considering. Implementing. Enacting. Operating. Presenting. Seizing. With care. With precision. With abandon. With precaution. With tension. With unease. With trouble. With thought. With heed. With appreciation. With pleasure. Of things. Of places. Of people. Through time. Through space. Through materials. By means direct and by means circuitous. Since ever. Since we choose for it to be so. From complexity. Towards simplicity. As well as places between. Anon.

Working with Bodies in Flight invariably followed a similar approach, an accustomed rhythm. Turning up at a tech run or dress rehearsal, taking the photographs 'live'; with few, if any, images being set up specifically. For me, entering this rehearsal space felt like receiving a

FIGURE 37.2: *Skinworks*: contact sheets. Image courtesy of Edward Dimsdale.

gift – bodies in space, in movement, in stasis, on screens, served up to be photographed. I would feel licensed to take photographs from anywhere, from any perspective, inserting myself into the performance space and becoming an actor. Movement, as a stimulus, is always compelling for the stilling insistence of a photographer.

3RD PHOTOGRAPH: *WHO BY FIRE – A MEMORY (2004)*

Colour is accidental, a hypothesis; colour is an experience of rejection; a deceptive lure; an apparatus that contrives to control and subordinate the manifested content of any photographic image. Or so I have told myself, generally preferring the more austere distribution of monochromatic tonality (an apparatus itself) to the easier pleasures of the colour

FIGURE 37.3: *Who By Fire*: performers Polly Frame, Doug Bott, Graeme Rose, Neil Johnson, Tim Atack and Benjamin Clough. Photo: Edward Dimsdale.

spectrum. For *Who By Fire*, however, it seemed appropriate to document the show in colour. The reason for this is that different camera formats possess different authorities – and the respective sizes and proportions of the negatives or positive images from respective camera formats insist upon different requirements. I was using a Pentax 6×7 camera, which means that the resulting negative is 6 cm wide and 7 cm long, both wider than that of a 35 mm camera. The larger the negative, the more that colour seems to be the choice of film – or so it has always seemed to me. Beyond the format, the colour cast of this image has very little in common with the colour temperatures experienced in the theatre space at the time of taking the photograph. Indeed, the image, as it appears in this publication, has little in common with the print I am looking at as I write this. Colour is exotic, esoteric and subversive. Colour must be experienced to be believed, and in each instance, it is the particularity of that specific experience that counts.

Who By Fire was an unusually intense convergence of the elements that characterize Bodies in Flight's work, in which the formation of the still image also became a central concern of the work. During the performance, the performers would slow to a halt, coalescing into tableaux, moments which were drawn in contrast to the extended periods of dynamic movement (sometimes languid, sometimes frenzied). The emergence of this *becoming-picture,* arising from Bodies in Flight's twin conceptual and choreographic drives, signalled an increasing confluence with my own interest in the still image.

4TH PHOTOGRAPH:
MODEL LOVE – A LOVERS' MANUAL (2008–11)

If I were to choose a single image to represent the totality of 30 years of collaboration with Bodies in Flight, it would be this photograph of a close-up of a face, with bookbinding string and table lamp, a piece of photographic documentation from the first durational performance installation of *Model Love – A Lovers' Manual* at the Battersea Arts Centre in London. This was the first time that the company had worked with a photographer as a collaborator, rather than simply a photographer, as documenter or a generator of publicity material. Working alongside and between the company, I produced three bespoke photo-books, which became the dispersed, multiple-located centres of the work. We began with three location shoots – a woodland lake, a hotel room and a library. In each, a set of power relations were imagined, drawing variously on forms of looking and differing perspectives, as well as from themes drawn from mythology, voyeurism and ecstatic experience.

FIGURE 37.4: *Model Love*: installation Battersea Arts Centre. Photo: Edward Dimsdale.

These shoots became the basis for three very different books of photographs, and three performers (who featured in each of the three books) then interacted with the books in various ways – for example, the images of one book were sewn together from loose images into sequential (consequential) being, while another was subjected to autopsy – anatomized, subjected to forensic scrutiny. In another performance, one of the books was lowered slowly – *Deus Ex Machina*-like – onto the stage. For the company, the focus on the photographic image was a useful laboratory for exploring how ready-to-hand technologies of image-making produce multiple self-portraits with multiple potential performances of self. For my own part, I was more interested in using the contexts of theatrical performance as an experimental space to examine the performance of the photograph – any photograph – and of the drives that compel the taking and making of photographic images.

5ᵀᴴ PHOTOGRAPH

One of the performance strategies employed in *Model Love* would involve a figure (Graeme Rose), hunched over a small, dense book, containing a sequence of images of what appeared to be a tawdry three-way tryst in a business-traveller hotel. This book, prosaically known as Book 2 (and more pretentiously thought of, by me, as *Thanatos*, evoking Freud's concept of the Death Drive) would be placed on a brightly lit visualizer (also known as a digital document viewer), a piece of equipment which can send video to a data projector. In this way, the projected images would be cast onto a screen on the other side of the performance space, and as the figure would slowly turn the pages, muttering dark observances to himself, the fractured narratives could be experienced in two places at once, on both horizontal and vertical axes, both large and small in scale, and both actual (on the visualizer) and mediated (projected onto the screen). The figure would ignore certain images, and certain sequences, passing over them, while lingering over others, even physically caressing them. Then, pulling on latex gloves and taking up a scalpel, the figure would begin to cut directly into the soft surface of the paper, carving out discrete visual elements; and the book would start to be taken apart, cut after cut, with the newly eviscerated elements re-positioned in the space of the projection. This live collaging, improvised throughout the duration of the performance, would be accompanied by typographical and textual interventions, striving to make sense of the re-formulated visual elements. The words were snatches of the dark mutterings made visible; the arrows were the attempts to reveal undisclosed affinities.

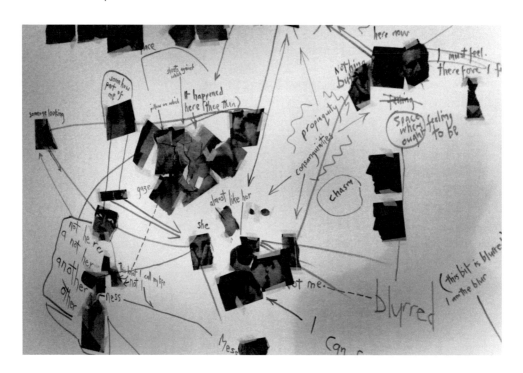

Whilst I have spent much of the last 25 years lecturing on photography, showing images (only very rarely my own) and discussing them (usually at some length), making use of (mostly) my own words, for this durational performance-lecture on photography, I was dumb, providing only the images, having to relinquish any control over how they might be deployed. The words were not my words, although I recognized my own ideas through them in ways I had never understood them previously. It is, to date, the most insightful, the truest, the best lecture on photography that I have n/ever delivered.

6TH PHOTOGRAPH

This is a final image from the first theatrical presentation of *Model Love*, in which the audience was invited on stage at the end of the show, to view the books that had been both the performance's objects and subjects. They could also select, to take home, a postage stamp-sized photogravure image, printed on newsprint, scattered across the floor.

FIGURE 37.5: *Model Love*: installation Battersea Arts Centre. Photo: Edward Dimsdale.

FIGURE 37.6: *Model Love*: audience examining the books after the performance, Arnolfini. Photo: Edward Dimsdale.

For the most part, the difference between seeing something and saying something about that experience appears to be simply a matter of convenience; of relatively frictionless translation, arriving at an equivalence that is generally perfectly adequate for the purpose of everyday survival. However, the distance between what we see and what we can say about it expands in exponential proportion as we reflect upon the matter: the visible establishes its own province, which is irreducible to the efforts of the legible, or the linguistic, to foreclose meaning. Working with Bodies in Flight has allowed me – a photographer – to go into spaces between the *see-able* and *say-able* that I might never have had access to otherwise, in order to be able to think about the photographic image, and explore it experimentally, in ways that themselves can be described as *otherwise* (see Jones and Dimsdale 2018). These collaborations have convinced me of the necessity of engaging in interdisciplinary, intermedial experimentation, in which the ultimate benefit of interaction, of exploring shared hinterlands and cultivating interstitial spaces, opens up the potential for intra-active, emergent transformations (Barad 2007), brought about within individual practices.

References

Barad, Karen (2007), *Meeting the Universe Halfway: Quantum Physics and the Entanglement of Matter and Meaning*, Durham: Duke University Press.

Foucault, Michel (1966), *The Order of Things – An Archaeology of the Human Sciences*, New York: Vintage.

Jones, Simon and Dimsdale, Edward (2018), 'Unsettling materialities: The indexical relationship of photography and theatre in Bodies in Flight's *Model Love*', *Journal of Photography and Culture*, 11:2, pp. 153–67.

Further Reading

Anderson, Joel (2015), *Theatre & Photography*, Basingstoke: Palgrave Macmillan.

Reason, Matthew (2006), *Documentation, Disappearance and the Representation of Live Performance*, Basingstoke: Palgrave Macmillan.

Bodies in Flight

38
Hymn (2009)

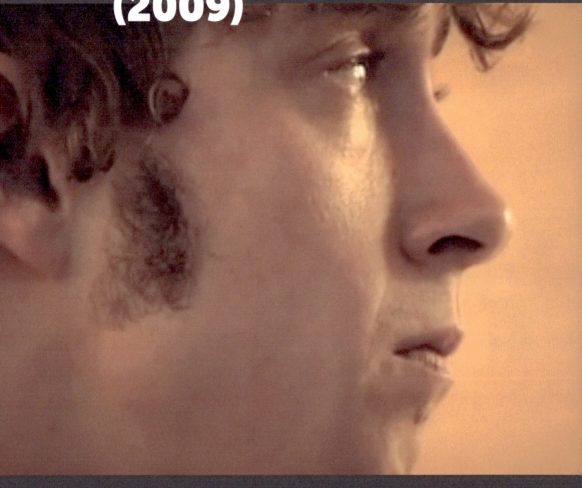

FIGURE 38.1: *Hymn*: performer Tom Wainwright. Video still courtesy of Tony Judge.

FIGURE 38.2: *Hymn*: performer Tom Wainwright. Video still courtesy of Tony Judge.

FIGURE 38.3: *Hymn*: performer Tom Wainwright. Video still courtesy of Tony Judge.

Hymn is an 11-minute, single-screen video that takes choreographic material from *Model Love* and a song from *Who By Fire*, to foreground for the first time the queer sensibility within much of Bodies in Flight's work. Sara's 'open-book' choreography from the first scene of *Model Love* is reworked as an explicit queer fantasy, set to a lament for lost youth, originally sung by Polly Frame in *Who By Fire* to a 'dead' lover, here re-recorded by Tim Atack as a same-sex torch song. Along with Sara's *Triptych*, Simon's *Hymn* acknowledged the depth of our long-term collaboration that allows each co-director to return to elements of previous shows to discover and focus upon aspects of the material of particular personal meaning. These early 'side-projects' led directly to *Do the Wild Thing! Redux* with its focus on individual artists 're-entering', re-discovering and re-imagining the unfinished business of our (joint) 'back catalogue'.

ANGEL TECH song music, EDWARD DIMSDALE photography, CATHERINE DYSON performer, SARA GIDDENS choreography, SIMON JONES camera, director and text, TONY JUDGE post-production, GRAEME ROSE performer, TOM WAINWRIGHT performer.

Extracts exhibited: Quake (Dèda, Derby), *Flesh & Text: 30 Years of Bodies in Flight* (Wickham Theatre, Bristol), Lakeside Arts (Nottingham), PR1 Gallery (Preston).

2009–Present

The Third Series

Opening Out Towards Co-creating the Portfolio Work

Way back in 1989, the first flight had been energized by a desire to escape the 'confines' of text as playscript; however, in fleeing 'motive' and 'intention', we were also in some sense running away from our audiences. Reviewing the NRLA the following year, John Jordan focused on this aspect in our next show.

'*The incessant throwing of scraps of dislocated information at the audience was, in a sense, most successfully accomplished by the invited company Bodies in Flight, whose performance* Exhibit, *undoubtedly a stylish piece of physical theatre, was one of the festival's most powerful uses of theatricality [...] whose contents amounted to a shopping list of issues – "Sex, Boys, Violence, Girls, Politics" – about which absolutely nothing was said. When asked why the group had tried to cram so much into one work, the director disarmingly replied that they were rather more concerned with effect than with meaning*' (in *Performance*, 63, March 1991).

To be careless of how audiences responded was necessarily folded into the heady irresponsibility of those first few shows. It was not until *Rough* (1992) that we turned for the first time to face our audiences and address them directly.

With that simple yet profound move, we became concerned with the relation between our audience's everyday and the 'world' we created in the performance event. Earlier works had jammed the one crudely up against the other. Henceforth, we would explicitly guide audiences from that everyday into the world of the work with what we called 'inductions', literally – *leadings in*. As part of those inductions, later shows (*Skinworks*, *Who By Fire*, *Model Love*) would use found material from the internet or performers' own experiences to create bridges into the works' 'extraordinarinesses'. Viewed from this perspective, Bodies in Flight's current series merely extends what these earlier inductions prefigured: the relating of the audience's everyday to the work's fictional situation. However, in acknowledging the audience, in staring into their eyes, it became impossible not to see them *as persons*, to see their investment in the work as a profound gift, a call which we were obliged to answer.

As a consequence, *Dream→Work/Dream→Walk*, which included oral-history interviews with inhabitants of places through which the show walked and with whom we occasionally interacted on their streets, was followed by *Gymnast* and *Life Class*, which were made with communities bringing their skill sets, concerns and experiences directly into the devising workshop. We controversially understood this 'co-creating' to be a bringing together of wills, to hold open that group's sense of itself *as a community alongside* our wills as artists, not to allow either set of wills to hold sway over the other. This required us to open up our methodology and our concerns to them; to spend time building trust and encountering their everydayness *as practice*: for instance, how streets were walked; how routines emerged from training exercises and how weekly dance clubs contributed to health and mental well-being. From the earliest series, we had always been focused on critiquing 'commonsense' or 'everydayness', rather than specific 'issues' or 'ideologies'. We had explicitly recognized this in our second series of cross-media collaborations: Sara's micro-choreography deconstructing everyday gestures; Simon's writing investigating from the inside commonsense notions and feelings. Now we brought that 'everyday' and 'commonsense' directly into the making of the work by way of the embodied experiences and knowledges of the different communities with whom we collaborated.

As performance-makers, our processes of abstracting and aestheticizing were strengthened by and anchored in this open relation to each community's know-how and know-why, for all to see. This opening out of our practice, producing multiple perspectives on commonplace experience, helped us to fashion a new idea of community that was specifically realized in the performance event itself, in-between actuality and imagination, the everyday and the possible. Furthermore, because the work now had a fundamental responsibility to a community, and thence a responsiveness to what it encountered in its making, the envelope of what each work could do necessarily extended into a 'portfolio' of outputs. New 'editions' were sited in different locations and responded to communities' and producers' different priorities. The material was re-mediatized to reach new audiences. In turn, this led to returning to and 're-entering' previous material to find new meanings in new contexts and media. This counter-intuitively gave us opportunities to make more personal, 'satellite' works alongside these community engagements – *Triptych*, *Hymn*, *Still Moving: Moving Still* and most recently *Unbox Me!* In these ways, Bodies in Flight's practice was opened out not only to other persons and communities but also through space and time to multiple sites and new pasts and futures as part of an endless re-invention of what any one work could become.

39 Dream→Work/ Dream→Walk (2009–16)

PUBLICITY COPY
Dream→Work
Every working day millions of us get up still half asleep, look in the bathroom mirror and start the daily task of putting on a public face: we try to work out what on earth we are doing – with our lives, with the lives of others, our lovers, children, friends, or just the must-dos of the day ahead. As we commute to work, this daily day-to-day construction of self continues through a strange overlaying of both public and private spaces: what happens on the street with what happens in our heads. Only when we get to the workplace are we finally ready to play 'ourselves'.

Dream→Walk/Skegness Edition
Off to Skeggy! Freed from the daily grind for a day, a week or a fortnight in caravan or B&B! Fun in the sun, sea and sand! Commissioned by Dance4 as part of Big Dance 2012, Bodies in Flight makes a welcome return to SO Festival. Their seaside walk celebrates the Great British Seaside Holiday. Accessible for any age group, the walk will take you from the station, along the Grand Parade, to the sea, exploring through a sensory mix of soundscape, movement and performance the funny, intimate and sometimes profound experiences we all have when we holiday by the seaside.
The walk lasts 35 minutes. You will be provided with a headset to experience the specially composed soundscape and guided by the performers along this dream walk.
This is an outdoor walking commission, please dress accordingly.

TIM ATACK musician, POLLY FRAME performer, SARA GIDDENS choreography/co-direction, SAM HALMARACK music/sound-score, NEIL JOHNSON music/sound-score, SIMON JONES original text/co-direction, GRAEME ROSE performer, TOM WAINWRIGHT performer.

With: TONY JUDGE video documentation, DUNCAN SPEAKMAN audio consultant.

Performed: Singapore Arts Festival (2009), Nottdance (Nottingham 2009), Mayfest (Bristol 2010), Wirksworth Festival (2011), SO Festival (Skegness 2012 & 2013), Productive Margins (Cardiff 2015), Know Your Bristol On the Move (Bristol 2016).

FIGURE 39.1: *Dream→Walk* Wirksworth: performer Graeme Rose. Photo: Tony Judge.

FIGURE 39.2 (next): *Dream→Work* Singapore: route map. Courtesy of the University of Bristol Theatre Collection.

FIGURE 39.3 (next): *Dream→Work* Singapore: performers Sam Halmarack and Polly Frame. Photo: Yuen Chee Wai.

FIGURE 39.4 (next): *Dream→Work* Bristol: performer Tom Wainwright. Photo: Tina Remiz.

FIGURE 39.5 (next): *Dream→Walk* Skegness: performer Graeme Rose. Photo: Simon Jones.

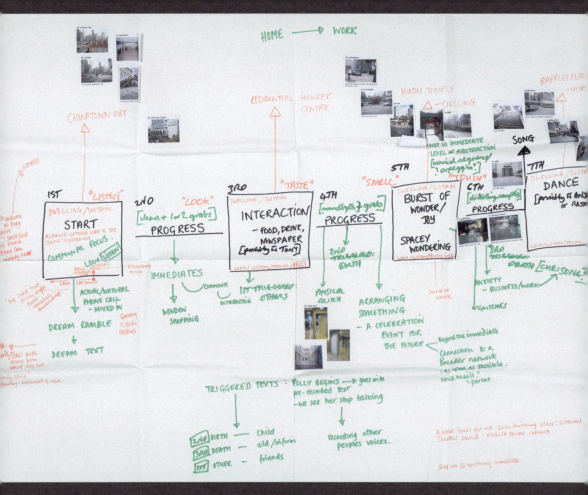

Our original aim had been to take our method of investigating the everyday out onto the streets, to join and mingle amongst commuters as they went to work. Collaborating again with spell#7 in Singapore, we took on the role of ex-pat worker, as spell#7 played the local going back home. We moved that ex-pat back to the United Kingdom to Nottingham and Bristol, to disappear into the commuting crowds, and then suddenly through song and dance appear amongst them as performer. With each new edition, as we made the work, people would come up to us on the streets and share stories of their towns: these approaches changed the direction of the project. Over seven years and seven editions, it morphed

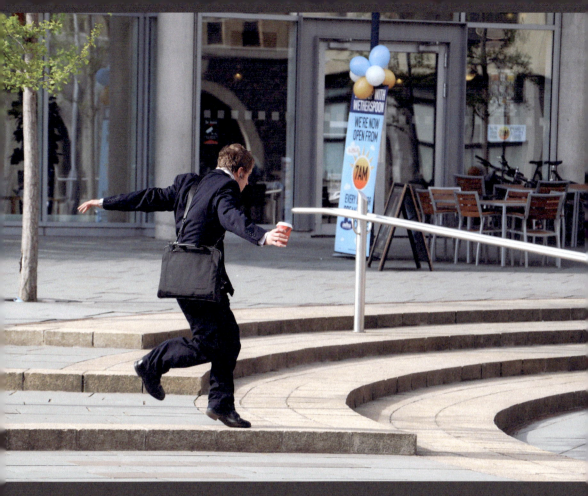

from being about the experience of commuting to explore place and identity through the memories of local inhabitants, from the global city of Singapore to the British seaside of Skegness, from the miners' strike of 1984/85 to recollections of circus animals on the streets of Bristol. In each place, the work was made anew, inhabitants were interviewed about their memories of a place and their hopes for the future. Interviewing the young and the very old from a diverse mix of communities, we responded to the briefs of local producers who variously wanted to draw attention to their town's architectural history, the 30-year commemoration of the miners' strike, the life of West St in Bedminster (Bristol).

40
Gymnast (2011–13)

Figure 40.1: *Gymnast* Arnolfini: gymnasts Joshua Avallone, Nicole Andrew, Sophie Gaunt and Night Bus Choir singers. Photo: Tony Judge.

Figure 40.2: *Gymnast*: poster. Courtesy of Tony Judge.

PUBLICITY COPY

Bodies in Flight in their 17th performance project GYMNAST delves into our fascination with the athlete's drive to physical excellence, their supreme attention to bodily task, the high point on the parallel bars, the thousands of minute adjustments needed to hold that still. In collaboration with video artist Tony Judge and composer Jen Bell and Night Bus Choir, GYMNAST uses the training session as both source and structure, from warm-up routines to the display of gymnastic exercises, from novice to expert, to explore the continuing power of the Olympian ideal of athlete as interface between human and superhuman, the mortal and the divine.

This project responded to the 2012 London Games by exploring the athlete's drive and determination to acquire the skills necessary to achieve physical excellence, both from the insider's point of view – the trainee gymnast, and from the spectator's – the admiration we feel in watching the achievement of physical mastery. Using the gymnast's training session as both source and structure, we developed a micro-choreography revealing the beauty of the gymnast's supreme attention to bodily tasks, placed alongside new writing set to music and sung by a choir. In parallel, Tony Judge created the video consisting of interviews and sequences capturing the training regime and micro-choreography of the gymnasts' movements. The work was presented in various forms: as a multi-screen video installation, sometimes with live gymnastics and/or live choir; as a theatre performance or as a gymnasium presentation. Four videos were selected by the BBC for their Big Screens contribution to the Cultural Olympiad and shown at 22 locations nationwide in the run-up to the Games.

NICOLE ANDREW gymnast, JOSHUA AVALLONE gymnast, JENNIFER BELL composer/conductor, SOPHIE GAUNT gymnast, SARA GIDDENS choreographer/co-director, SAM HALMARACK composer/post-production, SIMON JONES lyrics/co-director, TONY JUDGE video/photography/artwork, BEN TAYLOR gymnast.
THE NIGHT BUS CHOIR: Martin Bailey, Dominic Cauldwell, Jamie Darwen, Bertie Goffe, Lucy Goldsack, Kate Howson, Alex Kalinowska, Andy Marshall, Adrian Mantle, Phaedra Mawle, Alex Reid, Ruth Russell, Gemma Smart, Jan Swann and Katy Wilkes.

On video: gymnasts and coaches from the following clubs – Alfreton Leisure Centre Gymnastics, Amber Valley Gymnastics Club, Notts Gymnastics Academy, Sharley Park Girls Gymnastics Club, The Belgian Gymnastics Federation, Tibshelf Gymnastics Club.

Performed: Ferment/Bristol Old Vic, Surface Gallery (Nottingham), Arnolfini (Bristol), Atkins Gallery (Hinckley), Mayfest/City of Bristol Gymnastics, Rushcliffe Academy (Nottingham), BBC Big Screens (nationwide).

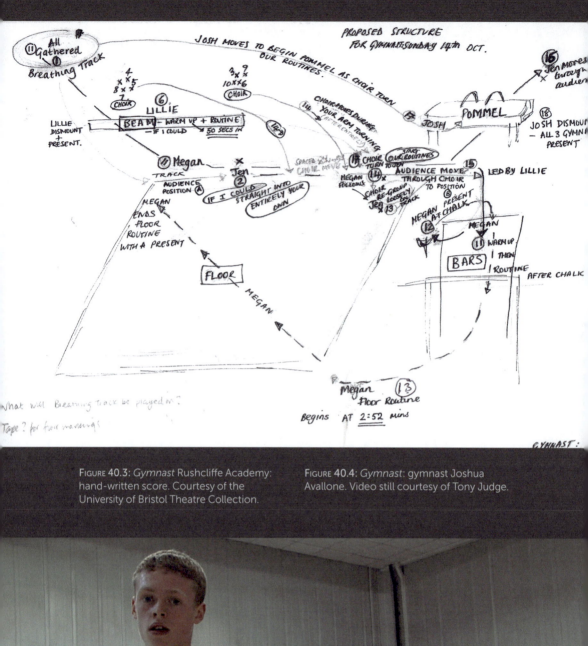

FIGURE 40.3: *Gymnast* Rushcliffe Academy: hand-written score. Courtesy of the University of Bristol Theatre Collection.

FIGURE 40.4: *Gymnast*: gymnast Joshua Avallone. Video still courtesy of Tony Judge.

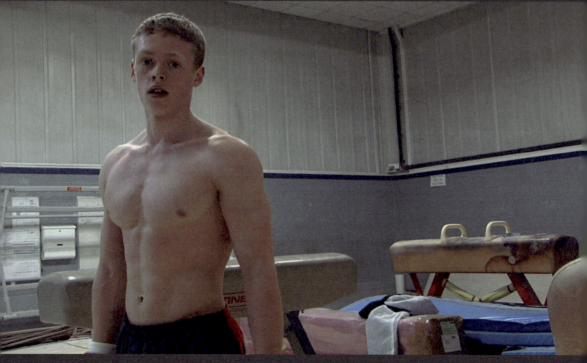

Figure 40.5: *Gymnast* Surface Gallery: gymnast Joshua Avallone and Night Bus Choir singers. Photo: Tony Judge.

Figure 40.6: *Gymnast* Mayfest: gymnast Joshua Avallone, Nicole Andrew, Sophie Gaunt and Night Bus Choir singers. Video still courtesy of Tony Judge.

41

A Place That Is Intelligent, A Little Bit Punk Even ... But Always Human

SUZANNAH BEDFORD

SUZANNAH BEDFORD worked with theatre companies Out of Joint, Talawa and Greenwich and Lewisham Young People's Theatre. On returning to Nottingham, she joined the dance team at Arts Council England, where she developed a relationship with Bodies in Flight over several years. Joining the regeneration charity, The Renewal Trust, enabled her to set up the pioneering project entitled Place, *a community-led commissioning approach to working collaboratively with artists and local communities. She is currently the director of the community arts organization, City Arts Nottingham.*

In this writing, Suzannah considers the new perspectives brought to Gymnast *and* Life Class *by Bodies in Flight's participants.*

I first came across Bodies in Flight when I joined the Visual and Performing Arts Department at Trent Polytechnic, as a secretary, back in 1991. Sara was a performance and dance lecturer on the Creative Arts BA at Victoria Studios, a course, which for me, as someone who did not come from a background with 'access to arts', felt like another world, with music drifting into the stairwell, dance and sculpture. Looking back, I realize now that the benchmark had been set high for me in terms of performance. Out of the Creative Arts course, a number of seminal live art and performance companies emerged, and its studio spaces like the Powerhouse introduced audiences in Nottingham to companies including Gob Squad, Forced Entertainment and Bodies in Flight. This was a special time for me. If I couldn't make work like this,

I wanted to be around Nottingham's incredible performance scene: we had Now Festival and Nott Dance; at the same time, Nottingham Playhouse was under the artistic directorship of Ruth Mackenzie, sharing some of the programming from London's International Festival of Theatre, which meant we got to see mid-scale dance companies including V-TOL and Wim Vandekeybus. Even amongst these companies, I remember seeing Bodies in Flight. I recall the feeling: something attractive, assembling in front of me, pushing my thinking, not always comfortable. Then, unfolding into something even more beautiful, rich and poignant, like a peony, at its most beautiful as it unfurls and then fades.

Inspired by my time at Trent Polytechnic, I studied literature, then went on to London to work in theatre, coming back to Nottingham about ten years later. Yet live art remained a significant part of my own personal aesthetic. The fact that Nott Dance, Lakeside, and companies like Bodies in Flight were here made it possible to leave London, knowing that I would still find quality, ground-breaking performance. When I joined the dance team at Arts Council East Midlands, live art didn't seem to have a home. Because I had a passion for this work and these companies, I became responsible for those relationships and insisted upon including them in the performing arts portfolio. Amongst the inspiring conversations with Sara and Simon in project meetings over those years, I particularly enjoyed conversations around their ambitions for *Gymnast*, a response to the London Olympic Games, a performance bringing together film, a choir and the skill of local gymnasts. Every time my appraisal came around, I'd be reminded that live art wasn't in my job description. But I knew this company's work was precious. Even if we couldn't get what we wanted, I wouldn't give them up!

Now, as a creative producer, I make arts projects with communities, with a focus on excellence, developing relationships with under-served and under-valued communities in Nottingham's inner-city neighbourhoods. Working in St Ann's and Sneinton, I pioneered new, community-led ways of working with artists, ways that I am continuing to explore in my current role as Director of City Arts in Nottingham. So, I know what a huge achievement it is to involve people in challenging and experimental work, and this is what Bodies in Flight does so well with projects like *Gymnast* and *Life Class*. I have witnessed their voice evolve and mature. This is a company to grow up with: from their provocative and radical youth – though always profound – their work has gradually gained more layers and depth. I always knew that Bodies in Flight was unafraid to challenge us, making work that holds us whilst we reach a new awareness, always aesthetically beautiful and considered.

But now for me, it's their way of bringing people into the work that feels so natural and yet takes their work in new and unexpected directions. Of course, working with professional collaborators – dancers and filmmakers – ensures that the performances are created and performed to the highest standards. Yet the performers are now not always the main focus of the shows: sometimes they become a channel; their movement giving physical form to the voices of people. It is a symbiotic relationship, elevating the everyday through the skills of the artist, and local people themselves becoming the performers. Working in partnership with gymnastic societies, *Gymnast* shone a light on the extraordinary skill of the athlete. The gymnasts became the performers: by placing them in an art gallery, their exceptional skills were given new meaning, and their practice routines became a visceral choreography. In the same project, by placing performances in gymnastic halls, art is less remote, it reaches new audiences because it is more relevant to those groups. Serenaded by a choir throughout, Bodies in Flight wove seemingly disparate elements together into a beautiful and unexpected storytelling whole. The music, the words, the movement, film – distinct and yet more than the sum of their parts.

Working with local people, with non-artists, is not straightforward: it requires an integrity about honouring who they are, their voice and their contribution. It can run the risk of seeming tokenistic, focusing on the 'real' artists with community members as peripheral. Finding the right groups to connect with can take time, lots of research and, importantly, relationship building. When I saw the performance of *Life Class* at Lakeside Arts Centre (Nottingham), I knew that Bodies in Flight had got this right. The theatre venue was laid out like a community centre hall, with plastic chairs around the edges, and party streamers strewn around. I felt like I was in a neighbourhood space, filled with the human warmth that usually only community spaces seem to radiate. The professional performers and social dancers worked together to recount stories of love, engagement, marriage, of bonds that seem to belong to another generation, another time and place. The effect was transporting, with the participants woven into the fabric of the performance seamlessly, demonstrating that Bodies in Flight understands that participants have something to say. Without them, *Life Class* would have been a beautiful and engaging dance duet. With them, bringing their own skills as ballroom dancers, it added layers of time, age, class and relevance for different audiences.

My experience of engaging communities in the making of art and performance helps me understand just how much trust participants need to have in the artist or company, in order for them to agree to be taken out of their comfort zone. The clarity of Bodies in Flight's vision and their offer to communities is key. This in itself is not always as easy as it sounds when work is devised. Fundamentally, the artists have to be of a standard, a high enough quality, for people to take a risk and put themselves in front of an audience. Bodies in Flight have the courage of their own conviction to share their vision with participants. Together they create artworks that are truly unique, performances that linger in the consciousness years after the live moment. Bodies in Flight have always made beautiful art. Now they invite people into a place that is intelligent, a little bit punk even, but most importantly, for me, a place that is human, where we can recognize both our limitations and our potential, at a safe remove, through the power of their extraordinary artworks.

Further Reading

Ayers, Robert and Butler, David (1991), *Live Art*, Sunderland: AN Publications.

Doherty, Claire (ed.) (2009), *Situation*, Cambridge, MA: MIT Press.

42

Mayfest and Mayk: From Festival to Co-creation

MATTHEW AUSTIN IN CONVERSATION WITH SIMON JONES

MAYK is one of the country's leading live performance-producing organizations. Based in Bristol but working internationally, MAYK's mission is to make important, unexpected, revelatory work with visionary artists that changes our experience of the world and each other. The work of the organization year-round is to create dynamic meeting points for participation in world-class live performances, both in and out of traditional art spaces. Led by Kate Yedigaroff and Matthew Austin, MAYK was established in 2011 and continues to make a space for a holistic long-term approach to creating memorable experiences that are accessible to lots of people. MAYK curates and produces Mayfest – Bristol's international festival of theatre, and was a lead partner on Horizon, a showcase of performance created in England, alongside BAC, FABRIC, Fierce, GIFT and Transform.

Here Matthew Austin discusses Bodies in Flight's developing partnership with Mayfest.

SIMON:
Bodies in Flight first worked with Mayfest on *Who By Fire*.

MATTHEW:
I actually have a clear memory of that show. I remember really loving it. Mayfest was in its second year. It emerged from the desire of Simon Reade and David Farr, joint artistic directors of Bristol Old Vic, to find a way to satisfy more experimental, local artists, because their focus in the main house was very much on modern adaptations of classic texts.

The first programme in 2003 was more national, whereas in 2004 there was a Bristol focus, sitting alongside what Arnolfini Gallery was doing at that time. I think there was a really interesting crossover between companies working between these two venues, such as The Special Guests, who were Associate Artists at Arnolfini, but also presenting at Bristol Old Vic. And I felt it was right for *Who By Fire* to be sitting in a theatre context, even though in the rest of the programme, it was one of the more experimental works.

SIMON:
Can I ask about the crossover of companies between venues? I sensed that the labelling and placing of work was crucial, driven by sensible factors, like the limited audience for what was described as live art.

MATTHEW:
Mayfest's original remit was very much about physical and visual theatre. But we never really liked that term, and we've always resisted too much categorization. Even now we don't badge work by genre because it feels important to us that people make up their own minds about what it is or isn't. Although labelling can be helpful when thinking about funding, labelling something as 'live art' might be off-putting to some audiences.

SIMON:
Did it help that you were working within Bristol Old Vic, a nationally recognized theatre?

MATTHEW:
Yes, I think it did because the programme felt more radical within that context. Prior to Simon and David, none of that work was being seen at Bristol Old Vic. It had been more writer-led. Whereas in the context of Arnolfini or the National Review of Live Art, it didn't feel that radical. So, we've always enjoyed the slightly playful rubbing up against that institution.

SIMON:
What was the ambition of those early programmes in terms of audience development? Were you reaching out to audiences of the main house shows?

MATTHEW:
I think there was the desire to build an entirely new audience. In the first year 2003, tickets were £10. And then the second year, we decided to make everything £5; and that doubled the audience. We worked really hard to promote it beyond Bristol Old Vic's audience. We went to places that presented live music or to contemporary art centres, like Arnolfini, or art-cinema venues, like Watershed, to say, look, there is something for you at Bristol Old Vic now.

SIMON:
With our second partnership on *Dream→Work/Dream→Home* (2010), two shifts were occurring in Mayfest's programming. Firstly, can you remember the motivations for moving out of the traditional theatre space? Because, for me, that's been one of Mayfest's most successful aspects – its use of a wide range of other spaces in the city, that then interestingly folds back on your choice to use the main house at Bristol Old Vic. The other aspect is the internationalism, that took Mayfest beyond its original Bristol focus.

MATTHEW:
In 2008, Bristol Old Vic closed for a year, pushing us to make that jump. We secured our first funding from Arts Council England, and from that point, we began to think of Mayfest as a cross-city festival. In 2010, we did a show called *Electric Hotel*, sited on the harbourside in a specially constructed outdoor space, which felt like we were declaring Mayfest a festival for Bristol. *Dream→Work/Dream→Home* were ambulatory works around the city, alongside Duncan Speakman's *My World Is Empty Without You*. It was exciting we were saying that Mayfest is sited across the city, not just a venue. However, sometimes it felt like audiences have been more excited about the site's potential, rather than the work. So, we tried to resist the site as a gimmick. Around then also, the Pervasive Media Studio at Watershed was starting, with an emphasis on digital technology, and an interest in site-based work engaging with the public. This encouraged us to do more stuff that's not in theatres. And that offers lots of opportunities for audience development too, as you've removed a barrier to people attending: they don't have to enter a building they might find intimidating or 'not for them'. 2022's programme was also heavily site-based, and perhaps that's reflective of where Bristol is now, with venues like Bristol Old Vic having worked hard at broadening the work they stage. So now, there's less need for us to be an agitator in that way. It feels more complementary.

Over those first few years after 2008, Mayfest moved from being a showcase of work largely by local artists to being an opportunity to bring in more international and national voices to the city, to inspire artists here. We still felt quite new, so working internationally was a scary thing – stressful and expensive, but important as there wasn't anyone else in the city programming international theatre. Your collaboration with spell#7 from Singapore is a good example of the local and the international working together.

SIMON:
With *Electric Hotel* in the Waterfront Square, are there costs to going out into the city? It's in a public space, so a lot more volatile. I was highly aware of that myself, moving from the safety of a black box or gallery to the streets of Bristol and Singapore.

MATTHEW:
When I look back at that year in particular, I'm amazed at how young and relatively inexperienced we were. Today, I probably wouldn't take the risks that we took then with such a tiny team. Now we take more care than maybe we did then. It was a huge learning curve because sited work does take more energy, more work and more money. When you're working with a theatre, you can hand the show over. But the minute you move into a non-theatre space, indoors or out, your role as a producer becomes more responsible. It's easier to put the show in, say, the Arnolfini: here's the technician; off you go. Whereas outdoors, there are more variables and more risk. And so, yeah, that is definitely a challenge. One that's often quite fun, where the payoff is bigger. It was more important to make sure that the artists were having a good time and felt looked after and cared for than to overstretch ourselves.

SIMON:
How does this strategy connect with MAYK's role in producing new work?

MATTHEW:
In 2004, Theatre Bristol, an organization set up to develop the theatre ecology in the city, emerged as Bristol was becoming known for its concentration of artists and young theatre-makers. And around that time there were several development schemes – the kind of programmes that help artists get an idea off the ground. However, we noticed that there wasn't anywhere for artists to go once they'd proved an idea. It felt like there was a ceiling for artists in Bristol, who weren't able to go beyond the city and tour. Companies, like Bodies in Flight, Uninvited Guests and Action Hero were making brilliant work, then finding it hard to sustain that into a longer life. We set up MAYK to

help artists take their work into production and distribution. Mayfest was a platform for presentation, but we wanted to be more involved in the making process. We wanted to help things live longer. It took a few years to figure out what the relationship between the work we were producing and the festival was, and how we could use the festival to give projects a kickstart. We very definitely didn't want to start a producing factory. We wanted it to be a small number of artists whom we could work with carefully.

SIMON:
Interestingly, at the same point for us, our project *Dream→Work* evolved into *Dream→Walk*, which worked more closely with different communities, putting together their memories of place. This led to our decision in our next project *Gymnast* to work directly with two different communities from the outset – social choirs and élite gymnasts, in the build-up to the London Olympics. I'm interested in your thoughts on the participatory turn in the arts more generally, and specifically the role of Arts Council England's strategy in privileging this approach, for instance, the recent strategy which blurs the distinction between artist and participant (see Reference).

MATTHEW:
I think there are lots of brilliant things about this approach – how it opens up culture for new audiences, how it shifts hierarchies and the potential for new co-created work, but I do worry about the position of the artist in this strategy. Where do artists go who have a more experimental practice – the weird shit? It feels harder to describe that work in terms of a 'community' or it being 'relevant'. And I think that's the challenge. With *Gymnast*, that was the beginning of making co-created work for us.

SIMON:
I recall we only began to understand the impact of collaborating with those two different communities after the work was performed. For instance, the gymnasts had material that they put together in a particular way. Sara wanted to put together a piece where half a dozen routines were synchronized on a series of beams, which they would never have done because they were used to working individually. After the performance, their coach came up and asked if they could use that piece in their Christmas show. Of course, we said yes. Also, the choir carried on using their material from the work. It felt very much like we wanted to bring these two cultures together, but there was a

lot of work in organizing the meshing of their expectations as different communities. The legacy of that was very significant for us.

MATTHEW:

That is something that we would now build into our co-created projects as a festival. So that it didn't feel like the show happened, and then nothing else happened. When I was thinking of *Gymnast*, I wondered what we could have done afterwards to maintain a relationship with the gym. It becomes more about a longer-term relationship than simply doing a show. So, it's good to hear that there was that continuation. *Gymnast* also chimed with Bristol City Council encouraging arts organizations to work in neighbourhoods. We were asking how we move a festival that was largely in the city centre into much wider locations. I remember at the time having conversations about how far out the gymnasium venue was, on the edge of the city, and would people go. Now I think we would have a different conversation about putting more effort into promoting it to the people who lived in that area, rather than encouraging audiences out from the centre.

Reference

Arts Council England, 'Let's create', https://www.artscouncil.org.uk/lets-create. Accessed 9 May 2024.

43
Do the Wild Thing! Redux (2012)

Figure 43.1: *Do the Wild Thing! Redux*: installation and performance. Photo: Tony Judge.

Figure 43.2: *I'd Like to Call You Joe Tonight*: performer James D Kent. Still courtesy of Tony Judge.

Figure 43.3: *Do the Wild Thing! Redux*: installation and performance combining *Muse*, performer Dan Elloway. Photo: Carl Newland.

Commissioned by Performing Documents, this project saw four of the original collaborators return to their archives of *Do the Wild Thing!* by working independently until the day of installing the work in Arnolfini Light Studio. Each produced a separate new work in their own medium – dance,

photography, text and video. Like a hologram, shattered, we offered a set of different perspectives, (literally) *through-seeings* on to the object (of the 'original' performance) that was no longer there.

Sara Giddens' *Still Moving: Moving Still* was a durational dance duet, exploring still-ing as a choreographic strategy, performed a number of times over *Redux*'s opening weekend.

In *Make the Fixed Volatile, and Make the Volatile Fixed*, Edward Dimsdale reworked one photographic technology through the frame of another, specifically re-figuring old photogravure techniques with the digital.

In *I'd Like to Call You Joe Tonight*, Tony Judge exploded the single perspective of the 1996 multi-camera video document by harnessing the potential of high-resolution imaging and hard-drive synchronization, to produce a three-screen video work that reinvented the show from each of its actors' points of view.

Simon Jones' *Muse*, as an installation and prose work, explored the bonds between flesh and text in the 1996 performance. One of the show's original performers read from a limited-edition book that mused upon the relationship of writer to performer.

TOM BAILEY performer, EDWARD DIMSDALE photography, DAN ELLOWAY performer, SARA GIDDENS choreography, SIMON JONES writer, TONY JUDGE film director/editor, MARTHA KING performer.

On video: CHRIS BIANCHI performer, POLLY FRAME performer, JAMES D. KENT performer.

With: MARTIN BLACKHAM 1st assistant director, JAKE CHANNON set technician, TERRY FLAXTON director of photography, PAUL GEARY runner, ADAM DJ LAITY focus puller, PETER MILNER camera operator, JONATHAN SCOTT audio recording, PAM TAIT wardrobe.

Exhibited: Arnolfini (Bristol).

44
Still Moving: Moving Still (2012–18)

Originally part of *Do the Wild Thing! Redux*, *Still Moving: Moving Still* was further developed by Sara and re-staged at Nottingham Contemporary as part of the Dance in Galleries season (2013), curated by Dance4, and then commissioned by DanceXchange for the Birmingham International Dance Festival and performed at Birmingham Conservatoire of Music (2018).

Still-ing (2017), a seven-screen video installation, emerging out of and including documentary footage from *Still Moving: Moving Still*, was shown at *Talking, Thinking, Dancing*, hosted by Dance4 (The International Centre for Choreography, Nottingham), alongside a series of experiential workshops, *Still Small Acts*, developed for the *Between Spaces* symposium (University of Chichester), *Practice-as-Research NOW* conference (University of Galway), *Slowing and Still-ing* symposium (Birmingham), *Contra: Dance and Conflict* (University of Malta), *Rethinking Research: Disrupting and Challenging Research Practices Conference* (Coventry University), Centre for Excellence in Learning and Teaching Conference (CELT) Conference at The University of Central Lancashire; and as a case study of practice as research in performance at the first Dance in Galleries season curated by Dance4 and the International Centre for Choreography at Lakeside Arts, Nottingham.

SARA GIDDENS director and choreographer, ELLA JUDGE performer, MARTHA KING performer, USHA MAHENTHIRALINGHAM performer, PARMJIT SAGOO performer, JEN SUMNER performer, RUTH SPENCER performer, JUSTYNA URBANCZYK performer, KERSTIN WELLHOFER performer, and guests.

With: MARTIN BLACKHAM camera operator, TONY JUDGE video.

FIGURE 44.1: *Still Moving: Moving Still* Nottingham Contemporary: sited performance. Photo: Tony Judge.

FIGURE 44.2: *Still Moving: Moving Still* Birmingham International Dance Festival: sited performance. Photo: Tony Judge.

FIGURE 44.3: *Still Moving: Moving Still* Nottingham Contemporary: sited performance. Photo: Tony Judge.

45
Developing a Portfolio
SARA GIDDENS

In this Flight, I reflect upon our response to ever-more diverse platforms and audiences and our strategies for survival: how performance and its ecology of developing and funding work has become more complicated in the last decade or so; how that complexity has become enfolded with our methodology to sustain for as long as possible an openness towards the mix of materials and media in any one work. As a consequence, our practice has opened out to both how material can be re-used and re-purposed across different media, and how diverse communities can engage with our devising process. Projects have developed from single outputs, mainly performances, to a portfolio of outputs, responding to funders and partners; single 'versions' have become 'editions' allowing material to re-invent itself in response to new opportunities. I conclude by returning to my opening Flight in recognition of a process of ongoing return and re-invention.

In the late 1980s and for much of the 90s we created shows that could be broadly categorized as experimental theatre. I do not recall us ever needing to categorize our work for ourselves, only to enable us to apply for funding, or to market our work to producers and venues. Then Arts Council England explicitly encouraged experimentation: we ticked the 'developing the art-form' box on our applications to them. Experimental theatre as a category seemed to give us freedom to focus on the art, to make art for art's sake. I am not sure that freedom is afforded to small-scale performance-makers now. Over the years the category has changed to reflect the external theatre ecology. We have variously been classified as live art, combined arts, dance or drama, as the funders' and producers' priorities changed. However, we always felt, and continue to feel, we were and are in-between such culturally and politically fluid categories. Our work may have a certain style or signature, but it consistently shifts in emphasis and in the balance and range of materials employed within it. Undoubtedly, this fluidity has been difficult for some funders and producers (see Richard Dufty's Chapter 11, 'From Fan-Boy to Programmer'). For a while, in the late

90s, even the two co-directors being based in different counties of the United Kingdom became problematic for some funders: yet now collaborating with partners across regions and beyond is encouraged and applauded.

As our investment in dialogues between artists and their media (see Chapter 9, 'Working Alongside') and the extension of our duet with technology developed, we found ourselves almost by accident moving beyond the 'single' work and into 'portfolio' projects, articulated either through different media or as a series of bespoke editions of the same work (*Dream→Work/ Dream→Walk*). However, it was our CD-ROM *Flesh & Text* that not only extended our relatively new-found desire to share our work, both the shows and how we made them, beyond the live event, but also shifted our thinking, necessitating as it did the need to break material down into manageable chunks so it could be digitized and re-used (see Tony Judge's Chapter 32, 'The Transmediated Image'). So much so, that the following show *Skinworks* opened out from a performance to a series of linked outputs, employing different media, including a radio broadcast, installation and lecture-demonstrations. After our 'rock opera' *Who By Fire*, made in collaboration with the band Angel Tech, blurred the distinctions between who did what on stage, I felt I could do more with the choreographic material. So, I made *Triptych*, our first stand-alone video work with filmmaker Tony Judge, inspired by and even incorporating a small section from the live performance. Made specifically for film, it incorporated location footage shot for, but not necessarily used in, the theatre show.

Now such strategies of re-using, re-purposing and re-working material seem so clear-cut, so decisive. In reality, this shift happened gradually, as a considered response to our commitment to inviting and remaining open to both a mixing of ideas, materials and people and *how* we worked with them, through multiple outcomes and media, within the specific and shifting, regional, national and international funding contexts and concerns. Indeed, *Model Love* was the first project to intentionally design multiple outcomes from the outset: through our collaboration with photographer Edward Dimsdale, the installation versions and performance editions actively explored an openness and willingness to re-use and re-purpose.

This shift from a 'single' work into multi-platforms was significant both strategically and methodologically. We found that following material through each medium foregrounded the delicious and delicate impossibility of work that itself exists between media: something remains or reveals itself that cannot be fully determined or expressed through the performance or event itself (see Chapter 20, 'Set-up and Situation'). As our experience of making *Triptych* from footage gathered for *Who By Fire* aptly demonstrates, there is always something left over that requires, or at least invites, that specific medium to reshape or reconstruct itself, somehow to go further in its own way. Indeed, our contribution to Performing Documents: *Redux* at Arnolfini began from the express desire to re-purpose the original physical, textual, photo- and video-graphic materials made for *Do the Wild Thing!* into four complementary, but stand-alone artworks, situated across different parts of the building, with each strand being led by one of the four original collaborators, each taking the material further along their own way.

The shift towards a portfolio, both helped and necessitated us to develop a more open and flexible method, a means of co-creating materials through a multiplicity of multi-nodal collaborations. In turn, these allowed us to be more responsive to a wider range of creative and funding opportunities. Since Arts Council England project funding had been, and continues to be, our major source of funding, we needed to position ourselves in a place that would enable us to respond in articulate and innovative ways to its and others' increasingly diverse and contingent invitations. Alongside scaling down their involvement in artists' development (until the pandemic forced a new wave of small 'developing your creative practice' grants), Arts Council England's strategy changed from an artist- to an audience-participant-centred focus. So, we invested in robust and lasting relationships with key regional and national organizations such as Dance4/ FABRIC and created *Gymnast*, made with élite and amateur gymnasts, in direct response to the London 2012 Olympic Games. This signalled the broadening of our reach, beyond theatres and galleries into gymnasia, and our desire to extend our collaborations with different communities of skill, to attract increasingly diverse audiences and funders: e.g., through the commissioned screen-based works for the 'BBC Big Screens', erected in 22 towns and cities across the UK for the games and generating a footfall of 3.4 million.

This move towards a multiplicity and variety of outputs, alongside our increased openness to producers' priorities, sat comfortably alongside our commitment to dwelling. Drawn from Martin Heidegger's ([1951] 1978) work, dwelling made sense to us in a way that previous theorizations had not (see Chapter 18, 'The Magnificent Minutiae'). Through dwelling, our practice and our method had found its theory; and we readily extended this beyond people and places into ideas and proposals. Indeed, *Dream→Work*, originally set in the early-morning commute, morphed into *Dream→Walk* in response to both the integration of dwelling into our methodology and producers' callouts. When we began *Dream→Work* in Singapore in 2009, we had wanted to explore anonymity in 'global cities'. However, through the process of dwelling with residents and passers-by and staying open to their reflections and narratives, the work ended up being increasingly local and intimate, with their stories forming a very significant part of each bespoke work.

The Wirksworth edition of *Dream→Walk* answered the commissioner's request to engage with the architectural and built environment; and the Skegness edition, made for the SO festival in collaboration with Dance4, placed holiday-making in the 1950s and 1960s at its core. The recorded experiences and memories of locals in Wirksworth and holidaymakers in Skegness were placed at the heart of each edition and accessed as part of bespoke soundscapes through individual earpieces supplied to audience members. The *Dream→Walk* we made for the Connected Communities festival was devised and sited in the central retail district of Cardiff and marked a point exactly thirty years since the miners' strike. By placing reflections from members of the Butetown Riverside Grangetown Communities First Group alongside marketing copy for the brand new hyper-modern shopping zone, this edition deepened our on-going exploration of how layers of history are sedimented into a specific location, not only by its built environment, but also through its inhabitants' everyday use of buildings and streets. In the 2016 West Street edition, which marked a return to Bristol, we were commissioned to employ pre-existing oral histories. So, we decided to place these alongside new interviews capturing young people's hopes for the future of the area, because we wanted to counter the tendency of these oral histories to lionize the past as a golden age. Although unpopular with some, we felt that we needed to address the future of communities, as much as their pasts.

Not surprisingly, the cross-over between our lives as artists and pedagogues, and particularly our experience as flexible, responsive and knowledgeable creative facilitators, became ever more pertinent the more we extended our work outwards. *Life Class* continued our externally facing engagement with and commitment to co-creating with community groups, this time through a collaboration with older movers, tea and social dancers, and local choirs (see Chapter 48, 'The Dare of Other Voices'). After live performances in Bristol and Nottingham (2019), the second phase of the work was due to begin just as the global pandemic hit. As a consequence, this edition morphed dramatically away from live performance into bespoke online and video versions. When we did return to develop the work for Lancashire Encounter Festival (Preston) in 2021, the participants' reflections upon their experiences during the pandemic, particularly their frustrations with not being allowed to dance and sing together face-to-face, and their creative solutions in overcoming this enforced isolation, became an unexpected, but crucial part of the show. We used the accompanying video documentaries, capturing the making alongside excerpts from the show and the participants' reflections upon the process, to extend the work's impact beyond its immediate setting and communities, thus opening up new opportunities for the project.

We have travelled a long way, metaphorically and literally, since our early days and the somewhat arbitrary definition as an experimental theatre company; yet more than thirty years on, co-creating with others to create challenging and relevant artworks is what continues to drive us. Having an open, responsive and transformative mode of working across environments and media, and engaging with multiple agencies across diverse communities, has been critical to these concerns. Working in-between and across platforms has led us to the creation of both complementary and stand-alone artworks. This, coupled with our commitment to working with a diversity of communities and community groups, has extended both our depth and range, enriching and empowering one of our signature concerns - the extraordinary ordinary, and proving the essential strength and importance of our focus on the everyday. It is hard to overstate how much more complex planning, devising and performing work that is co-created with community participants actually is. Certainly, the amount of time we get to make the work, in whatever forms, has shrunk in proportion to the time spent administrating, and particularly writing funding bids to raise money. However, once through the bureaucracy, this current period of opening out to ever more diverse co-creators and audiences has been richly rewarding.

This writing is an example of the complexity of my location, as a creator, unconcealed within a network of apparent complementarities, reflecting upon the multiple roles that Simon and I occupy, including those of co-director, choreographer, writer, facilitator, broker, project manager and administrator. Inevitably, like us all, I bring my own particular and idiosyncratic range of roles and voices, of thoughts, moves, influences and registers to this mix, coupled with a willingness and ability to expand the practice on our terms, within and, sometimes, outwith funders' priorities. I hope that I have found a way to touch upon both the how and why we have developed and successfully articulated a portfolio of flexible and innovative approaches and outcomes. It feels important to have expressed some of our central strategies for survival here. Not because we have a 'toolbox' that is ready to be lifted from a shelf and applied by others, not even because such strategies are so keenly entwined with our histories and methodologies, but because sharing these might encourage and support others to make, and keep making, art from their own unique perspectives and experiences, inevitably making connections to their yet unknown(s). As I end, I return to my beginning – Chapter 1, 'Unconcealing This Maker's Voice' with a somewhat arresting feeling that, through this writing, I have come to know this territory of creating, resourcing and making anew, as if 'for the first time' (Eliot 1974: 209) with a newly found respect and wonder. Dwell well.

References

Eliot, T. S. ([1944] 1974), *The Four Quartets*, London: Faber.

Heidegger, Martin ([1951] 1978), 'Building Dwelling Thinking', in D. Farrell Krell, (ed.), *Basic Writings*, London: Routledge.

46
Life Class (2019–22)

FIGURE 46.1: *Life Class*: performer Graeme Rose and participant Beth Holland. Photo: Scott Sawyer.

FIGURE 46.2: *Life Class*: poster. Courtesy of Tony Judge.

FIGURE 46.3 (next): *Life Class*: performer Morven Macbeth, participant Barry Winship, performer Graeme Rose and participant Betty Winship. Photo: Scott Sawyer.

FIGURE 46.4 (next): *Life Class*: participants Barbara J Clark, Beth Holland, Colin Moore, Barry and Betty Winship, Sheila Sims, and performer Graeme Rose. Photo: Scott Sawyer.

FIGURE 46.5 (next): *Life Class*: performers Morven Macbeth and Graeme Rose. Photo: Scott Sawyer.

FIGURE 46.6 (next): *Life Class*: participant Barbara J Clark, performer Graeme Rose, and participants Betty and Barry Winship. Photo: Scott Sawyer.

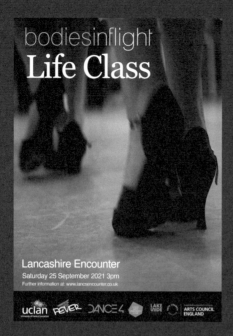

PUBLICITY COPY

Life Class *draws upon the Tea Dance to celebrate our greatest, most memorable, most requested role – ourselves, and asks how we ended up playing the part … in this scene … with these lines … and wonders – who's this playing opposite? Through poetic text and detailed choreography, inspired in part from work with Tea Dancers and community choirs, this new performance explores how our response to the call of the other determines who we are: how it makes us us.*

Taking as its starting point the fictional encounter between two lovers at a dance many years ago, our twentieth work extends our collaborations with different communities to work with a group of senior social dancers to explore the role that dance has played in their lives, and how one incident in a person's life can change its direction forever. Thirty years ago, Bodies in Flight began its artistic journey with the child's game of playing dead, focusing on performance's uncanny need to concretize what is possible to imagine. Today, we return to the most basic performance situation: beginning with two people on stage in front of an audience facing one another; we return to the duet and to the mixing of texts, both verbatim and imagined; to the mixing of bodies – performers and social dancers, singers and audiences; as yet another iteration of our exploration of performance's fundamental processes – a constant return to beginnings: to imagine the world anew.

In addition to performances in theatres and community venues, two sibling works were developed: a two-screen video installation re-imagining the ecstatic 'Third Circle' of the original theatre piece – *You Are Present to Me Now* – continued the face-to-face roots of the original work; and *Life Class: A Dialogue* – an audio work exploiting the heightened intimacy of binaural recording to locate the listener in the middle of the couple's sometimes bitter, sometimes loving lifetime's conversation.

JON AVEYARD sound, SOPHIE-LEIGH BARROW assistant choreographer, SARA GIDDENS choreographer/co-director, CELIA HAMMERSLEY assistant choreographer, NEIL JOHNSON composer/sound, SIMON JONES writer/co-director, TONY JUDGE video/ web design, MORVEN MACBETH performer, CHLOE MORRISEY assistant choreographer, GRAEME ROSE performer.

Tea Dancers: Barbara J Clark, Beth Holland, Rachael Holland, Bev and Paul Kershaw, Irene and Allan Molyneux, Colin Moore, Julie Parkinson, Sheila Sims, June and John Wilkes, Barry and Betty Winship.

With: Keith Adams, Colin and Pat Chappel, Doug Church, Margaret Howe, Brenda Hughes, Margaret McDade, Elisabeth Mooney, Maureen Morgan, Val White.

Singers: Jon Aveyard, Jill Brass, Rachel Emmett, Jezz Fleet, Richard Flewitt, Ian Harris, Hilda Hawkins, Ruth Hawley, Moira Hill, Germina Jauzelon, Angela Kay, Sigrid Pach, Allan Pickup, Dave Pitt, Annie Quill,

Robin Reece-Crawford, Angela Smallwood, Kathleen Tattersall, Sarah Trevers, Janice Weston-Smith.

Performed: Wickham Theatre (Bristol), Lakeside Arts (Nottingham), Lancashire Encounter/ Fever Dance (Preston).

You are Present to Me Now: SAM ALDERTON production manager, HAMZA ASHRAF focus puller, JON AVEYARD sound artist, GEORGIE BROWN second unit camera, FRANCO FEDERICO camera grip, SARA GIDDENS choreographer, NEIL JOHNSON composer, SIMON JONES writer, TONY JUDGE director/ editor, MORVEN MACBETH performer, OLLY MITCHELL key grip, HARRY PHIPPS sound recordist, GRAEME ROSE performer, JOE SAVAGE Steadicam operator, ROB WORSEY colour grading.

Exhibited: Leeds Arts University, Middle Floor Gallery (Leeds), PR1 Gallery (Preston).

Text extracts

SIMON JONES

After making Dream→Walk *on the streets of various towns and cities, I wanted very much to return to the theatre, to the most basic theatrical set-up of performer facing performer in front of an audience. That formed the beginnings of* Life Class's *situation: a couple investigating the history of their relationship, starting counter-intuitively at its bitter end and rewinding to its ecstatic start. To this, Sara added the specific milieu of the 'tea dance'. And as we worked with the communities of elderly tea-dancers, their memories, senses of loss and of hope became woven into the couple's reverse narrative. Technically, continuing my interest in the performative edges of language, I wanted the text to push in its scale and complexity the performers' capacities to deliver it: long passages were followed by extended call-and-response dialogues, each challenging performers Morven Macbeth and Graeme Rose in different ways.*

1ˢᵗ CIRCLE

MAN: Hey, you. I conjure you … and there you are. You're a figment of my imagination. I can do to you as I will … any force … any whim as I would … were you real. But you are not real. Not really here. Always somewhere else … in your head … off with the fairies … or on your phone. Is this a haunting? Are we ghosts? Tears in the fabric? Little condensed pellets of all the poison and the bad that happened in this club … when the camera only recorded the good times … the camaraderie … the affairs. But you are not even a ghost … since then you would once have had to have been alive. I've danced with you. We have made love … made children … but never really been together in the same world … never really shared the idle time … or occupied the common ground. You got in my way, yes.

WOMAN: We have agreed on that, at least.

MAN: All those times I called for you … and you came … and sat there before me … so attentive … so there for me … I got on a roll … and made up the entirety of you … from this … spook …

WOMAN: … whatever …

[...]

MAN: He wants to tell her he loves her. He sort of has the words ready … here … [POINT TO HEAD] all bundled together in a singularity of love … a potentiality. But he cannot bring himself to speak his love. It feels to him as if the words … if said out loud … would say too much. The love would be too much … for either him … or her … or both … to bear. And so, he declines. He will not speak for fear his love … once spoken … will just be too much … for the world … for reality. So, what he most keenly feels here … [POINT TO HEART] as if it were the quintessence of him … his signature … will remain unsaid as if it had never been … as if it could never have been. And he must live with that. And she must live without that. That never said love.

WOMAN: On the other hand … maybe just as likely the reason … he will not speak … is that this his love … once uttered … would sound pathetic … only ringing true in the hollow of its very own tiny space. No room for her to respond. It will astound, not in the expansiveness of its reach … or the gasp of its dare … but in the squint of its scope … and the brevity of its elaboration. Wow, was that it? She'll think that.

MAN: She won't say it.

WOMAN: But she will think it. No point rubbing salt into the wounds. How little is his love. Such a little journey it travels. Such a little room it stalks. And with such a little splash it breaks upon the shore of her consideration. How could he have thought it could conceivably have taken purchase in the storehouse of her heart?

MAN: How could he have ever thought otherwise?

WOMAN: You feel your life is like those deleted scenes they shove on to DVDs to make them seem better value for money. You know … the scenes that never made it into the real film … the one people were prepared to pay to see. And when you can be bothered to look at them … when your Saturday night really is that soul-destroying … what do you see? Well … they do sort of add something to the story. They're partially treated … you know … the colour's not quite right … they didn't waste time grading it like the real film.

	And the sound's not all there … it's kind of thin. And the rhythm's all wrong cos they worked so hard to hone that down to make the real film feel whole … like nothing else is needed. This deleted scene just feels … out of step … not a part of the world … as they say … of the film. And that is how you feel your life has played out … at times … not every screening … but most repeats … at the dead of night … on the – you might joke – niche channels. Like an unfinished scene … not incomplete because there's so much left to do … but discarded because there's nothing left to be done. It doesn't quite gel … it's only telling us things we already know … or don't need to know … in a less amusing way … with less economy of effort …
MAN:	… less panache …
WOMAN:	… a redundancy that threatens to draw attention to the weaknesses that inevitably lie hidden in the whole … amongst the real the film needs to convince us of … threatening to reveal its world as just another make-believe … just another put-up job. So, if you want a hit, better to forsake the scene to save the film. And boy, do you want a hit.

[…]

MAN:	Sitting here … sometimes … I know … you look at me and think, because you loved me, of all the others whom you did not love … who passed you by … whose caresses you never felt … from whose kind words and graceful interventions you never benefitted. This lover would have had depth and mould-breaking inventiveness when it came to the care they would have taken of you as you came and went … and the courage and enterprise they would have mustered every time you strode out to meet the world. This other would have spent their life upon you … and for such an exorbitant sacrifice you would have rendered yours up wholesale in exchange … to this … imaginary being. And then, because of him, you hate me, don't you? Me who loved you without condition … whose love you embraced so freely and so wittingly. I dare to speak what you feel but are too afraid to utter … lest in mouthing your fears, you summon them up

	from down below … make yourself in deed the creature you've always felt at heart you are. If my cruelty hadn't worded him into being, he would be lurking still about your heart … or maybe you would have forgotten him and made up an entirely other you …
WOMAN:	… a happy one …
MAN:	… who, as a child, skipped along the lane and caught the sun under her chin with that buttercup … the one whose imaginary lover marinated himself in the honeyed nectar of her life-force … whose children gathered round them at the beginning and the end of each day … as if their presence banished time … that one …
WOMAN:	… the happy one …
MAN:	… the one my remorseless unpicking never left space for … amongst the interminable trial of words … to appear as a mere image in your own head, let alone to simply come into being. You hate me, for the lives loving me meant you could not live. You're sorry, but that is just how you sometimes feel … while looking longingly at me …
WOMAN:	… in some idle moment …
MAN:	… when it seems that time is without succession and all is suspended … looking at me … me looking at you … you are overcome by all the other lives you ought to have lived. No mercy then for lovers. No end to torment in love's blisses. Even then … in the heat … to think of what else might have been … in whose arms else you could have languished. Even there in the depths of our embrace … which we two …
WOMAN:	… only of all the multitude …
MAN:	… can … must … share … where all the differentiating seems to be resolved … all the separatenesses joined … all the incompletenesses made whole …
WOMAN:	… what dread …
MAN:	… that there in that embrace of love we re-enact our own worlds … two apart … two alone. You whisper in my ear … forgive me, my one and only love …
WOMAN:	… my world …
MAN:	… my nowhere-else but here and now. My obligation and my choice. My destiny and my life.

[…]

2ᴺᴰ CIRCLE

WOMAN: Do you remember? I shall never forget. Where you there? The account of the death of a parent …
MAN: … or was it a lover?
WOMAN: … or a child … and how that cleft a body … my body … into three. It was as if I became three entirely differentiated beings. The one you would expect … the grieving child …
MAN: … lover …
WOMAN: … parent … traumatized to suffer this disappearance of the greatest source of love that could ever have been felt. The other standing there in the hospital ward … for let's say it happened there … cogitating on the mechanics of what would now need to be done … who would now need the unfailing support … the go-to for all the business that death drums up. And then … there was this third … this outsider … witnessing the scene as if from a distance … though right there in the room … a drone … with an unblinking stare … fascinated to be so close to another's final job. And it did not matter how very dear to me this parent … lover … child … had been … how much I had wished this time could have been indefinitely postponed … the curious one took their place in the room … jostled the other me's … but all of us separate … existing in distinct worlds … each with their own rhythm and mood somehow earthing into the main event. I cannot say … if these selves … because they felt more than parts … if these selves have come back together since. Maybe they had never been one. Maybe that was the illusion … the use of the first person … as if constant iteration would produce a one-and-only me …
MAN: … practice makes perfect.
WOMAN: Maybe up until that gouging, tearing passing, it had been possible to hold on to the fantasy … of me passing as myself … one passing cleaving another. Shall I ever be that old me again? Did I ever know who that was? And anyway I hear you say … what does any of it matter when death will undo us all before too long?

[…]

3ʳᴰ CIRCLE

WOMAN: You are …
MAN: … present …
WOMAN: … to me …
MAN: … now …
WOMAN: … absent though you are.
MAN: Present …
WOMAN: … in your blazing self …
MAN: … though surely gone.
WOMAN: Secure in here [INDICATE HEART].
MAN: Chattering away in here [EAR].
WOMAN: Filling this [HEAD] brim-full with occasions. Without you, I could not be.
MAN: My first … my one and only … is nothing without your second …
WOMAN: … without this one facing this other.
MAN: Without this coincidence, how could there be an instance?
WOMAN: And a place for that instance to happen in?
MAN: It's all measured here …
WOMAN: … in this in-between. Or at least …
MAN: … it all begins with us …
WOMAN: … the leap across the gap between one and two …
MAN: … the earthing and the projecting …
WOMAN: … the facing.
MAN: And though I guess I shall never really come to know who you are …
WOMAN: … this difference opens up all the possibilities of me …
MAN: … this forever asymmetry of you and me …
WOMAN: … which can never be settled …
MAN: … never accounted for …
WOMAN: … never truly and finally and fully answered …
MAN: … the asymmetry of that gesture of love …
WOMAN: … even of the recognition I have heard you cry or seen you wince in pain …
MAN: … even in that recognition no settlement …
WOMAN: … no community …
MAN: … searching in your looks …
WOMAN: … that offhand remark you made before you went upstairs …
MAN: … never done with …

WOMAN: … looking for the same in this difference …
MAN: … a different same.

[…]

WOMAN: What if you will never be fully present to me until you are gone?
MAN: That you take my being here …
WOMAN: … for granted.
MAN: Or that this being present is somehow lacking …
WOMAN: … not the real thing …
MAN: … not enough.
WOMAN: And so only in desertion or death …
MAN: … in the rupture of that loss …
WOMAN: … do you become there for me …
MAN: … in remembering I materialize …
WOMAN: … appear sitting in your chair …
MAN: … in the familiar way …
WOMAN: … appear.
MAN: But now … maybe …
WOMAN: … you are already a trick of the light …
MAN: … a fancy in the blur.
WOMAN: All the detail …
MAN: … all the decisions …
WOMAN: … the manner …
MAN: … just smoke and mirrors hiding the real show …
WOMAN: … that you are not actually here until you are no longer here …
MAN: … never in body … in flesh …
WOMAN: … only ever truly in this heart …
MAN: … or traces of electrical activity amongst the synapses of your brain.
WOMAN: Imagine if that were true.
MAN: So, all this would only be a rehearsal for the main event … my going …
WOMAN: … the parting.
MAN: But necessary, of course. Because without that stuff …
WOMAN: … the comings and goings …
MAN: … the downtime …
WOMAN: … the hopes etc …
MAN: … the practical existence …
WOMAN: … without all that, there would be no mutuality …

MAN: … no heartache …
WOMAN: … no joy … when you have finally gone …
MAN: … as I must surely finally go …
WOMAN: … and only then you will oblige me to feel you alongside in the room …
MAN: … I will appear to you …
WOMAN: … like that first time …
MAN: … when I was all unknown …
WOMAN: … all future …
MAN: … all possibility to you.
WOMAN: All relations henceforward relate to that relation …
MAN: … me and you …
WOMAN: … in that room … more present now …
MAN: … years on …
WOMAN: … than then.
MAN: More present with each succeeding day as those other possibilities …
WOMAN: … manifolded within it …
MAN: … fail to materialize …
WOMAN: … fall on the slippery surface of our everyday …
MAN: … as fact and history swarm around …
WOMAN: … to crowd us out of this present …
MAN: … with what can never now be done …
WOMAN: … so, the presence of that first look returned …
MAN: … becomes …
WOMAN: … more real …
MAN: … more felt than feeling …
WOMAN: … more alive than life.

47

Making and Breaking, Failing and Faking

MORVEN MACBETH

MORVEN MACBETH is an actor, theatre-maker and facilitator based in Scotland. She is an Associate Practitioner with the UK theatre company imitating the dog, whose work explores the boundaries between theatre and technology. Morven has toured extensively both nationally and internationally, performing as well as facilitating workshop programmes and leading residencies. Her other work in theatre includes Opening Skinner's Box *(Improbable),* Bring the Happy *(Invisible Flock) and* Called to Account *(Tricycle Theatre).* Life Class *was her first project with Bodies in Flight.*

Here, Morven writes about her experience of making and performing Life Class.

As an actor and theatre-maker, I like to think that I am cast in certain roles or asked to join a company for a project because I am a good collaborator. If the creative process has an emphasis on, and value given to, welcoming each person into the space (whether that's a rehearsal room, a dance studio, or a table read-through of a play text), whether you're an actor, a sound designer, a non-professional participant joining a project, then that's where I am my best self. *Life Class* was my first time being invited to work with Bodies in Flight, specifically with co-artistic directors Sara Giddens and Simon Jones, and with their long-term collaborator Graeme Rose. I had worked with Graeme before, on an imitating the dog show called *The Zero Hour*, so knew him not only to be a wonderful actor but also someone for whom the collaborative process is key.

Interrupted by the pandemic, we made the show first in 2019 in Nottingham, and then again in Preston in 2021. I found myself in a beautiful sunlit studio in the Dance4 building in the centre of Nottingham, taking our first read-through of the text. It was unlike any text I had worked with before: deeply poetic, richly layered, complex, funny and moving. In my experience, creative projects come to a person, as a maker, contributor, participant or audience member: they meet us at a particular moment in our lives. I was at a point in my own life where I was reflecting on what a partnership between two people means, questioning my understanding of where love fits into that, what kind of love that might be (thank you, bell hooks) and what the wrecking ball of grief does to any and all of that philosophical stuff anyway. The stories I was interested in as a theatre-maker (and audience member) were changing, and I came to *Life Class* with new curiosities. As a writer, Simon is incredibly generous and open when working with performers; and we talked and read and talked some more, slowly interrogating the text and the voices therein. It struck me that this process was not so much about building characters, but rather a matter of feeling one's way, as a performer, inside a rich and complex structure, and together giving voice to this poetic, discursive, philosophical study of life and death, of what it is to be in relation to, in relationship with, another.

The dialogue between flesh and text is, of course, central to the company's work; and the two must necessarily develop in a unison which steadily reveals itself. The layers of Simon's text began folding their way into Sara's intricate choreography, as we opened up the conversation into its own physicality, its own rising and falling, its own muscularity. This choreographic language was developed around established sequences from social dances, in particular the tango. Learning to tango on one's own, positioned in the space metres away from Graeme as we circled each other, was an exercise in shedding completely what my body 'knew', and creating something recognizable as a couple's dance, but now simultaneously broken and united, disjointed and synergetic. Sara and Simon's vocabulary, developed over 30 years of making live performance together, comes into its own, one director giving way to the other, one process embracing the other, layer upon layer, wrapping around the other, much like learning a new choreography, having danced together for years.

So, having reached a certain point in the development of the piece, how would we invite six social dancers into the room, all completely new to making theatre performance? Graeme and Sara had already been working with and getting to know the participants who had agreed to be part of the project, interviewing them about their experience of dance, what part it had played throughout their lives, as well as joining in and dancing with them in their weekly sessions at the Nottingham Mechanics Institute. Alongside all of this, the company recorded each dancer, through film and audio, so that their movement and voices could offer further visual and aural layers to the final production and associated outputs.

Meeting the dancers, whose average age was around 70, at their social club for the first time was such a warm, welcoming experience. They were delighted to see Graeme again and made me feel at home immediately, inviting us to dance with them, chat and have a cuppa. Introducing myself around the room, what struck me in the conversations was how important dancing was to each person. For some couples, it was often central to how they met, at a dance when they were in their early twenties; and it was something they had always enjoyed together, becoming a regular fixture in their social lives now they were both retired. For others, they had met their partner, in dance and in romance, at this very club, only recently. For the women who came to dance without a male partner (and in this context, it was nearly always women), they found friendship and a ready acceptance of dancing in either role, leading or following. Of the verbatim texts, which were integral to the success of *Life Class* as a piece of live performance, I grew particularly fond of the way in which dancing (and married) couple Barry and Betty's recorded voices punctuated what we called the 'First Circle'. The audience is being guided into the world of the show, and Graeme as Man has just opened with an exquisitely vicious diatribe, delivered to Beth, one of the social dancers from the club, seated in the space opposite him, very deliberately having lowered her head as the Man started to speak. The final line of this opening speech follows:

MAN: I have staked my life on an invention … this bubble … let me pop you … you over there … silent … moody … disgruntled … unhappy you.

At this moment, I enter the space, wearing an outdoor coat, and walk at speed across it, stopping very suddenly. Beth and I look at each other. Neither of us looks at Man. I turn and exit the space, resuming my pace, and Beth again lowers her head. We hear the disembodied voices of Barry and Betty, laughing about what they call 'the domestics', the arguments that occasionally flare up on the dancefloor at the club:

BARRY: A lot of them used to have domestics … where you don't do it right, the wife … you don't do it right, I'm not coming with you anymore … and we used to be there, and you stood on me toe once … so I took me shoe off, threw it in middle of the hall and said if you want to get in me shoes, you can have 'em … and they all used to laugh …
BETTY: If we went wrong, we used to laugh …

BARRY:	... and that's how we dealt with it. We've never really had a domestic.
BETTY:	No.
BARRY:	If we go wrong, we laugh. But some of 'em ... you've done it wrong ... you know ... but that got 'em when we threw the shoe in the middle, didn't it?

At this fragile stage in any piece of live performance, as an audience is grappling with 'the rules' of the show and instinctively seeking out boundaries, offering up the space to laugh is often vital, and in the case of *Life Class*, it gifted us immediate access to the humour, albeit often darker in nature, threaded through the piece.

Something that came up again and again was how 'ordinary' they considered themselves and their dancing to be, that this was just a part of their lives week in, week out, just something they did, really no big deal. And talking to them, and later performing with them, I had to agree on one level: dancing, moving their bodies to music, was indeed something they just did. What was extraordinary to me was the palpable joy just beaming from them when they danced, both with each other and as part of a company of performers, working with Sara, Simon, Graeme and me in the rehearsal room and in the performance space, as they became an integral part of the production. This relationship between the apparently 'ordinary' and 'extraordinary' is at the centre of Sara's choreographic work with Bodies in Flight, how what we might consider to be everyday gestures, the tiniest of seemingly involuntary or habitual movements, can reveal, amplify and expose so much. This resonated with Nick Cave's recently published conversations with journalist Seán O'Hagan – *Faith, Hope and Carnage*:

> The luminous and shocking beauty of the everyday is something I try to remain alert to, if only as an antidote to the chronic cynicism and disenchantment that seems to surround everything these days. It tells me that, despite how debased or corrupt we are told humanity is and how degraded the world has become, it just keeps on being beautiful. It can't help it.
> (2022: 30)

As a performer, I was both fascinated and profoundly impacted by the ways in which the older dancers' bodies moved; their energy, their skill, their instincts and how our bodies change as we age. As I reflect upon the process of making *Life Class* and the participants we worked so closely with, I think of my own body changing, from my five-year-old self, a wee girl playing with puppets and making up dances and stories in the Highlands of Scotland, my body as a teenager discovering contemporary dance, and my body now as an actor in my mid-forties and its resilience, its strength, its memories. And yes, its aches and pains and griefs. It strikes me how utterly unique we all are, and yet broadly the same. Our stories, our desires, our triumphs, our failures, our weaknesses, our wonder: the common ground is always there to be found and to be shared, and this surely is what brings us back, time and again, and in spite of its obvious shortcomings, to the theatre.

References

Cave, Nick and O'Hagan, Seán (2022), *Faith, Hope and Carnage*, Edinburgh and London: Canongate Books.

hooks, bell (2001), *All About Love: New Visions*, New York: HarperCollins.

Further Reading

Bailes, Sara Jane (2010), *Performance Theatre and the Poetics of Failure*, London: Routledge.

Samuel, Julia (2017), *Grief Works*, London: Penguin Life.

Van Der Kolk, Bessel (2014), *The Body Keeps the Score*, New York and London: Penguin Books.

48

The Dare of Other Voices – From Verbatim to Co-creation

SIMON JONES

In this Flight, I explore what happens when the closed loop of our devising methodology is opened out to working with non-professional participants. I reflect on how our principle of opening up and dwelling in the gaps amongst the different kinds of material in the performance was strengthened through co-creation with participants from different groups; how their very presence on stage roots the work and its unconcealing of everydayness into a specific lived community, becoming an intensification of the necessary trust between performer and auditor-spectator. I talk about how the dare and risk entailed in stepping out on stage is differently experienced by the participant as opposed to the performer; and how the participant's trust in us as collaborators must be answered by me as a writer. I conclude by proposing that such co-created performance affords art a new kind of political efficacy.

> Preserving the work means standing within the openness of beings that happens in the work. This 'standing-within' of preservation, however, is a knowing. [...] He who truly knows beings knows what he wills to do in the midst of them. [...] [T]he essence of *Existenz* is out-standing standing-within the essential sunderance of the clearing of beings.
> (Heidegger 1978: 192, original emphasis)

In Chapter 13, 'Speaking in Texts', I describe a relationship between writer and performer: my job is to find expressions, to phrase my feelings and thoughts, sometimes pushing the limits of what might be possible to perform; the performer's to find a way of communicating those expressions to an audience. Ideally, I would write with no audience in mind, no aim or teleology; the performer would seek to commune with their audience. All this would be achieved in the privacy of the rehearsal space, made public only after intensive effort and reflection. This Flight explores what happens when the closed loop of this devising methodology is opened out to working with non-professional participants, and so, profoundly altered and enriched. We began opening our process to other voices because the situation required it: in *Skinworks*, the chatroom environment was invoked by video clips of remote participants variously presenting real or fictionalized 'online' posts; in *Model Love*, posts from dating sites were integrated verbatim, that is — exactly as they were written, into the text and used as song lyrics.

The textual contributions from these others, often explicitly outside the process of making, helped audiences move from their own worlds into the work's situation: what might otherwise be alienating and off-putting was approached gently by way of 'relatable' soundbites. They solved the problem of how to induce, literally — lead the audience into the work, a bridge between their everyday and the performance: for instance, *Who By Fire*, with its exploration of mortality, opens with the performers re-telling stories of absurd deaths that they had heard, their rhythm and easy interchange, the gentleness of their voices, readily evoking the feeling of a party winding up around the kitchen table in the early hours of the morning. Then with *Dream→Work*, an ambulatory, place-specific performance, we found ourselves forced to go further with this inclusion of others' voices: our original focus — the anonymity and interchangeability of so-called 'global city' spaces with their international technocratic workforce — quickly encountered locals questioning what we were doing on 'their' streets. They wanted to share with us anecdotes and concerns anchored in the specificity of where we were walking. Our process was obliged to respond to this appearance and insistence of the 'other': we collected these oral histories of each locale where the work was sited and integrated them into the flow of action and text in each performance walk. In this way, the work was surprisingly and progressively transformed from being about the anonymous (work-)space of late capitalism to the embedded experiences of inhabitants: *Dream→Work* became *Dream→Walk*.

In these situations, the collaborators became dialoguers — interviewers, using their skills at communicating — communing with their audiences, either as performers, sound artists or video-makers, to find a shared language with the participant, soliciting their feelings and thoughts, gathering their memories and hopes. As a writer, my job became twofold: to be the interlocutor between their expressions and our audiences; and then to find the resonances between those expressions and my own text. Ethically, the first was primarily a matter of respect; the second was a question of wills. I respected their participation by using their expressions word for word – verbatim, but organizing them in a way that invited the wider audience to find easy points of reference, such as grouping soundbites thematically, or giving an anecdote space for its context and relevance to unfold. Then I sequenced them alongside my text so that insights involved in both resonated as deeply as possible. At this point in the process, I did not meet the participants in person, because I found it helped this task if I was not distracted by the 'noise' of personal interaction. I could use the alienating medium of audio recordings to listen to what they said as if I were an audience member hearing it for the first time in performance – not dissimilar to the job I asked of performers encountering my text. My ethical responsibility towards these interviewees reversed the 'carelessness' with which I usually treated the audience when writing my own text: what I felt was the intent and truth of their words had to be conveyed in the most unambiguous manner.

With our next project – *Gymnast*, we extended our devising process to co-create the work with élite and amateur gymnasts, to devise in their spaces, and variously present the work in galleries, theatres and gymnasia. Through an extended series of workshop sessions with the gymnasts at their training sessions, video-maker Tony Judge explored a range of video material from fly-on-the-wall documentary to staged-for-camera routines to to-camera interviews. Again, I began alone with this interview material, before actually meeting the participants in person. This allowed me to acknowledge the deeper force of their expressions, how their hopes and passions speak out, often in the smallest phrase, or hesitancy, or unguarded exuberance, which I then juxtaposed with the signature of my own text: for instance, the athletes' precise insights into their training regime, the underpinning optimism of their ambition, set alongside acapella songs whose lyrics explored how the spectator idealizes the gymnast's capabilities. These two mutually exclusive points of view were jointly created: the down-to-earth pragmatism, delivered by these teenage athletes in the conventions and decorum of video-interview soundbites, in relation to the live choir, singing about the impossibility of achieving a perfect routine, of bodies being absolutely still, bodies defying gravity (see Chapter 36, 'Finding Suspension').

Thus, the work opened up a space between the video and the song, the lone gymnast/protagonist and the choir/polis, for the audience to dwell on the relationship between the everyday and the sublime, the resilience and the dare. Each different kind of text, verbatim – lyric, is voiced differently in different media, each expressing themselves fully in their own way: neither could be read off against the other, because each opened up their own perspective on the gymnast, from the inside of the athlete's practice and from the outside of the spectator's gaze. I think of this as a 'contestation' of wills, not in the common-sense way of one will dominating another, but how Heidegger describes art, in which wills strive in their differences to produce clearer and more intense expressions of themselves.

> In setting up a world and setting forth the earth, the [art]work is an instigating of [...] strife [where 'opponents raise each other into the self-assertion of their essential natures [...] each opponent carries the other beyond itself' (1978: 174)]. This does not happen so that the work should at the same time settle and put an end to strife by an insipid argument, but so that the strife may remain a strife. [...] It is because the strife arrives at its high point in the simplicity of intimacy that the unity of the work comes about in the instigation of strife.
> ([1936] 1978: 175, my gloss)

By combining text with verbatim, Bodies in Flight's developing methodology responded to the so-called 'participatory turn' in the arts more generally, becoming with every project more a co-creating between professional artists and community participants. However, unlike many artists, who quite properly attend to questions of issues, rights, justice and fairness, that is, *how to become a citizen*, we became interested in a problem that both precedes our daily necessity to act as citizens and exceeds it: *how to become a person*. At a time when structurally the artist is being co-opted into a state function, intended to placate mainly marginalized communities and eventually pacify their complaints, we realized that co-creation provided us with new opportunities to affirm our manifesto from our beginnings in 1990 (see Chapter 6, '*Love Is …*'): namely, that art's unique work is to express the problem of the person, since art is the only place in civil society where the person can appear *publicly* and talk about its problems. In all other places, even on the psychoanalyst's couch, it must appear as the citizen, concerned or anarchic; it can only have an opinion with respect to the social, its 'place' in the world. Whereas art alone expresses the person's genuine solitariness, who does not necessarily crave nor need a civil bond.

With our next work – *Life Class*, we sought a more involved co-creation by bringing together professional performers (Morven Macbeth and Graeme Rose) and amateur social dancers at the outset of the devising, with the explicit focus on their community of senior social dancers: here their skills were not at stake, but the part dance played in their lives, their health and well-being, and beyond that – their reflections on love and relationships. Dance was both metaphor and weekly practice. Alongside this, as a dramaturg, I had wanted to return to the stage, after our previous works being on the streets or in gymnasia or galleries: specifically, I wanted to respond to Marina Abramovic's *The Artist Is Present* (MOMA, New York, 2010) and her claim that it was not 'theatrical'. We began by replicating her 'non-theatrical' set-up: artist – participant face-to-face in a gallery before a crowd of visitors, with our own theatrical set-up: performer–participant on stage before spectators. In this set-up, we placed the situation of a couple of social dancers who confront the history of their marriage, but in reverse, starting at its bitter end, and ending in its blissful beginning across a dance floor. Within this set-up/situation, the social dancers would participate throughout the devising process and in performance *as themselves, as persons.*

In Lakeside Arts (Nottingham), this was literally personified by Beth Holland, organizer of the Nottingham Osteoporosis Dancing Club, walking onto the empty stage and opening the show, with audience on both sides as they would have been in the club's weekly sessions. In doing this action, standing alone centre stage, her courage produced a tension with her physical frailty, which Graeme's entrance and assured actions *as artist* amplified. She directed Graeme to set the chairs and take her coat, and Neil Johnson (sound artist) to start the track of verbatim reminiscences. As they sat facing one another, Graeme *performed* the first text of bitter recrimination, calling Beth 'a spook', and she simply and magnificently responded by appearing *as person.* His performed challenge was met with her lived dare. In this most simple of theatrical situations, the face-to-face, *Life Class* answered *performing* with *being.* We wove the highly crafted dialogue between Graeme and Morven with the participants' oral histories of social dance in their youth, as well as the health benefits of dance as exercise. In the 'Second Circle', we heard the social dancer's powerful, simple statements on the loss of partners, widowhood and living with grieving, as they silently stood there on stage. Against which, Morven spoke a text imagining a partner's death and the irreversible impact of grief: the fictional set alongside the actual; the experienced working alongside the imagined: (again) both retained their own voices and in consort intensified one another's insights in a direct and mutually respectful dignity.

If the problem of the person is *occasioned* by society, by acting as a citizen, provoked into realizing it has this problem with its personhood by the inevitable *mixing with other persons*, then, this is not about 'becoming an individual' or 'expressing one's self' or 'achieving one's potential'. The individual is, of course, a social construct whose appearance shows how the social shifts its frames of reference from time to time, in order to provide an easily graspable, ready-to-hand solution for everyday living. No, finally, *the person is not an individual*, describable by way of class, ethnicity, gender, sexuality or body-mass: *a person is a style*; and the problem of the person is precisely how to realize and *sustain* a style amongst the competing styles of others who make up their world. One particular juxtaposition of styles from *Life Class* marked how the appearance of the person on stage (in an artwork) obliges us to confront the limitations of the social: two couples sat at the sides facing each other, practically occupying the audience's point of view, Graeme – Morven, Barry Winship – Betty Winship. Barry suddenly interrupts the text with an off-the-cuff anecdote about witnessing couples on the dance floor having a 'domestic', an obvious comment on the 'dramatic' recriminations being played out. His untrained and unamplified voice required the audience to lean into what he was saying; his conversational register contrasted with the performers' crafted and amplified text. The dialoguing as an opening-up of space(iousness) between artist and participant was made explicit in both set-up and situation: his authenticity, as in his presenting his own personhood, at ease *in the set-up*, wise *about the situation*, all the more telling alongside the artist's performed craft.

In *Life Class*, by combining verbatim and text, in the co-presence of artists and participants, their appearing face-to-face, performing facing being, we felt we were approaching how performance allows the person to appear before the citizen: *before* in two senses: in front of them, standing suddenly before them *in space* – performer and social-dancer; and preceding them, having a life previous, before them *in time* – the rewound narrative of married life and the deep reminiscences of social worlds now lost to us. We learnt that by opening up the privacy of our devising to these others, together we are able to make a performance that exceeds the theatrical and obliges us to attend to *the person in society*: the person on stage dares us citizens to shed our civil protection and, as a gathering, approach this (new) person *as persons*, each solitary in the crowd, encouraged to find our own way – Beth centre stage. So, in performance, we pose the problem of personhood in this particular way, not only *before* the citizen, but *amongst* citizens: the temporary disruption of a dare before returning to the everyday, but not quite in the same way, that is, with a style now not quite one's own, or rather, one's own style obliged to answer the call and tremble at the touch of another's – the person-to-person of the human. Fittingly, *Life Class* concludes with a dance lesson for anyone from the audience who wants to participate: unsurprisingly, everyone joins in!

References

Heidegger, Martin ([1936] 1978), 'The origin of the work of art', in D. Farrell Krell (ed.), *Basic Writings*, London: Routledge, Kegan & Paul.

49
Unbox Me! (2023)

Figure **49.1**: *Unbox Me!*: performer Graeme Rose. Video still: Jacob Rose.

PUBLICITY COPY

This brand-new work-in-progress – Unbox Me! *begins at that moment when a parcel arrives at your door: will its contents live up to your expectations? Fulfil the functions required of it? Maybe even your dreams? Dare you open it to find out? In this one-person show, Bodies in Flight continue their innovative, visceral and playful exploration of identity in our contemporary world of next-day delivery and endless credit, life as consumption or life as metaverse.*

Responding to a commission by the Department of Theatre, as part of the seventy-fifth-anniversary celebrations of the founding of the Department of Drama at the University of Bristol, *Unbox Me!* depicts a 'typical' 'gig worker', a delivery driver, returning to his run-down lodgings after a long shift. Surrounded by opened parcels, he tries to make contact with a remote family and world through his mobile phone: he cannot; so, he streams the plaintive sounds of Patsy Cline's *Crazy* – the whole world is, indeed, at his fingertips. Then he notices an unopened package, and the piece shifts through a series of performance modes and frames, culminating in a fierce, anarchic, solitary dance of defiance. *Unbox Me!* exemplified the benefits of holding our non-collaboration open over an extended series of projects (see Chapter 28 'Being In-Between: Collaboration as Non-collaboration'): its complexity and richness issuing directly from our methodology amongst long-term collaborators, resulting in an endless capacity to transform and become anew, *to live again.*

SARA GIDDENS dramaturgy, SIMON JONES direction/text, GRAEME ROSE performer, BRUCE SHARP lighting/video rig, FRANCESCO BENTIVEGNA sound design.

With: TIM ATACK music re-recording (original song music ANGEL TECH/lyrics SIMON JONES), BETH BRANSOME theatre technician, ELLEN HEALY theatre intern, TONY JUDGE video editing, JACOB ROSE video camera.

Performed: Wickham Theatre (Bristol).

Bodies in Flight

Afterword
PAUL RUSS

PAUL RUSS *is artistic director and chief executive of FABRIC, the Midlands dance development organization formed by the merger of Dance4 in Nottingham and DanceXchange in Birmingham in 2022. He holds responsibility for the strategic and artistic direction of FABRIC, including the realization of Nottdance and Birmingham International Dance festival, and a wide range of artist and art-form development programmes and strategic training and engagement activities.*

Here he reflects on his thirty-year friendship with Bodies in Flight, as witness, mentee, commissioner and presenter.

I hear reflections about bodies … bodies that have been watched in flight …

I carry so many nerves, anticipation, unknowns. I'm welcomed by bodies that are in tandem … connected … in love … in fear … in a dance. I must watch it. A young eager mind exploded by the complex modes in which this work, *Do the Wild Thing!* (1996 – Now Festival, Nottingham) confronts me. Only reading about such work before, only dreaming I would see it. Well, I'm suddenly thrown into an experience that explodes my brain, confuses and stimulates my body. I throw perceptions out of the window and witness. I feel looked after, confronted by the intimacy, challenged by a new kind of dancing. I knew I was forming new thoughts about what I could do and what I might want to say.

Almost thirty years ago, gulp. I carry with me the work, feelings, energy and the name.

I find myself in a lift in Derby. An invitation to witness the emerging ideas of a new performance – *Dream→Work* (2009). I listen to complements about my blue shoes. I'm sampling new ideas, early thoughts and actions. I have that wonderful buzz (I always feel) when trusted to be with artists and ideas at such an early stage. I acknowledge my influence in this moment. I realize it feels a little weird, a place that requires me to really care and be my most open. I know this company: now I'm in this moment with them.

If you've not been to Skeggy, then my advice is: go, you'll have a lovely day. As a child, I enjoyed many family holidays there. But today I'm here for a new iteration of *Dream→Walk* (2012). I'm following this man, an out-of-the-ordinary man for the town centre. Those of us following this man do so with intrigue and excitement. Hearing the familiar, seeing the strange and absurd, smelling chips and the sea. We rest on the sand and watch him enter the sea. We weep, we miss him ... But he's still there.

In 2013, as a commissioning partner in the Collaborative Doctoral Project of Sara Giddens, I've been invited into the temporary studio we currently occupy at Dance4. I'm welcomed to dwell some more. Gurgling pipes, mats, blankets and cushions. We talk about the experience of quiet, suspension, of silence and violence. The deep joy and fear in pausing ... actively waiting ... dwelling. I jump with glee, with giggles, with nerves. I'm with my friend and mentor ... a continual inspiration and guide. I leave with joy.

I am grateful for Bodies in Flight being a constant presence in my life. Their thirst to reveal the unknown perspective, to explore perception through a collaborative enquiry that expanded my perspectives as a student whilst at Nottingham Trent University in the 1990s. Sara cared for our young minds and bodies. Importantly for me, she enabled me to be with and in vulnerable conversations with artists and participants in a creative process.

With the heaviest heart, I acknowledge that Sara has now passed away and this wonderful collaboration has come to a sad and abrupt end. However, the experiences both Sara and Simon have created over three decades continue to challenge, inform and influence my purpose, my approach and continue to contribute to a curatorial approach and body of work. Sara and Simon, your collaboration made and continues to have a profound impact on me and, I trust, others too. I'm struck by the tenacious spirit in which you carefully nurtured ideas, imaginatively collaborated and were able to hold and explore uncertainty. A gracious ambition that realized wonderful genre-defying work.

As a curator and a custodian of an archive that I have the privilege to evolve, I've been delighted to further a personal connection to the work of Bodies in Flight, and to professionally continue to cite their practice in the programmes of dance emanating from Dance4 and its partners. I've seen work from many artists, invited research and presented choreographic works co-created with non-professionals, building a body of work and an organizational archive that strives to embolden the public through dance. Bodies in Flight has brought their open-hearted and collaborative practice to the heart of our curatorial practice. Their artworks draw their structure, poetics and narrative from the breadth of community voices and relationships that they nurture and celebrate. Our collaboration, the challenge and trust we have developed, informs my personal and organizational approach in holding dialogues, making invitations and critiquing ideas that result in more voices being central to the creation, realization and sharing of choreographic/ dance works at Dance4, now FABRIC. We are an organization that has and will continue to value ideas that place curiosity, disruption and joy at the centre of work we bring about with artists and communities. Bodies in Flight has no doubt paved the way for more to be possible now and in the future for our organization and for the field.

Long before the funding system saw and recognized the value of creating space for the voice of the non-professional to inform the ideas, research and artworks that shape the cultural offer in communities across the country, Bodies in Flight has been inviting, listening, facilitating, embedding and revealing the voices and lives of communities here in Nottingham, across the United Kingdom and beyond. *Dream→Walk, Gymnast* and *Life Class* are life-changing experiences for their non-professional collaborators. The work they have created and shared holds a contemporary relevance, beautifully informing us about lives at the beginning, somewhere through and at the later stages of life, showing what they believe counts and how they wish to care and be together.

In my opinion, there is clearly still more for the company to do. However, let's take a breath and acknowledge that their contribution has brought wonder and challenge to many. I see how their work expands what dance is and means to people, how their non-professional co-creators think about dance and feel heard. I see practices that activate public discourses, bring people and lives together, who might never meet, let alone be friends. For many years, Bodies in Flight have been unpacking ideas and approaches now more common in dance and performance: how important this is.

I'm honoured to have the opportunity to contribute in a very small way to this moment and to have been privileged to present work from Bodies in Flight to audiences in Nottingham and the Midlands. This book is a testament to the strength of the work they have created over more than thirty years, and to their contribution to the fields of dance, choreography, performance, new writing and theatre.

Figure P.1: *Life Class*: performers Morven Macbeth and Graeme Rose. Photo: Scott Sawyer.

Postscript

SIMON JONES

Just as we were finishing work on this book, having reflected on the many projects we had done together since 1990, my dear collaborator Sara Giddens died. I cannot write what that loss means to me, but I can let this book, and particularly the words she wrote, speak to that wonderful time working together on making performance. We began this book with an image taken during work on *Constants*: one of very few we have of us in the act of collaborating. In 1997, the world of making small-scale experimental performance seemed rich and full of possibilities: the Arts Council readily funded work focused on developing the art form; there were many promoters and venues in both major cities and small towns ready to take a chance on a relatively unknown company; and as importantly, there were audiences prepared to experience new work with fresh ideas. Now, in 2025, that ecology does not appear so robust: audiences are starved of opportunities to experience new work outside of occasional festivals; and there is only a patchy, underfunded infrastructure to nurture and support the new, emerging generation of performance-makers, let alone sustain the careers of experienced artists. So, making this kind of work becomes even more an act of both faith and will: despite this, we hope this book has inspired you to such acts.

Returning to an image first conjured in Andrew Quick's 'Foreword' and variously throughout this book, it seems fitting to end with Sheila's final text from *Constants*, as she sits in the dead centre of the shared performance space:

> She will have said when the time comes, do you think me will turn in on itself, like the patterning of a shell? Like all nature goes that way. Turn and turn in, ever inwards. And never arrive. So maybe me like so. Me gets so small it cannot be seen, cannot be felt in the room. And keeps turning in on its own deep space, keeping me me, as this flesh fails, must surely fail, and you pronounce me dead and cry for me, who suddenly gets so small I cannot be measured, but must be assumed, in the minds of those who loved me, still to remain somewhere elsewhere untouchable, as theoretical me. So tiny I am, to all intents and purposes, and for all considerate hearts, everywhere.

Bodies in Flight

Figures

F.1:	*Constants* rehearsal (Arnolfini, Bristol): Patricia Breatnach, David Gilbert, Darren Bourne, Sheila Gilbert, Caroline Rye, Sara Giddens and Simon Jones. Photo: Edward Dimsdale.	xii
2.1:	*Deadplay*: performer Barnaby Power. Photograph: courtesy of Bodies in Flight.	12
2.2:	*Deadplay*: poster. Courtesy of the University of Bristol Theatre Collection.	13
2.3:	*Deadplay*: performers Justin O'Shaughnessy and Barnaby Power. Image from contact sheet courtesy of the University of Bristol Theatre Collection.	14
2.4:	*Deadplay* VHS video still: performers Justin O'Shaughnessy, Rachel Feuchtwang, Barnaby Power and Martin Plunkett. Image: Tony Judge.	14
2.5:	*Deadplay*: opening page of the performance score. Image courtesy of the University of Bristol Theatre Collection.	15
4.1:	*Exhibit*: performers featuring Lucy Baldwyn. Photo: Jon Carnall.	20
4.2:	*Exhibit*: poster. Courtesy of the University of Bristol Theatre Collection.	21
4.3:	*Exhibit*: performers featuring Charlotte Watkins. Photo: Jon Carnall.	22
4.4:	*Exhibit*: performers Lucy Baldwyn and Barnaby Power. Photo: Jon Carnall.	22
4.5:	*Exhibit*: performers featuring Lucy Baldwyn. Photo: Jon Carnall.	23
4.6:	*Exhibit*: performers Charlotte Watkins, Simon Pegg, Lucy Baldwyn and Chris Ratcliff. Photo: Jon Carnall.	23
6.1:	*Love Is Natural and Real but Not for You my Love*: performers Justin O'Shaughnessy, Katherine Porter and Ursula Lea. Photo: Lucy Baldwyn.	26
6.2:	*Love Is Natural and Real but Not for You my Love*: postcard. Courtesy of the University of Bristol Theatre Collection.	27
6.3:	*Love Is Natural and Real but Not for You my Love* 'energy graph'. Image courtesy of the University of Bristol Theatre Collection.	28

6.4:	*Love Is Natural and Real but Not for You my Love*: performers Justin O'Shaughnessy, Ursula Lea, Katherine Porter and Nitin Chandra Ganatra. Photo: Lucy Baldwyn.	28
6.5:	*Love Is Natural and Real but Not for You my Love*: performers Nitin Chandra Ganatra, Katherine Porter, Ursula Lea and Justin O'Shaughnessy. Photo: Lucy Baldwyn.	29
8.1:	*iwannabewolfman*: performers Simon Pegg, Charlotte Watkins, Lucy Baldwyn and Barnaby Power. Photo: Edward Dimsdale.	38
8.2:	*iwannabewolfman*: poster artwork. Courtesy of the University of Bristol Theatre Collection.	39
8.3:	*iwannabewolfman*: performers Charlotte Watkins, Barnaby Power and Lucy Baldwyn. Photo: Edward Dimsdale.	40
8.4:	*iwannabewolfman*: performers Simon Pegg, Charlotte Watkins, Barnaby Power and Lucy Baldwyn. Photo: Edward Dimsdale.	40
8.5:	*iwannabewolfman*: performers Simon Pegg, Barnaby Power, Katherine Porter and Charlotte Watkins. Photo: Edward Dimsdale.	41
8.6:	*iwannabewolfman*: performers Charlotte Watkins, Barnaby Power, Simon Pegg and Lucy Baldwyn. Photo: Edward Dimsdale.	41
10.1:	*Rough*: performers Graeme Rose, Simon Pegg and Charlotte Watkins. Photo: Edward Dimsdale.	50
10.2:	*Rough*: postcard. Courtesy of the University of Bristol Theatre Collection.	51
10.3:	*Rough*: performers Graeme Rose, Katherine Porter, Simon Pegg and Charlotte Watkins. Photo: Edward Dimsdale.	52
10.4:	*Rough*: performers Graeme Rose, Simon Pegg, Charlotte Watkins and Katherine Porter. Photo: Edward Dimsdale.	52
10.5:	*Rough*: performers Simon Pegg and Graeme Rose. Photo: Edward Dimsdale.	53
10.6:	*Rough*: performers Katherine Porter, Simon Pegg and Charlotte Watkins. Photo: Edward Dimsdale.	53
14.1:	*Beautiful Losers*: performers Charlotte Watkins and Jon Carnall. Scan from original slide. Photo: Bridget Mazzey.	78
14.2:	*Beautiful Losers*: postcard. Courtesy of the University of Bristol Theatre Collection.	79
14.3:	*Beautiful Losers*: performers Charlotte Watkins and Jon Carnall. Scan from original slide. Photo: Bridget Mazzey.	80
14.4:	*Beautiful Losers*: performers Jon Carnall and Charlotte Watkins. Scan from original slide. Photo: Bridget Mazzey.	80

14.5: *Beautiful Losers*: performers Charlotte Watkins and Jon Carnall. Scan from original slide. Photo: Bridget Mazzey. — 81

14.6: *Beautiful Losers*: performer Jon Carnall. Scan from original slide. Photo: Bridget Mazzey. — 81

16.1: *Littluns Wake*: performers Jon Carnall and Charlotte Watkins. Photo: Edward Dimsdale. — 96

16.2: *Littluns Wake*: poster. Courtesy of the University of Bristol Theatre Collection. — 97

16.3: *Littluns Wake*: performer Charlotte Watkins. Photo: Edward Dimsdale. — 98

16.4: *Littluns Wake*: performer Jon Carnall. Photo: Edward Dimsdale. — 98

16.5: *Littluns Wake*: performer Dean Byfield. Photo: Edward Dimsdale. — 99

16.6: *Littluns Wake*: performers Dean Byfield and Jon Carnall. Scan from original slide. Photo: Bridget Mazzey. — 99

17.1: *Do the Wild Thing!*: performers Jane Devoy and Dan Elloway. Photo: Edward Dimsdale. — 104

17.2: *Do the Wild Thing!*: postcard. Courtesy of the University of Bristol Theatre Collection. — 105

17.3: *Do the Wild Thing!*: design ground plan of the stage by Bridget Mazzey. Courtesy of the University of Bristol Theatre Collection. — 106

17.4: *Do the Wild Thing!*: performers Jane Devoy and Dan Elloway. Photo: Edward Dimsdale. — 106

17.5: *Do the Wild Thing!*: performers Jane Devoy and Dan Elloway. Photo: Edward Dimsdale. — 107

17.6: *Do the Wild Thing!*: performers Jane Devoy, Dan Elloway and Jon Carnall. Photo: Edward Dimsdale. — 107

19.1: *Constants*: performer Sheila Gilbert. Photo: Edward Dimsdale. — 124

19.2: *Constants*: postcard. Courtesy of the University of Bristol Theatre Collection. — 125

19.3: *Constants*: performers Patricia Breatnach and Sheila Gilbert. Photo: Edward Dimsdale. — 126

19.4: *Constants*: performer Patricia Breatnach. Photo: Edward Dimsdale. — 126

19.5: *Constants*: sound artist Darren Bourne, performer Patricia Breatnach. Photo: Edward Dimsdale. — 127

19.6: *Constants*: performers Patricia Breatnach and Sheila Gilbert. Photo: Edward Dimsdale. — 127

21.1: *DeliverUs*: performers Mark Adams and Polly Frame. Photo: Edward Dimsdale. — 134

21.2: *DeliverUs*: postcard. Courtesy of the University of Bristol Theatre Collection.	135
21.3: *DeliverUs*: performers Mark Adams and Polly Frame. Photo: Edward Dimsdale.	136
21.4: *DeliverUs*: performers Mark Adams and Polly Frame. Photo: Edward Dimsdale.	136
21.5: *DeliverUs*: performer Polly Frame. Photo: Edward Dimsdale.	137
21.6: *DeliverUs*: performers Mark Adams and Polly Frame. Photo: Edward Dimsdale.	137
24.1: *Double Happiness*: performers Marianne Wee, Benjamin Clough, Dan Elloway and Kaylene Tan. Photo: Edward Dimsdale.	158
24.2: *Double Happiness*: postcard. Courtesy of the University of Bristol Theatre Collection.	159
24.3: *Double Happiness*: performer Marianne Wee. Photo: Edward Dimsdale.	160
24.4: *Double Happiness*: performers Marianne Wee and Benjamin Clough. Photo: Edward Dimsdale.	160
24.5: *Double Happiness*: sonic artist Chong Li Chuan, video operator Ben Davies, lighting operator Jessica Morris, performer Kaylene Tan. Photo: Edward Dimsdale.	161
24.6: *Double Happiness*: performers Marianne Wee and Dan Elloway. Photo: Edward Dimsdale.	161
25.1: *Beautiful Losers*: performers Gerald Chew, Kaylene Tan and musician George Chua. Photo courtesy of spell#7.	162
25.2: *Beautiful Losers*: performers Gerald Chew and Kaylene Tan. Photo courtesy of spell#7.	162
25.3: *Beautiful Losers*: performers Gerald Chew and Kaylene Tan. Photo courtesy of spell#7.	162
25.4: *Beautiful Losers*: performer Kaylene Tan. Photo courtesy of spell#7.	162
26.1: *Flesh & Text*: CD-ROM architecture schematic plan with handwritten annotations. Courtesy of the University of Bristol Theatre Collection.	168
26.2: *Flesh & Text*: CD-ROM cover. Courtesy of the University of Bristol Theatre Collection.	169
27.1: *Skinworks*: performer Polly Frame. Photo: Edward Dimsdale.	170
27.2: *Skinworks*: postcard. Courtesy of the University of Bristol Theatre Collection.	171
27.3: *Skinworks*: performers Polly Frame, Doug Bott, Tim Atack, Kaylene Tan and Neil Johnson. Photo: Edward Dimsdale.	172

27.4: *Skinworks*: performer Polly Frame. Photo: Edward Dimsdale. 172
27.5: *Skinworks*: performers Neil Johnson, Polly Frame and 173
Graeme Rose. Photo: Edward Dimsdale.
27.6: *Skinworks*: performer Kaylene Tan. Photo: Edward Dimsdale. 173
29.1: *Who By Fire*: performers Benjamin Clough, Tim Atack, 190
Doug Bott, Polly Frame and Graeme Rose.
Photo: Edward Dimsdale.
29.2: *Who By Fire*: postcard. Courtesy of the University of 191
Bristol Theatre Collection.
29.3: *Who By Fire*: performers Polly Frame, Neil Johnson, Doug 192
Bott, Benjamin Clough, Graeme Rose and Tim Atack.
Photo: Edward Dimsdale.
29.4: *Who By Fire*: performers Tim Atack and Benjamin Clough. 192
Photo: Edward Dimsdale.
29.5: *Who By Fire*: performer Graeme Rose. 193
Photo: Edward Dimsdale.
29.6: *Who By Fire*: performers Doug Bott, Neil Johnson, 193
Polly Frame, Graeme Rose and Tim Atack.
Photo: Edward Dimsdale.
31.1: *Triptych*: video montage. Still courtesy of Tony Judge. 202
31.2: *Triptych*: video montage. Still courtesy of Tony Judge. 202
31.3: *Triptych*: video montage. Still courtesy of Tony Judge. 202
33.1: *The Secrecy of Saints*: performer Polly Frame. 210
Photo: Edward Dimsdale.
33.2: *The Secrecy of Saints*: postcard. Courtesy of the University 211
of Bristol Theatre Collection.
33.3: *The Secrecy of Saints*: performers Polly Frame and 212
Neil Johnson. Photo: Edward Dimsdale.
33.4: *The Secrecy of Saints*: performers Neil Johnson and 212
Polly Frame. Photo: Edward Dimsdale.
33.5: *The Secrecy of Saints*: performer Polly Frame. 213
Photo: Edward Dimsdale.
33.6: *The Secrecy of Saints*: performers Polly Frame and 213
Neil Johnson. Photo: Edward Dimsdale.
34.1: *Model Love*: performer Tom Wainwright. 222
Photo: Edward Dimsdale.
34.2: *Model Love*: postcard. Courtesy of the University of 223
Bristol Theatre Collection.
34.3: *Model Love*: Book Two. Image courtesy of 224
Edward Dimsdale.
34.4: *Model Love*: performers Sam Halmarack, Graeme Rose, 224
Catherine Dyson and Tom Wainwright.
Photo: Edward Dimsdale.

34.5: *Model Love*: performers Sam Halmarack and Graeme Rose. Photo: Edward Dimsdale. — 225

34.6: *Model Love*: performers Tom Wainwright, Catherine Dyson and Graeme Rose. Photo: Edward Dimsdale. — 225

37.1: *iwannabewolfman*: performers Charlotte Watkins, Katherine Porter, Simon Pegg, Jon Carnall and Barnaby Power. Photo: Edward Dimsdale. — 244

37.2: *Skinworks*: contact sheets. Image courtesy of Edward Dimsdale. — 246

37.3: *Who By Fire*: performers Polly Frame, Doug Bott, Graeme Rose, Neil Johnson, Tim Atack and Benjamin Clough. Photo: Edward Dimsdale. — 247

37.4: *Model Love*: installation Battersea Arts Centre. Photo: Edward Dimsdale. — 249

37.5: *Model Love*: installation Battersea Arts Centre. Photo: Edward Dimsdale. — 250

37.6: *Model Love*: audience examining the books after the performance, Arnolfini. Photo: Edward Dimsdale. — 251

38.1: *Hymn*: performer Tom Wainwright. Video still courtesy of Tony Judge. — 254

38.2: *Hymn*: performer Tom Wainwright. Video still courtesy of Tony Judge. — 255

38.3: *Hymn*: performer Tom Wainwright. Video still courtesy of Tony Judge. — 255

39.1: *Dream→Walk* Wirksworth: performer Graeme Rose. Photo: Tony Judge. — 260

39.2: *Dream→Work* Singapore: route map. Courtesy of the University of Bristol Theatre Collection. — 262

39.3: *Dream→Work* Singapore: performers Sam Halmarack and Polly Frame. Photo: Yuen Chee Wai. — 262

39.4: *Dream→Work* Bristol: performer Tom Wainwright. Photo: Tina Remiz. — 263

39.5: *Dream→Walk* Skegness: performer Graeme Rose. Photo: Simon Jones. — 263

40.1: *Gymnast* Arnolfini: gymnasts Joshua Avallone, Nicole Andrew, Sophie Gaunt and Night Bus Choir singers. Photo: Tony Judge. — 264

40.2: *Gymnast*: poster. Courtesy of Tony Judge. — 265

40.3: *Gymnast* Rushcliffe Academy: hand-written score. Courtesy of the University of Bristol Theatre Collection. — 266

40.4: *Gymnast*: gymnast Joshua Avallone. Video still courtesy of Tony Judge. — 266

40.5:	*Gymnast* Surface Gallery: gymnast Joshua Avallone and Night Bus Choir singers. Photo: Tony Judge.	267
40.6:	*Gymnast* Mayfest: gymnast Joshua Avallone, Nicole Andrew, Sophie Gaunt and Night Bus Choir singers. Video still courtesy of Tony Judge.	267
43.1:	*Do the Wild Thing! Redux*: installation and performance. Photo: Tony Judge.	278
43.2:	*I'd Like to Call You Joe Tonight*: performer James D Kent. Still courtesy of Tony Judge.	278
43.3:	*Do the Wild Thing! Redux*: installation and performance combining *Muse*, performer Dan Elloway. Photo: Carl Newland.	278
44.1:	*Still Moving: Moving Still* Nottingham Contemporary: sited performance. Photo: Tony Judge.	280
44.2:	*Still Moving: Moving Still* Birmingham International Dance Festival: sited performance. Photo: Tony Judge.	280
44.3:	*Still Moving: Moving Still* Nottingham Contemporary: sited performance. Photo: Tony Judge.	280
46.1:	*Life Class*: performer Graeme Rose and participant Beth Holland. Photo: Scott Sawyer.	288
46.2:	*Life Class*: poster. Courtesy of Tony Judge.	289
46.3:	*Life Class*: performer Morven Macbeth, participant Barry Winship, performer Graeme Rose and participant Betty Winship. Photo: Scott Sawyer.	290
46.4:	*Life Class*: participants Barbara J Clark, Beth Holland, Colin Moore, Barry and Betty Winship, Sheila Sims, and performer Graeme Rose. Photo: Scott Sawyer.	290
46.5:	*Life Class*: performers Morven Macbeth and Graeme Rose. Photo: Scott Sawyer.	261
46.6:	*Life Class*: participant Barbara J Clark, performer Graeme Rose, and participants Betty and Barry Winship. Photo: Scott Sawyer.	261
49.1:	*Unbox Me!*: performer Graeme Rose. Video still: Jacob Rose.	312
P.1:	*Life Class*: performers Morven Macbeth and Graeme Rose. Photo: Scott Sawyer.	318

Bodies in Flight

Index

Note: Page numbers in italics indicate figures.

2012 London Games 265, 269, 284

A
A Bout de Souffle (Breathless) 131, 135
Abramovic, Marina 309
Act Without Words 1 234
Action Hero 276
Adams, Mark *134, 136–37*
Andrew, Nicole *264, 266*
Angel Tech 64, 75, 194, 196–200
archives xiv, 35, 149–50, 186–87, 205 see also documentation
Arnolfini Gallery (Bristol) 18, 273
Arts Council East Midlands/England 269, 274, 276, 282, 284, 319
Atack, Tim *172, 190, 192–93, 247*, 255
audiences 46–47, 76–77, 145, 152, 258–59
Avallone, Joshua 206–07, *264, 266–67*

B
Bad Seeds 199
Bailey, Tom 120–21
Baldwyn, Lucy *20, 22–23, 38, 40–41*
Bargeld, Blixa 199
Barker, Howard xxi–iii
Bataille, Georges xxiii
Battersea Arts Centre (BAC) 64–65
BBC Big Screens 265, 284
Beautiful Losers 11, 63, 76, 90–92, 129, 163–67
Beauty#2 105, 129
Beckett, Samuel xxii–iii, 214, 234–35
Blow Up 226
Bott, Doug *172, 190, 192–93,* 196, 198, 199, *247*
Bourne, Darren *127*
Breatnach, Patricia xxiv, 44, *126–27*, 131
Bristol Old Vic 272–74
Butetown Riverside Grangetown Communities First Group 285
Byfield, Dean *99*

C
Cage, John 93, 116, 198
Carnall, Jon *78, 80–81, 96, 98–99, 107,* 115, 244
Cave, Nick 199
Chew, Gerald 163, 165–66
choreography 1–5, 67–68, 146, 206–07, 237–42, 301 see also dance
Chua, George 166
Clark, Barbara J *290–91*
Clough, Benjamin *158, 160,* 165, *190, 192–93,* 197, *247*
Coldplay 199
collaboration xiv, 1–4, 42–45, 164–65, 182–88, 252, 300–04, 316 see also non-collaboration
communities xxvi, 317 see also participants
Constants xxiv, 43, 44, 46, 93, 120, 130–31, 319
Cunningham, Merce 116

D

dance 1–3, 44–46, 289, 301–03, 309, 315–17 *see also choreography*

Dance4/FABRIC 2, 284, 300, 315–17

Deadplay xix–xxi, 12–19, 24–25, 72, 128, 204

DeliverUs xxii, xxv, 46, 76, 120, 131–32, 147–48, 149–56

de-second-naturing 121

Department of Drama, The (University of Bristol) 16–19, 30, 63, 313

Devoy, Jane *104*, *106–07*, 115–17, 119–20, 130

Dimsdale, Edward 116, 235, 237, 283

direct address 51, 54, 76, 82

Do the Wild Thing! xi, xiv, xxii, 46, 102, 115–20, 129, 138, 169, 186, 231, 237, 279, 284, 315

Do the Wild Thing! Redux 120, 186–87, 207–08, 255, 281, 284

documentation xv, 27, 169, 204–05, 245

Double Happiness xxii, xxv, 164–65, 187

Dream→Work/Dream→Walk xxvi, 47, 117, 120, 133, 214, 231, 258–59, 274–76, 283, 284–85, 292, 306, 315–17

duetting xiv, 36, 42–43, 45–47, 102, 184–85 *see also set-up and situation*

dwelling 118–21, 133, 150, 182, 185–86, 241, 284–85, 307–08, 316 *see also in-between*

Dyson, Catherine *224–25*

E

edition 259, 262–63, 283–86 *see also portfolio work; re-use*

Electric Hotel 274–75

Eliot, T. S. 238

Elloway, Dan *104*, *106–07*, 115–17, 119–20, 130, *161*, 165, *278*

Eno, Brian 91

everyday, the xiv, 45–47, 68, 76, 94, 115, 117, 120–21, 194–95, 214, 237, 242, 258–59, 262–63, 270, 286, 303, 306, 307, 310 *see also participants*

Exhibit xx, 11, 24–25, 27, 72, 258

F

Feuchtwang, Rachel *14*

Flesh & Text CD–ROM xv, 43, 150, 205, 283

Forced Entertainment 187, 268

Frame, Polly 64, *74–75*, *134*, *136–37*, *170*, *172–73*, *190*, *192–93*, 199, *210*, *212–13*, 214, *247*, 255, *261*

G

Ganatra, Nitin Chandra *28–29*

Gaunt, Sophie *264*, *266*

Gilbert, Sheila xxiv, 46, 93, *124*, 125, *126–27*, 130–31, 205, 319

Gob Squad 268

Greig, David 144

Gymnast xxvi, 46–47, 206–07, 240–41, 258–259, 268–71, 276–77, 284, 307–08, 317

H

Halmarack, Sam *224–25*, *261*

Hamlet 143–45

Heidegger, Martin 1, 3, 32–33, 118–19, 234–35 *see also phenomenology*

Holland, Beth *288*, *290*, 302, 309–10

Hymn 223, 259

I

I'd Like to Call You Joe Tonight 207–08, 279

iwannabewolfman xxii, 11, 73, 90, 118, 129, 244–45

in-between 1–4, 31, 77, 102, 121, 183–86, 241, 286, 307–08 *see also dwelling*

J

Johnson, Neil *172–73*, *192*, 196, 199, 212–13, *247*, 309
Judge, Ella 205–06
Judge, Tony 265, 283, 307

K

Kaprow, Allan 117
Kent, James D. *278*
King, Martha 120–21
Krapp's Last Tape 235

L

Lancashire Encounter Festival 285
Lea, Ursula *26*, *28–29*
Life Class xxvi, 46–47, 70, 76, 120, 258–59, 269–71, 285–86, 300–04, 308–11, 317
Life Class: A Dialogue 289
Littluns Wake xxii, 11, 46, 92–93
live art 11, 19, 25, 269, 273, 282
London International Festival of Theatre 269
Love Is Natural and Real but Not for You my Love xxii, 11, 32, 43, 75

M

Macbeth 143
Macbeth, Morven 70, *290–91*, 292, 308–10, *318*
Make the Fixed Volatile, and Make the Volatile Fixed 279
Massive Attack 198
Mazzey, Bridget 116, 129–30
micro-choreography 115–18, 152, 265 *see also* choreography
Million Tiny Glitches, A 199
Model Love xxv, 47, 64, 116, 187, 231–36, 237–39, 248–51, 255, 258, 283, 306
Moore, Colin *290*
Mountain Goats 199
Muse 279

music 75, 90–94, 196–200 *see also* technologies

N

National Review of Live Art, The xix, 10, 13, 18–19, 21, 24, 128, 204, 258, 273
Naturalistic drama 129
Neilson, Anthony 25
Night Bus Choir *264*, *266*
non-collaboration 34–36, 102, 182–88, 313 *see also* collaboration
Not I 214, 233, 234
Nott Dance 269, 315
Nottingham Osteoporosis Dancing Club 309
Now Festival 269

O

On the Exhale 145
O'Shaughnessy, Justin *14*, *26*, *28–29*

P

Parsifal xx, 13, 17, 18, 25
participants 270–71, 276–77, 284, 301–03, 305–11 *see also* communities
Paynter, John 93
Pegg, Simon *23*, *38*, *40–41*, 50, 52–53, 74, *244*
phenomenology 1, 4, 32–36, 43–44, 102, 238–39 *see also* philosophizing
philosophizing 30–36 *see also* phenomenology
physical theatre xx, 13, 45, 273
Plaid 198
Plunkett, Martin *14*
Porter, Katherine *26*, *28–29*, *41*, *52–53*, 73, *244*
portfolio work 133, 171, 206–07, 214, 223, 259, 283–86

Power, Barnaby *12, 14, 22, 38, 40–41, 244*
practice-as-research 2, 30–31, 36, 102, 105, 281
promenade performance 90–91, 92–93, 120 *see also* sited performance

R

Ratcliff, Chris *22–23*
re-entering xiv, 203, 208, 255, 259 *see also* edition; portfolio work; re-use
re-use xvi, 182, 204–08, 211, 283–85 *see also* edition; portfolio work; re-entering
Rose, Graeme *50, 52–53,* 64, 74, *173, 190, 192–93,* 199, 206, *224–25, 226, 247,* 249–50, *260, 262, 288, 290–91,* 292, 300–03, 308–10, *312, 318*
Rough xxii, 11, 63, 66, 70, 73–74, 75–76, 164, 187, 258
Rye, Caroline 125, 130–31, 135, 153

S

scenography 128–32 *see also* set-up and situation
Secrecy of Saints, The xxv, 76, 144–45, 147, 187
set-up and situation 35, 75–76, 108, 310
Sims, Sheila *290*
sited performance xiv, 79, 82, 93, 102, 166–67, 274–75 *see also* set-up and situation
Skinworks xxv, 46, 64, 74–75, 76, 82, 145–46, 194, 197, 246–47, 258, 283, 306
Sleepdogs 196
Sleeping Beauty, The 239
Speakman, Duncan 274
spell#7 162–67, 262, 275

Still Moving: Moving Still 47, 117, 120–21, 242, 259, 279
still-ing 117, 120–21, 203, 237–42, 247 *see also* choreography; dwelling

T

Tan, Kaylene 64, 74–75, *158, 161, 172–73*
technologies xiv, xxiv–v, 102, 147–48, 185, 204–08, 234–35, 249
digital xv, 159, 163–64, 169, 205, 232–33, 249
photography 222–25, 226, 231–36, 243–52
sound 93–94
video 120, 125, 131–32, 135, 138, 147–48, 151–55, 205–08, 211
virtual xiv, 159, 171
text 4, 11, 54, 67–68, 143–48, 164–66, 300–01 *see also* verbatim; writing
Theatre Bristol 275
Tinder 232–33
Triptych 206, 255, 259, 283

U

Unbox Me! 187, 259
Uninvited Guests 276

V

Vandekeybus, Wim 17
Vanishing Point 25
verbatim 302, 306, 307–10 *see also* text
virtual online environment xiv *see also* technologies
Visual and Performing Arts Department (Trent Polytechnic) 268–69

W

Wainwright, Tom *222, 224–25,* 237–39, *262*

Watkins, Charlotte *22–23, 38, 40–41, 50, 52–53,* 73, *78, 80–81, 96, 98,* 244
Wee, Marianne *158, 160–61,* 165
Wishart, Trevor 93
Who By Fire xxv, 64, 70, 75, 146–48, 187, 196–200, 205–06, 211, 247–48, 255, 258, 272–74, 283, 306
Winship, Barry and Betty *290–91,* 302–03, 310
writing 32, 72–73, 75–77, 153, 306–07
    see also verbatim; text

Y

yoga 44, 118, 240
You Are Present to Me Now 289